NATURE

NATURE

An Environmental Cosmology

Joseph Grange

STATE UNIVERSITY OF NEW YORK PRESS

Production by Ruth Fisher
Marketing by Bernadette LaManna

Published by
State University of New York Press, Albany

Printed in the United States of America

For information, address the State University of New York Press,
State University Plaza, Albany, NY 12246

Library of Congress Cataloging-in-Publication Data

Grange, Joseph, 1940–
Nature : an environmental cosmology / Joseph Grange.
p. cm.
Includes bibliographical references and index.
ISBN 0-7914-3347-1 (hc : alk. paper). – ISBN 0-7914-3348-X (pb) :
alk. paper)
1. Philosophy of nature. 2. Environmental ethics. I. Title.
BD581.G55 1997
113–dc20 96-41494
CIP

10 9 8 7 6 5 4 3 2 1

To
the people of the South Bronx, the people of Southern Maine, and the people of Connemara, Ireland

CONTENTS

Part Three. An Ethical Vision

PREFACE

This work marks the beginning of a speculative effort to understand in a systematic way the entwined realities that jointly make up our contemporary environment. Those realities are represented by the signs, "City & Nature." As experiences, the city and nature are felt with high degrees of intensity. So great is their presence in our lives that they appear to represent opposed realities. On the one hand, there is the city standing for all that is civilized, human, and worthy of the term "culture." On the other hand, there is nature representing all that is living, fresh, unspoiled, and vital. At the same time, there is the city understood as the very sign of the wicked, a sinful, corrupt, and decadent artifact—source of all our woes. Equally present is nature as mindless force threatening our precarious lives with overwhelming, sudden, and destructive power. And so we have come to understand our environment as torn in two. It is a split world, a dual universe whose essential unity ever escapes us.

As practiced for the last decade, the discipline of environmental ethics has focused on just such a division of reality into the natural and the human. I will argue against such an interpretation by constructing an environmental cosmology that envisions reality as a process of emergent events, each of which has its own intrinsic value as well as its causal influence on other parts of reality. The division of the world into the natural and the artificial will be seen as having no metaphysical ultimacy. In fact, I will argue that this distinction has outlived its usefulness and is now a positive hindrance to the construction of a comprehensive, adequate, and applicable environmental ethics. City and nature name two dimensions of a real unity: The achievement of value in the temporal world.

In exploring this underlying axiological matrix, I take as my model the work of Alfred North Whitehead. His *Process and Reality* remains the metaphysical masterpiece of the twentieth century and continues to point the way toward doing philosophy that reaps important knowledge and rewards. But I would not have my work regarded as one more exegetical exercise on the intricacies of Whitehead's cosmological system. Such scholasticism has done much to embalm his thought. Rather, I seek the pragmatic significance of systematic speculative philosophy. In other words, I believe that cosmology has important things to say about both the generic features as well as the actual worth of the natural and built environments. The application of thought is as important as the principles guiding its development. Therefore, the cosmological system and its categoreal scheme is entirely my own and stands or falls on its own merits. The ultimate test of its efficacy is always the pragmatic one: Does it help us to understand nature more fully and therefore take better care of our environmental heritage?

Equally important as exemplar and inspiration is the effort of those process thinkers who have sought to advance Whitehead's vision by reconstructing it in the light of comparative philosophy and contemporary experience. I refer especially to the labors of Robert Neville, David Hall, and George Allan. Each in his own way has advanced the project of systematic philosophy. Robert Neville has demonstrated the sheer power of order and goodness as primary traits of the real. David Hall has stressed the centrality of spontaneity, freshness and surprise in an emergent cosmos. George Allan has made palpable the dense richness of temporal succession—past, present, and to come—in its respective mesocosmic settings.

It is characteristic of cosmology that it seeks a togetherness of parts that is more than their ontological sum. In so doing cosmology rejects the claim of positivism that there is a final and irreducible distinction to be made between fact and value. The philosophic tradition is filled with distinguished thinkers who uphold this perspective. These philosophers, both Eastern and Western, understand reality as expressive modalities of the good. In the midst of its growing ecological concern, humanity needs to return to such a view. It is to regain the feel of such historical weight that I bring into this argument so many seemingly disparate thinkers. What Lao-Tzu and Confucius, Spinoza, and Whitehead share is a deep and profound respect for the environment, which makes our humanity possible. In turn, this respect is grounded in axiologically rooted thinking.

While a sense of this axiological tradition needs to inform our environmental thinking, it is not sufficient of itself to revive our impoverished consciousness. Environmental cosmology must find direct application in the everyday world. If the reader tires of the difficult initial work of constructing an environmental cosmology, I hope patience will inform flagging energies. In systematic philosophy the rewards are often long in coming but when they do arrive, they are substantial and sustainable.

Three factors have shaped this book. First, there is the sense that we remain worthy heirs of a great tradition, that of philosophy as the pursuit of wisdom. Second, I believe that thought is not nearly as enfeebled as contemporary critics would have us believe. Last, a systematic presentation of the most important traits of environmental reality is not only possible but also necessary if humanity is to regain, retain, and employ that deft sense of environmental sensitivity which once graced our being.

As the twentieth century moves toward its completion, it has become customary to view the city and nature as opposed dimensions of experience. Furthermore, this general disjunction embraces a number of other more particular separations that trouble our culture. The distinctions drawn between the body and the mind, the genuine and the artificial, the vital and the mechanical, the organic and the technological, the natural and the built—all these fragmentations can be viewed as subsets of the wider problem of the relation between city and nature. In this sense the theme of city and nature serves to bring together many of the great public issues of the day. The question of value and its achievement, the place of the past, the present, and the future in human life, morality, justice, environmental ethics, and the meaning of creativity itself are but some of the questions embraced by this topic.

In its long march out of nature and into the city, civilization appears to have left behind most of what is included under the rubric of the natural. Or so the majority of cultural commentators would have us believe. For whether one aligns oneself with the party of nature and longs for the return of wilderness or one sides with the technical advances of the urban, the metaphysics remains the same. Both sides assert an absolute dichotomy between the city and nature. This study directly challenges that position. It sees this view as cosmologically naive and, what is worse, the source of much of the alienation that presently lacerates our cultural life. Stated more positively, this study sees the distinction between the city and nature as lacking in metaphysical ultimacy. As will be demonstrated throughout this study (and the work on urban cosmology I am developing), what binds these regions together turns out to be far more significant than what divides them.

Great civilizations are distinguished by their vision of what is important. Such a vision arises when an age has established a consistent perspective that promotes an understanding of the important aspects of reality. With the emergence of sustained articulations of this vision, there is accomplished a consolidation of importance, expression, perspective, and understanding. These four notions—importance, expression, understanding, and perspective—are entwined in every civilized age and comprise the major ways in which civilization organizes itself.[1] They are not necessarily conscious; in fact, they seldom receive direct attention. Nevertheless, they are implied in the very notion of civilization. Through them, we gain a sense of the general drift of an age, what orients its adventures, and how and why it claims its successes and produces its failures.

As themes, city and nature express a deep division in our sensibility. At the same time, we seem to sense a need to keep them together. Our inability to do so tells against the age. It is not that we lack information. Surely, no age has possessed such sophisticated knowledge about the workings of natural and urban experience. Nor is there an absence of political energy. Partisans on every side urge programs of reform. And certainly, there exists sufficient technological expertise to do something about our dilemma. Deep in our being we feel the need for both dimensions of experience.

It is wisdom that prevents us from excluding one or the other of these dimensions from our experience. Despite our biases, we rightly sense the importance of both and refuse to be without either. What is disturbing about contemporary culture is that we do not know how to achieve an appropriate balance between these seemingly opposed dimensions. It is the differences in the experiences that hold us: Their underlying identity eludes us. We lack a vision that sustains the unity of urban and natural experience.

Importance

Philosophy deals with ultimate notions. Four such notions have been singled out, the first of which is importance. An ultimate notion cannot be defined in terms more basic than itself. If it could, it would not be ultimate. As ultimate, importance signifies that which matters. What matters is that which makes a difference. Importance is therefore the ground of value. When we say that something is important, we are recognizing its inherent worth. City and nature are obviously important notions, but it is equally obvious that we do not know their worth. If we did, our ability to bring them together would show itself. That they remain an unresolved antithesis is a philosophic scandal.

Philosophy does more with ultimate notions than simply list them. It also must coordinate them so that the relations between them become evident and useful. When such coordination is achieved, then philosophy becomes systematic. City and nature require such coordination if the unity that binds them together is to become important to us. Without such a systematic view, the value of both experiences are at the mercy of forces that know little of their inherent worth. Intellectual responsibility demands systematic philosophy. This study of nature is the first step in building such a theory.

Expression

Importance emerges from the ways in which civilizations express themselves. Expression is the mode by which importance diffuses itself throughout the environment. There are many modes of expression because it is essentially a finite, limited, and selective process. Cities express importance and so does nature. In the realm of expression, drawing an ultimate distinction between the natural and the urban is highly questionable. No expression can exhaust importance. Nevertheless, without expression there could be nothing important since it would never show itself. A great culture develops and elaborates a stunning array of modes of expression. This is how we can judge its importance. So far, our culture has been unable to express city and nature in anything more than a series of oppositions. Yet these two regions of experience are at the heart of our civilization. Our failure to express the unity of city and nature may well be a sign of the imminent collapse of our sense of what is important. Once a civilization ceases to express a unified vision of importance, its internal divisions grow and its source of energy is sapped. Civilized expression degenerates into warring ideologies and philosophy is reduced to factions.

Understanding

Systematic philosophy views understanding as the effort to relate various parts of experience so that coherent patterns of importance emerge. It always involves a comprehensive vision. To understand is therefore to assign appropriate values to all the domains of experience. Its aim is to provide a perspective so grounded in wisdom that justice is accorded all elements of experience. A civilization that cannot grant to city and nature a just decision on their relative merits and interrelations does not understand them.

Perspective

Because it is always selective, expression arises out of a particular focus. When expression gains a certain cultural steadiness and strength, then importance is viewed from a definite perspective. A perspective is an angle of vision used to gain a consistent hold on importance. It is a pivot around which expressions of importance can develop. Perspective serves to create, control, and arrange dimensions of experience considered important. It is obvious that our contemporary perspective can do little more than reserve separate domains for city and nature. Our environmental history warns against the folly of "separate but equal" places for these important regions of experience. A perspective that expresses itself in the thought, values, and actions of a civilization amounts to the very definition of that civilization. If our civilized perspective can do no better than merely recognize these domains as separate, then surely its sense of importance lacks comprehensiveness. Perspective should let a culture weave together the various important strands of its experience so that a harmony of value can show forth its multiform textures. More specifically, I will argue that the perspective offered by the currently dominant philosophy of scientific materialism is seriously deficient in its capacity to adequately deal with the important aspects of environmental experience.

These four notions—importance, expression, understanding, and perspective—establish a matrix for an introductory coordination of the major themes of this study of city and nature. The issue of importance involves the relative merits and values of natural and urban experience. It is necessary to establish in what specific ways they spring from the same source of value and precisely how they differ from each other. Expression in its many modes will be a key to this endeavor. It is not the case that the urban and natural are only similar. Such a position would make them incomparable, for it would accept as given the fact that they are discontinuous. The disconnection of city and nature is the problem to be resolved. My argument arises from a commitment to a form of naturalism that sees mind as continuous with nature, the cultural arising from the natural, and the human as essentially one with the processes of the natural universe. As stated earlier, this study is restricted to the natural domain. It will take another work to do justice to the urban side of this continuous process.

The question, therefore, is how to distinguish among expression's many types without tearing them apart. It is the apparent divisions between the experiences that divides our culture. Understanding demands a unity that tolerates difference: Partisan thought may win quarrels but it grants no wisdom. What is required above all else is a perspective generous enough to permit the vast riches of both domains to be felt and coordinated within human experience. We need a perspective that will allow city and nature to express their respective importance in an understandable way. In short, we need a cosmology.

Parts of Chapter Ten appeared in *The Maine Scholar,* Volume 7, Autumn 1994. Chapter Eleven is based on an essay I wrote for *Research in Philosophy and Technology,* Volume 14, 1994.

I owe a special debt of gratitude to Professor Tom Boylan, former Dean of Humanities at University College, Galway, and presently Professor of Economics at that same institution. It was through his generosity that I was granted a Humanities Fellowship at University College, Galway. The cordial hospitality and intellectual support I received from the Galway Faculty enabled me to complete this study. My dedication names the people of Connemara because it was through them that I sensed the importance of environmental beauty for right living. I owe a similar debt to the people of the South Bronx, where I was born and raised, and the people of Southern Maine, where I have lived for the last quarter-century. I also thank Professor Pascal O'Gorman of Galway's Philosophy Faculty for the privilege of addressing his advanced seminar on modern culture and ethics. I have learned much from him and his students.

There are others whose support, encouragement and wisdom made this book possible. I thank George Caffentzis, Joseph Conforti, John Grange, Malachy Grange, Jeannette Haas, John Kinsella, Stu Lamont, Jessica Roberts, Yuri Van Mierlo, and Maria Zayas. Finally, I thank Joseph Grange and Margaret Grange, my mother and father. They each showed me in different ways the value of beauty as a guide for life.

ABBREVIATIONS

AI *Adventures of Ideas* (1933). New York: The Free Press, 1967.

CP *Collected Papers of C. S. Peirce,* edited by Charles Hartshorne and Paul Weiss. Cambridge, Mass.: Harvard University Press, 1931–58.

MT *Modes of Thought* (1938). New York: The Free Press, 1968.

PR *Process and Reality* (1929), corrected edition edited by David Ray Griffin and Donald W. Sherburne. New York: The Free Press, 1978.

RM *Religion in the Making.* New York: New American Library, 1974.

SMW *Science and the Modern World* (1925). New York: The Free Press, 1967.

S *Symbolism, Its Meaning and Effect* (1927). New York: The Fordham University Press, 1985.

Part One

Environmental Cosmology

Chapter One

The Cosmological Method

Cosmology is the philosophical discipline that aims to articulate the basic traits of existence in this world. It has a long, distinguished history, with contributors that include such masters of thought as Plato, Confucius, Spinoza, Leibniz, Hegel, and Whitehead. Eastern and Western religions have also struggled to articulate through general ideas their understanding of the basic traits of their worlds. What these very different cultural efforts have in common is a respect for the concrete, which shows itself in a judicious use of abstractions and a wise employment of a systematic order. The importance of the ultimate success or failure of these cultural efforts fades before their enduring legacy: At their height, great civilizations have always sought abstract comprehensiveness and concrete particularity. This zeal for the individual and the universal, the abstract and the concrete marks a basic desire of the human heart.

Cosmology begins when human beings refuse to settle for dualisms. One of the best examples of this refusal to divorce the abstract and the concrete are those moments in *The Sophist* when Plato faces the deepest of differences—that of the *Gigantomachia,* the battle between the giants of permanence and change. Whom to follow, the champions of Parmenides or the followers of Heraclitus?[1]

Stymied by the difference between understanding the really real as permanence or regarding it as ceaseless change, Plato refuses to fold his cards. Instead, he seeks another way around the dilemma. In so doing he suggests the attitude necessary for cosmological speculation: Like the child, we must have both. Being and Becoming are both necessary for a full account of the real world. Of course, children seek to have their cake and their ice cream and to eat both. But from the cosmological perspective it is no foolish wish. Civilizations grow through the search for a wider vision, one comprehensive enough to bypass dualisms. In the battle of the giants, theory starts by turning a weakness into a strength. It endorses the very tensions that defeat less generous philosophies and seeks to see farther by refusing simple-mindedness. "Awesome unmoving perfection" and "life and motion" must be brought together into a unity. Later, this effort to bring together that which seems to be apart will be recognized as both the heart of the category of contrast and the soul of beauty as a cosmological quality.

More formally speaking, cosmology carries out this service by constructing hypotheses about the world and then systematically seeking to show their adequacy and relevance for the issue under study. Now this is a decidedly non-post-modern endeavor and at first blush may appear altogether strange to a contemporary reader.[2] I ask for patience as we begin the hard work of laying out the essentials of the cosmological method.

The Speculative Matrix

In the first part of *Process and Reality,* Whitehead is at pains to define cosmology as a discipline that produces important knowledge.[3] The thinking characteristic of cosmology has both internal and external traits that distinguish it from other modes of philosophy. In terms of internal traits, it is speculative and entails several qualities necessary to ground thought in the proper matrix. In terms of external traits, speculative philosophy has a job to do in the real world. It must make a pragmatic difference to human beings as they negotiate their environments.

I begin with its internal traits by speaking of the matrix of thought, or as Whitehead more formally called it: "The Categoreal

Scheme." A matrix is akin to a mother, in that the health of the child is a reflection of the health of the mother. Much of the protection of the particular by the universal, the nourishing of the factual by the formal and the enhancement of concrete experience by reason of abstract thought depends upon the proper coordination of these characteristics.

Coherence

Whitehead claims that a successful cosmological scheme must exhibit three formal internal traits. In the first place, it must be coherent in the sense that no one thought in the system can be understood as self-sufficient in its meaning and definition. That which presents itself as isolated from other ideas in the system violates the integrity of the scheme: "It is the ideal of speculative philosophy that its fundamental notions shall not seem capable of abstraction from each other."[4] Thus, coherence signifies the web-like texture of the schema. It demands that we think of the fundamental ideas as so woven together that they require reference to each other for their complete understanding. This is not a strict Hegelian dialectic wherein opposites pass into each other. Rather the ideas are not self-sufficient in themselves for "it means that what is indefinable in one such notion cannot be abstracted from its relevance to the other notions."[5] The quality of coherence presupposes the fact that in an environment the becoming of every being is woven into the becoming of all its members. There is no isolated fact, value, achievement, expression, or perspective. Because of the interrelatedness of concrete environments, a complete abstraction is a theoretical impossibility. Once together, always together: So it goes in any environment whatsoever.

The Logically Vague

The second formal trait of the speculative matrix is its logical character. While logical here has its ordinary meaning of self-consistency, it also has the special meaning of being logically "vague." This most important quality requires careful articulation. In the first place, "vague" here does not mean ambiguous, fuzzy or lacking in formal definition. It is not an invitation to relativism and all the games that go with that sort of thinking. Neither is "vague" an invitation to sloppy thinking. Finally, "vague" does not mean the kind of contextualized thinking that distorts all normative measures and makes the world collapse into a heap of meaningless terms.

What "vague" does mean is best understood in contrast with the "general." A general applies to all things indifferently. Generals signify "alls" and "anys" and are characteristic of science in its quest for natural laws and those types of philosophy that seek universal formal systems applying indifferently to everything in the universe. By contrast, what is logically vague requires a reference to a concrete and experiential instantiation of its being for its full understanding. Thus application is required if the formal system is to take on a truth character and say something important about the real world.

It is the great genius of the American philosopher Charles Sanders Peirce to have recognized this logical quality and given it a place in his formal speculative matrix:

> A more scientific pair of definitions would be that anything is general in so far as the principle of excluded middle does apply to it and is vague in so far as the principle of contradiction does not apply to it.[6]

Much confusion and philosophic diatribe can be avoided if at the outset we settle on this definition of the vague. It says in effect that one can create a speculative matrix that requires application for its full understanding. Thus it is neither true nor false before being used. Further, it derives its defining power from its application and is not a logocentric net thrown over the world to marginalize difference and substitute the abstract for the concrete.

So when I characterize an environment as overlapping sets of integrated events, I am not declaring all environmental situations to be identical but rather insisting that a true understanding of the environment requires viewing it from the perspective of entwined sets of spacetime experiences. The precise kind of spacetime character and its precise environmental value and influence await the specifications of a variety of other disciplines, scientific and humane. Cosmological method establishes a vague matrix out of which meaningful and specific concrete truths can be derived. Peirce termed this logical quality "objectively" vague because its full truth depends upon its encounters with concrete, actual, historical situations and enactments. It is one thing to say that the really real are events in process of becoming; it is decidedly another matter to say precisely how a fawn in the woods or a skyscraper in a city are such events.

By means of the parameters of the vague, there is established an interpretive loop between thought and reality. Through the proper application of the matrix, the categories of the scheme provide a deeper understanding of reality and, at the same time, reality forces the categories to prove their worth. Sometimes our understanding of reality has to be adjusted; other times will see the speculative categories in need of reconstruction. Often it will be a mixture of both these outcomes. Reality is the measure of our interpretations, not the other way around. The cosmological method seeks to secure a midground between the universality of scientific laws and explanations and the apodeictic quality claimed by types of phenomenological philosophy seeking to grasp the various essences of the life world.[7]

In the place of science's "alls" and "anys," and over against phenomenology's recourse to "the things themselves," cosmology offers a heuristic hypothesis that promises to restore both continuity and specificity to our understanding of systems of reality. What a vague descriptive system has over scientific explanatory laws is that the causal and predictive power of science is empty of particular meaning. As Peirce saw, generals tend to generalize. On the other hand, phenomenological intuitions are necessarily blind to the need for systematic unity and hierarchical distinctions. They endorse the particular but lose sight of the continuity characteristic of all worlds, artificial and natural. As Whitehead maintained, pure induction leads only to the observation of the same. Difference is captured through theoretical unity. A practical appreciation of the logically vague is captured in the message of the popular bumper sticker: THINK GLOBALLY, ACT LOCALLY.

Intuitive Necessity

This brings us to the third formal internal trait of the speculative matrix. Such a scheme of thought must have the character of necessity. Whitehead expresses it this way: "...the philosophic scheme should be 'necessary,' in the sense of bearing in itself its own warrant of universality throughout all experience, provided that we confine ourselves to that which communicates with immediate matter of fact."[8] Of course, such a mode of communication is ideal and is never in fact fully realized. Still, necessary means that which communicates itself with a certain, intuitive necessity. If I say that the world is made of tent poles, the mind balks. If, on the other hand, I claim that the world is made of intertwined spacetime events, the mind is willing to further entertain this hypothesis.

As experienced in a cosmological scheme, necessity indicates that the mind of another has intuitively agreed to entertain in a thorough and determined manner the hypothesis in question. To sum up: Three formal internal traits must characterize the speculative matrix. It must exhibit a formal coherence that is logically vague yet semiotically evocative of our direct experience of the world.

Adequacy and Applicability

This reference to the real world brings us to the remaining two formal external traits. They concern the application of the cosmology to the domain of experience. When the matrix is applied to the domain of real experience, that application must exhibit the formal traits of adequacy and applicability. In this empirical dimension of cosmological thinking, the matrix demonstrates its usefulness for enlarging and deepening our scope of understanding. An environmental cosmology should apply indifferently to all major environmental situations and realities. "Indifferently" here means that "the texture of observed experience, as illustrating the philosophic scheme, is such that all related experience must exhibit the same texture."[9] In this cosmology, that will mean that all dimensions of environmental experience will share the character of being modes of feeling circumambient spacetime regions. When applied to environmental structures and values, feeling is an adequate category if such a perspective expresses the most important aspects of environmental being. Applicable, therefore, means that our understanding of the environment is enlarged, renewed, and made more accessible through the use of the speculative matrix. Through adequate application the abstract categories of the speculative matrix provide breadth of thought for the concrete world of environmental experience.[10]

The themes of adequacy and applicability recall the quality of vagueness discussed earlier. Here, by means of an adequate application the speculative matrix takes on the specificity required to render its abstractions concretely intelligible. This is primarily the work of the special sciences and the humane disciplines. The speculative matrix does indeed enlarge our understanding of environmental complexity by envisioning all beings as entwined unities of feeling. But different disciplines, for example, biology and geology, architecture and poetry, can take hold of such a vague and generic description and specify it concretely through their special research tools. What the speculative matrix prevents is narrowness of vision, the kind of specialized blindness that so readily infects research programs that deliberately confine themselves to minute areas of knowledge. Cosmology sides with common sense when it seeks to express the important unvarying features of our environmental being. But common sense is always being overthrown by the special sciences.[11]

The Environmental Hypothesis

Cosmology begins its program of speculation by forming a well-wrought hypothesis that can be applied to real experience. The formal statement of the environmental hypothesis is as follows:

> An environment is a unison of the becoming of value characterized by a fundamental unity that always issues into the creation of an inexhaustible newness.

As such an environment is a very special mode of togetherness, since it drives toward the creation of the new even as it sustains itself through the appropriation of the past. It is a multilayered system that uses the past so that the new can arrive in due space and time. It may support any number of subsystems and parallel systems. Some of these systems can be closed and repetitive, while others can be quite open to novelty. Environments are regions where many things go on simultaneously. Inhibitions, enhancements, eliminations, and causal influences are but some of the activities to be found in environmental domains. They can be stable or ephemeral, enduring or fleeting, fatal or life-giving.

Given such exceptional variety, it is important that the environmental hypothesis to be used in this study name all the essential features of any environment whatsoever. The formal statement names four factors that are essential to the functioning of all environments, natural or human: A unison of becoming, the achievement of value, fundamental unity, and creativity.

A Unison of Becoming

An environment exhibits a unison of becoming because it supports many modes of being at the same time. Its togetherness is not a simple togetherness of parts but rather a whole more than the sum of its parts that in some way or other provides for the birth, growth, and perishing of its members. Its unison is described in two ways. There is the environment itself which is a diachronic field that supports across its being any number of events in various stages of process. Following Whitehead, this environmental dimension can be given the name coordinate or morphological. It contains all those orders within which various environmental events may, can, or do appear. Diachronic is used to suggest the transverse temporal axis that operates throughout environmental domains. If spatial reality is to be emphasized this dimension can also be called the horizontal. In any environment there will be an extension of causal influence across its spatiotemporal expanse.

The second mode of the unison of becoming concerns the elements within the environment itself. These events, beings, or creatures can have their own relative independence such that they can be conceived of as individuals in their own right. Again following Whitehead's lead, this mode of the unison of becoming is termed the genetic or concrescent dimension. It contains those environmental elements that establish a dominant synchronic presence within the environmental field. These events grow together to form significant identities that focus the environmental field in one way or another. Again, if spatial reality is to be emphasized, these events can be called the vertical domain within environmental fields.[12]

In sum, environments create unisons of becoming through the weaving of vertical synchronic spacetime events onto horizontal diachronic spacetime regions. Whether emphasis is to be given to the synchronic or the diachronic, the vertical or the horizontal, is a matter for the special sciences and disciplines to decide. What counts is that an objectively vague environmental character, awaiting appropriate empirical specification, has been identified.

The Achievement of Value

The second factor in the formal hypothesis states that the unison of becoming in environmental regions results in the achievement of value. It is value and the terms of its achievement that is at the very heart of this attempt to construct a cosmological paradigm for an adequate environmental ethics. Since its beginnings in Descartes's philosophy, the fact/value distinction and its assorted variations has for too long stalled the process of getting on with a viable environmental philosophy. Whether the distinction is rooted in Hume's categories of matters-of-fact and matters-of-thought or is, more simply, merely held as a modernist metaphysical dogma, the result is the same. An interminable debate settles over the question of whether there is intrinsic value in the world or whether all such terms are subjective reactions to objective matters of fact.[13] We are still stuck in the era of scientific materialism and continue to inherit its unhelpful and outdated categoreal bifurcations.

Through the use of the hypothetic method of speculative philosophy I propose to get beyond this impasse. There are two reasons for such a move. In the first place, modernism's epistemological distinctions carry no warrant of metaphysical ultimacy. Their aim is methodological rather than ontological; therefore, they rest on a vast set of unexamined metaphysical assumptions.[14] Second, as we have seen, in cosmological speculation the final proof is in the fruitful application of the scheme. It is better to see if these categories illuminate something fundamental about urban and natural regions than to suffer one more failure of speculative nerve. Our cultural power to do something effective about environmental affairs hangs in the balance.

The hypothesis, therefore, is that whatever comes to be in environmental domains achieves a value. To be is always to be a value. What can this mean? Scientific materialism separates fact from value in the discussion of types of experience. This is largely due to its reliance on sense data as the only true form of empirically valid knowledge. This epistemological commitment then determines an ontological dogma. It is the fallacy of vacuous actuality. This theory of reality claims that nothing happens in the universe except the transfer of matter from spacetime zone to spacetime zone. It says that what is really real is the movement of extended things between objective points of reference. In Whitehead's words: "Nature... [is]...merely the hurrying of material, endlessly, meaninglessly."[15] In contrast to this dead world of facts sliding silently past each other, this environmental cosomology speculates that reality is shot through and through with emergences of value, units of experience that have a special mode of existence—one best called the achievement of value.

Further, we can specify in a vague way just how these units of value come into being. The hypothesis is that harmony is the essential structure assumed by each environmental being in its coming to be. Each event brings together into a unique perspective its relevant environmental conditions so as to express its particular and unique importance. As such, every environmental being has both essential and conditional features that it harmonizes in order to be just what it is in its special ecological niche. Its conditional features are those dimensions of its own special environmental setting that both contribute to and limit its coming to be. These conditional features provide a level of complexity to the being's achieved harmonic intensity. Its essential features are the unique ways in which it expresses its own identity in the midst of the welter of its environmental conditions. These contribute a level of simplicity to its achieved harmonic intensity. Thus, every environmental being is a contrast that holds together in a novel unity the oneness of its own being and the manyness of its environmental reality. The resultant achievement is its value.

Call each such achieved value "an environmental integrity." Then from this perspective, all actual things in the world can be seen as contrasts that emerge out of the relation established between a thing's identity and the differences in its relevant environment. Furthermore, each such value expresses a threefold perpective throughout its environmental region. It is a value for itself, a value for others in the environment and a value for the environment taken as a whole.

To recall the four basic ideas sketched in the preface: Expression, importance, perspective, and understanding and their mutual interrelations are the ultimate ideas binding together any adequate environmental cosmology. Therefore, in summary:

1. To be environmentally is to be an expression of value.
2. The importance of such a value is registered through its own harmonic experience as well as its environmental contributions.
3. Each environmental being is a perspective balancing simplicity and complexity of environmental presence.
4. Understanding such values requires a reference to their essential and conditional features.

Fundamental Unity

The third part of the environmental hypothesis states that a fundamental unity exists within all environmental regions. This unity is caused by the fact that relations within environmental domains are internal. They involve the real internal constitution of the entities concerned. Even though what is conditional for one entity can be essential for another, each entity is really and actually related to its environment. In fact, its obligation to fuse its being into one, final, determinate expression of value is carried out precisely by reason of its seizure of its environmental conditions. Each such grasping into a unity involves the internalization of environmental influences such that a unity funded through the mutual actions of environmental beings comes steadily into play.

Therefore, the unity of an environment is not an artificial one, consisting only of empty spatial and temporal relations. Rather it is fundamental in the sense that the bonds holding environmental beings together are fully part of their reality. Now, within particular environmental domains, unity can be tight or loose, narrow or broad. The unity is never the same in the sense of an abstract homogenized or "empty" container. Nor is the Aristotelian distinction between substantial and accidental form of any help. Rather, unity here means the way in which each entity actually uses the environment to form a unique, indissoluble presence. In their turn these integral fusions establish the bonds—weak or strong—that hold environments together.

This is not a theory that totalizes environments into types of unchanging geographies. The unity that is fundamental to an environment is a constantly shifting process that moves now this way, now that, in concert with the vagaries of its members. Thus it is better to understand an environment, in Whitehead's phrase, as a "Unison of Becoming," for it emphasizes the essential flexibility of environmental unity. A unison is a process and not a state of being. Accordingly, fundamental unity points toward the real presence of internal relations in the coming to be and fading away of environmental beings. Values shift and change as the internal relations between entities increase or decrease, simplify or become more complex.

The logically vague unity of an environment is specified by the actual values attained in the specific environments in question. Within its shifting borders, any environment plays host to and witnesses the ceaseless arrival and departure of competing, conflicting, and contrasting modalities of value. It is this quality of fundamental unity that makes ecology so close a relative to speculative cosmology. The environmental hypothesis provides a vague but real sketch of the important traits of environments which specific ecological domains then express in achieved values.

Creativity

The last part of the environmental hypothesis is in some ways the most important to remember and the most easy to forget. It says that all environments are governed by an ultimate category: Creativity. Now creativity does not here signify genius or artistic talent or any of the other "aesthetic" terms we customarily associate with it. Its real meaning involves the notion of newness, freshness, and originality. Creativity means that everything that comes to be is a unique, never-to-be-repeated instance of value. Creativity, therefore, signifies novelty. In Whitehead's famous phrase, it is "how the many become one and are increased by one."[16]

The one is the unique value formed out of the environmental many. This perspectival expression of importance holds together the environmental universe that marks the boundaries of its birth. It will never be present in exactly the same way again. It is a first and a last, an alpha and an omega. It is the real presence of creativity in the universe. It is what Heraclitus meant by "*panta rei,*" the endless flux of things. It is the source of the never-ending freshness of the world. It is the origin of its own being in that it creates itself out of the materials of its surroundings. It transcends its environment and therefore contributes a new expression to that same environment. It is immanent in its environment and therefore lets its own importance sink back into that same environment.

It is the most important dimension to remember about this environmental cosmology. For it announces the meaning of the universe: The creative advance into novelty. It is at the same time the easiest dimension to forget. For this creativity works silently and secretly. It is around us and within us. It does not necessarily show itself in big surprises. It is the astounding fact that the world is never the same once. It is the obvious fact that we cannot stop the world. It is a direct affront to our love of control. It is a reminder that we live in a universe larger than our own interests. It is a sign that we, too, shall pass. It cancels all notions of a perfection beyond all perfections. It gives the lie to all our dreams of progress even as it makes necessary the realization of at least some of those very same dreams.

It is what the Chinese call *Tao.* It is the source of the endless novelty that marks our natural and urban regions. It is the freshness of the flower in the morning and the spontaneity of children at an urban playground. In the words of Lao-Tzu: "Nameless, it is the source of the thousands of things" and "(named it is the 'Mother' of the thousands of things)."[17] As both nameless and named, creativity marks the beginning and the end of this study. For it invites us to explore the many names of *Tao* and at the very same time cautions us to respect its silent workings in city and nature. Such a vision of eagerness and restraint informs the environmental hypothesis which has now been articulated.

Building a Scheme of Environmental Categories

The complexity of the environmental hypothesis demands that its use be made workable through an adequate environmental categoreal scheme. In building such a scheme we must ask the question,

Environmental Categories	
Inscape	
Contrast	
Pattern	
Transmission:	Physical Conceptual Propositional Stillness

Figure 1.

what are the most vague but important characteristics of environments? The scheme should also point up the general traits of environments and show how these dimensions interrelate with each other across many different regions of experience and value (See figure 1). The scheme should exemplify precisely those qualities of coherence, necessity, and adequate applicability sketched earlier.

I suggest that there are four fundamental environmental categories: Inscape, Contrast, Pattern, and Transmission. Each category in its own way exhibits an important and irreducible dimension of environmental processes. Further, each category can only be fully understood when put into relation with the others. The extreme abstractness of the categories will diminish as their actual usefulness for environmental understanding becomes more and more apparent.

Category One: Inscape

This category states that the essential being of each and every environmental event or process is absolutely unique in its concreteness.

Its particularity springs from the way in which it houses its environmental universe. No two beings are exactly the same. This category expresses a radical environmental pluralism. It raises the individuality of beings to a preeminence that must be respected. The term itself is derived from the poetics of Gerard Manley Hopkins, himself a radical pluralist when it came to expressing the diversity of value inherent in nature.[18]

Further, this category of inscape makes clear the fact that value is the best term for the reality achieved by environmental events in their respective processes of coming to be. Inscape describes the special way in which beings carve their existence out of the background conditions provided by special environments. In terms of our earlier discussions, inscape is the impression made by environmental beings as they express their particular perspectives of importance.

In sum, inscape names that special way in which value emerges out of the welter of experience whenever a real concrete being comes into existence. It could be a mountain lion or a protozoa, a skyscraper or a bridge. Every concrete being sculpts out for itself a place in the universe wherein its own unique and irreplacable value is expressed. Inscape is the category used to describe the many ways in which this radical plurality of environmental values comes into being.

Category Two: Contrast

This category follows from the first. In its achievement of inscape each concrete being is compelled to take account of all the features of its environment. It does so by positively incorporating dimensions of its environment into its own inscape. But it cannot take on all the characteristics of its environment, for then it would not be itself but simply the environment as a whole. Therefore, it must be selective in what it allows in and what it rejects. It also must negate certain environmental dimensions in order to secure its special individual presence.

This obligation to take account of the environment in positive and negative ways lays a heavy burden on the creative potential of environmental beings. Obviously, one way to secure existence would be to reject in a massively uniform way the vast majority of environmental influences. Densely packed material objects like stones and planets tend to express their inscape in this manner (though on a microscopic level, they are maelstorms of activity). The other extreme would be to let in an almost limitless set of environmental influences. The ephemera of existence are characterized by such a shifting and uncertain character. Fogs lift and mental events come and go with surprising swiftness.

The category of contrast is the special way in which concrete beings expand their environmental limits and thereby make possible greater and greater degrees of reality. Contrast has a very special meaning. It does not mean to compare. It also does not mean to highlight one thing at the expense of another. Rather to contrast means: *To put into a unity with.* A contrast holds together parts of the environment that would more normally fly apart.

Perhaps the greatest example of a contrast is the unity maintained between the mental and physical sides of human beings. Normally, we expect them to pull apart. Where there is matter, there is no mind. Where there is mind, matter takes a back seat. In fact, entire philosophies and philosophical careers have been given over to explicating the incompatibility of these rival dimensions of being. Contrast is the way in which all such dualisms are naturally overcome.

Most environmental beings display some measure of contrast in their creative activities. But it is at the human level that contrast takes on a stable and enduring presence. Human civilization is itself one vast panorama of contrasts. As we study natural and urban environmental configurations, we shall see just how concretely contrast comes to play a crucial role in enlarging the borders of experience.

In organizing this environmental cosmology, great stress has been laid on the radical creativity inherent in its depths. The category of contrast allows us to see more specifically just how the environment organizes itself to procure greater and greater levels of creative activity. In speculating about the ultimate creative character of the universe, we came to the conclusion that it exhibited a never-ending plunge into novelty.

To account for this creativity, we must assume that there are two radically different dimensions in reality. We shall call one "Actuality" and the other "Possibility." The actual is the realm of the creative. It is what concretely takes place as creative environments evolve, take shape and pass away. On the other hand, the possible is what can be, what might be, what could be. Taken together, these phrases denote the essential reality of the possible. It is a realm that awaits actual concrete instantiation. It exists as a continuum having degrees of possibility ranging from the very likely to the almost impossible. In this sense possibility is the mirror opposite of actuality. For actuality always comes in individual packages whose determinate reality is incurably atomic. The actual dimension is limited to the inscape achieved by its members. To be a "this" is always at the same time not to be a "that."

The relation between the actual and the possible is at the heart of this environmental cosmology. Without the possible, there could be no novelty. Without the actual there could be no effective creativity. The two concepts require each other. The category of contrast involves the myriad ways in which the actual and the possible are brought together into specific environmental unities. Every mode of of contrast involves the establishment of some level of nexus between the actual and the possible. In addition, contrast plays a special role in the structural functioning of modes of consciousness, both animal and human. Finally, the felt experience of contrast is the foundation of all modes of ethical judgment including that of assessing environmental value. As a category, therefore, contrast is critical for the development of this environmental cosmology.

Category Three: Pattern

Environmental beings are not only solitary creatures. Rather they interlock with each other and often transmute themselves by reason of the patterned interactions they form with others in their neighborhood of being. Thus, emergent patterns can come into being that are far more powerful than the individual members that make them up. For example, nation states and biotic communities are examples of how patterns can serve to enlarge and radically alter the functioning of specific environmental realms.

The category of pattern is especially important for this cosmology since it designates those transformations in scale that occur in the environmentally significant region we have called the mesocosm—that midrange of activity within which city and nature work out their respective destinies. The category of pattern alerts us to look for those changes in perception, causal influence, and symbolic weight that occur when shifts to different levels of environmental interaction occur.

In particular, a pattern is a unique type of order. Its defining feature concerns the way in which it uses scale and proportion to achieve its end. Thus, a pattern always designates the way in which an order is brought to appropriate scale such that it weaves its members and environment together in a special way. Patterns are noticed by human beings because they evoke significant perceptual responses and emotional reactions. When pattern is used in this cosmology, it means precisely that form of order that evokes significant reaction.

Patterns grab attention and thereby demand that a certain level of respect be accorded them. For the most part, this power to gain respectful attention is the product of emphasizing the aesthetic order over the logical order. As we have discussed, there are many different kinds of order possible but among them two types stand out with a peculiar force.[19] The first type of pattern is "logical" pattern. This way of arranging the world dominates our reasoning powers and through it we seek to structure the world according to orders of importance. Logical order tends to push individuality and particularity into the background. It often neglects the first category of inscape. This is the reason why this environmental cosmology seeks to emphasize the second type of patterning—that which is based on the aesthetic pull of entities. By that I mean their power to call attention to themselves by reason of the strong patterns that make up their way of occupying a particular environmental niche.

The aesthetic order allows unique individuality to occupy a prominent foreground place in the gestalt of environmental processes. It structures its order so as to gain an openness for difference and uniqueness. It prefers the jagged edge of creativity to the smooth face of logical order. Most interesting urban and natural patterns feature this form of ordering through aesthetic sensibility. This notion of gaining attention and being respected introduces the final category of the environmental scheme. I term it transmission. It deals directly with the subject matter of aesthetic types of ordering—the content and impact of feelings.

Category Four: Transmission

The building of this categoreal scheme has now brought us to the point where we can name the fundamental and dynamic character of every environment whatsoever. It is our hypothesis that an environment is best understood as a region of feelings. These feelings come in various forms, shapes, and structures. Later on, the application of this categoreal scheme will show how these various structures and systems of feelings create different regions of environmental value.

For now, it is important that we discuss four fundamental types of feeling and how they transmit their influence along the lines of environmental regions. Given the process structure of every environment, all feelings reveal four fundamental spatiotemporal moods:

(i) Physical Feelings. These are feelings dominated by the past. These will be termed "physical feelings," because they represent the reenactment of the past in the present. Spatially, these feelings display a heaviness and density that mark the constraints of the past upon the present.

(ii) Conceptual Feelings. These are feelings dominated by the future. These will be termed "conceptual feelings," for they represent the presence of possibility as felt in the present. They stress the real immanence of the future in the present. They are therefore chiefly the outcome of thinking about one's environmental being and place. Spatially, these feelings have a certain glassy tone that marks the nearness of the future to the present.

(iii) Propositional Feelings. These are feelings that are a contrast of physical and conceptual feelings. These will be called "propositional feelings," because they can lure environmental beings into future choices. In spatiotemporal terms these feelings provide a sense of intriguing possibility such that real chances for novel experience begin to loom large as relevant and important possibilities.

(iv) Feelings of Stillness. These feelings are present when a certain fullness of achieved value is prolonged so that its duration can be felt. They are most especially the gift of environmental wholeness. These will be called feelings of "stillness." Spatially and temporally, these feelings transmit themselves as a sense of ambient surrounding such that an all-at-once tone attaches itself to their locus of engagement. The relationship between stillness and the experience of certain ideal environmental values is a matter of importance throughout this study.

The category of transmission marks out the ways in which changes come about in environmental regions. Physical feelings establish solid, dense material presences that maintain their felt presence in a massive and energetic manner throughout an environment. The looming presence of a mountain is an obvious example. When dominant, conceptual feelings provoke a mood of expectancy. The cheetah's chase of a gazelle displays in dramatic form the fluid presence of the future as it slips into an ever-narrowing present. The future rushes into the space of the present with an overwhelming force. Propositional feelings take over environments whenever plans are set afoot by reason of need, attraction, or desire. And so the herd sets out on the long trek toward better grazing lands. Lures for feeling hang over the spatiotemporal environment. Stillness pervades an environment when the fullness of a moment is sufficent for the coming to be of creatures. Animal satisfaction and human meditational repose exemplify this rare but fundamental mode of environmental feeling. A sense of circumambient spatiotemporal presence fills in the environmental field.

What is important to note in this final category of transmission is the shift away from an extreme materialist sketch of physical causation. In place of matter-in-motion we emphasize the felt reenactment of the past. Instead of reserving the mental solely to the human realm, we extend it (with appropriate reservations) across any number of environmental regions and let it signify the felt presence of the future as an effective force in environmental systems. Deliberation, choice, and the pressure of felt possible values are also given their niche in the environmental setting. Nature proposes many courses of action to its creatures. Finally, the feeling of fullness and satisfaction is not forgotten. For all creatures deserve their feelings of worth.

A Process Ever in Formation

This chapter has tried to set out in systematic fashion an elementary environmental cosmology. A speculative matrix, an environmental hypothesis, and a basic scheme of environmental categories have been put forth. Basically, I have been trying to bring together two opposed philosophical positions. I agree with Heraclitus that "all things are in flux." But I also agree with the philosophic tradition that says, when carefully examined this world of flux yields up a picture that makes some kind of sense. On the one hand, the world is ever changing. It is never the same once, let alone twice. On the other hand, there are enduring structures, categories, and forms of being pervading the environmental flux. It is not appropriate to respond to the ineluctable presence of change with irrational despair or a pose of benevolent intellectual indifference toward "A World Well Lost."[20] On the contrary, a process ever in formation invites us to weigh, appreciate, number, and remember its merits. That is the whole purpose of this axiological environmental cosmology.

My aim in this work is to enable us to prize environments—be they natural or human. To do so, one must know how they work, what makes them up, and what they do. This first chapter has taken several important steps toward providing an answer to these questions. In terms of how things work, I set forth the doctrine that the environment is a set of events that interlock, overlap, and transmit influences across a broad range of activites. A sophisticated theory of event metaphysics is therefore indispensable for environmental understanding. As regards the makeup of environmental regions, I offered the hypothesis that environmental beings are spatiotemporal events whose fundamental structure is that of a harmony of essential and conditional features. What these harmonies do is to achieve value in the sense of expressing their own unique perspective within the constraints of environmental obligations. Finally, I introduced the concept of feeling as the primary level of environmental structure and function. Events feel each other and thereby establish modes of intensity that span environmental regions granting them their special value and significance.

In particular, this cosmology has derived four fundamental categories that describe the essential traits characterizing environmental activities. The categories of inscape, contrast, pattern, and transmission mark out the vague but important ways in which environmental events carry out their functions. These categories also suggest the feeling tones infecting environmental regions dominated by one or all of these ways of environmental being. Each category asserts a modality of creativity—the ultimate character qualifying all environmental activities. Through this metaphysics of the actual and the possible we are able to gain a speculative grasp of the important traits that underlie the maelstrom of events making up environmental regions.

This cosmology offers a picture of natural and human environments as sharing a common mode of activity: Every environment is always a process ever in formation. So far, we have concentrated on the question of environmental activities. Another dimension now requires attention: The structures of environmental activity. When events harmonize environmentally, they put forth patterns that come to stabilize environments at certain levels and in particular directions. These tend to assume the role of markers or environmental anchors around which the events in a region tend to cluster. These structures provide the general character of environmental regions and are all-important for a correct understanding of the relation between broadly different environmental regions. We now move to an examination of these axiological formations.

Chapter Two

The Structures of Environmental Passage

When environments stabilize, they exhibit throughout their passage the presence of mesocosmic structures. These structures are the outcome of the category of pattern. It is the aim of this chapter to examine the genesis and meaning of these environmental stabilities. In particular, this chapter argues that the process whereby these structures come to be is the same as the achievement of value itself. There is an identity between what and how a thing is and the value that it expresses. The theme of this chapter is therefore the relation between structure, pattern, quality, and character.

My argument begins with an analysis of the concept of structure and then proceeds to the issue of normative measure. A renewed discussion of Plato's doctrine of participation fills out the relation between structure and value. The chapter concludes with a formal theory of the components of structural value and an examination of the value structures that tend to dominate natural and human environments.

Structure and Value

Structures are not idly-thrown-together heaps of matter. Rather, each structure is what it is because it patterns an ideal or series of ideals. When effectively realized, this actualized ideal is the defining quality of that structure. In terms of our categoreal scheme, structures are the ways in which patterns come into existence and exert widespread influences throughout environmental regions.

At first glance, it may seem silly or even bizarre to speak of structures as having ideals or realizing values. But that is the result of a certain cultural blindness inherited from an uncritical acceptance of positivism's fact/value dichotomy. Curing this blindness requires a recovery of the concepts of identity and truth. What makes something this rather than that? What is its identity? What is it to know the truth of something? Aristotle sees a direct relation between what a thing is (its reality) and how we are to speak of it (its truth).[1] We are not free to say whatever we wish when truth is at stake. Why is this so? The reason lies in the essential relation between a thing's being (or reality) and its truth. Something is what it is and is therefore no other. We call this its identity. To speak the truth of something is to express its identity. To say what is true is therefore to say what is real.

In discussing patterns and structures we seek to speak the truth about them. We now must ask about the identity of structures. What makes a structure the way it is? What is its truth? A structure brings together many different dimensions of the environment. It takes what is other to itself and brings it into its own being. It is a mixture. There is therefore an aim guiding the emergence of structural realities. This purpose leads it to bring the world together in just this certain way and no other.

More formally expressed, a structure fits the world together in its particular way through the influence of the ideal that it seeks to measure up to. It achieves its identity through the standard employed to measure out the appropriate relations that make up its identity. What is fit together is made fitting through the appropriation of a norm that rightly guides the patterning of the many into a good one. The relation between goodness and identity is a proportionate one. To the degree that a pattern expresses a good way to be, to that same degree it is more itself.

What this theory underscores is the way in which the identity of environmental beings is tied to the ideals they uphold. The reality of any entity is established by means of a structure that expresses patterns of fitness appropriate to specific environmental domains. The identity so attained expresses its special perspective of importance within the welter of environmental experience. When an environmental structure emerges and endures, it exhibits an essential integrity. This integrity is its identity because it has achieved its reality precisely by means of its effort to make actual what was once only possible.

The importance of speaking true things about environmental happenings becomes evident. To speak falsely about events making up environmental domains is to commit two faults at the same time. First, an unreal report of what is occurring is given out in place of what is really happening. Second, this distortion also masks the real achievements of value taking place in the environment. Both the worth of environmental reality and its truth depend upon recognizing the ideals upheld in those regions. Thus, the character exhibited by environmental structures becomes crucial in determining their truth and their worth. No assessment of environmental value can occur without the active presence of acute discernment. In practical terms this comes down to having the capacity for an aesthetic feel for the contours, patterns, and characters exhibited throughout the inscapes of environments.

As this discussion proceeds, an ever-closer connection between cosmology, ethics, and aesthetics becomes apparent. To speak of an ideal that fits together many different dimensions of an environment into an integrated whole is to assert the primacy of harmony as a condition for being real. The speculative scheme of categories sought to express this aesthetic dimension by stressing inscape, contrast, and patterns as the major modalities of environmental activity. Similarly, this cosmology asserts the strict relation between the identity of an environmental event and its goodness.

To speak of what a thing is, is always at the same time to express its respective value. What fits is a good way to be. But there are many degrees of goodness. And there are many forms of harmony. What is good in one environment can be decidedly destructive in another. Harmonies can displace achieved values as readily as they can enhance them. I am, therefore, not advocating a Leibnizian cosmos of advancing perfection. Neither does this cosmology accept as metaphysically ultimate the radical distinction between truths of fact and truths of value so beloved by contemporary scientific materialism. This entire effort has been directed toward finding a nuanced way of speaking about the subtle ways in which facts melt into environmental values and values becomes factical environmental presences. It takes only the slightest shift in perspective to turn a so-called material fact into a qualitative character that shifts the values of an entire environmental landscape. Just ask the residents of a neighborhood suffering the shock of urban renewal.[2] It is obvious that there are important measures at work within environmental regions. What is required is an art dedicated to the discovery and articulation of those measures.

Normative Measure

It is best to begin this discussion with a concrete example. Consider the important human act of purchasing a house. What do people do when they set out to buy a house? They select a set of measures which will enable them to identify the best possible house to purchase. Such measures include location, style, age, durability, efficiency in heating and cooling, proximity to schools, markets, and churches, price, resale value, and so forth. In using these measures, the prospective buyers would be identifying the house they really wanted to buy. Crucial to the entire process would be the degree to which the house in question measured up to these standards. Truth, reality, and value are aspects entwined in the process of identifying a fitting house.

Now, of course, one could be seriously mistaken in the selection of normative measures. Also, one could be quite correct in adopting certain standards and fail to locate a house that appropriately embodied them. Or as is more usually the case, one could find out that normative measures tend to contradict or even cancel each other. One normally could not have a large house and a low price at the same time. Indeed, the entire process of househunting is one long exercise in the choice, consideration, and application of appropriate normative measures. The point of the example is to make clear how ordinary and practical the concept of normative measure really is. It is not an abstruse philosophical doctrine that only a select few can understand. Rather, it is part and parcel of how we go about negotiating our worlds.

It took the special genius of Plato to raise the discussion of normative measure to a high art form. In such dialogues as *The Sophist* and *The Statesman,* he explored the many dimensions of the science of normative description. What is of concern for this work is the extraordinary way in which he anticipated the main lines of the argument now required to validate the emerging discourse of the disciplines of ecology, environmental ethics, and environmental philosophy in general. What they need is some way to sail between the two types of discourse that now dominate our culture. This is precisely the advantage held out by the theory of normative measure.

Call one type of discourse "objective" and the other "subjective." Public discourse is now dominated by objective thinking. Its essential marks are reliance upon the observable, the measurable, and the quantifiably reliable. It seeks quantitative expression and is satisfied when its results can be set forth in terms resonant with numerical calculation. Phrases such as "60 percent of all fish were shown to..." or "the correlation between median income and voter choice..." are representative types. Its prose is flat but confident; its tone serene and unquestionable. Most revealing is the fact that its conclusions are presented in the declarative mood so that the reader is given little choice in terms of reaction. A neutral display of fact-based information is presented: Reaction is neither desired nor expected. This is the world according to scientific materialism.

Subjective thinking, on the other hand, is value-laden and often employs the subjunctive mood as it seeks to engage the reader's attention. Its distinguishing features include hortatory appeals, emotional discourse, hyperbolic rhetoric, and sometimes rather shameless attempts to cajole, trap, and seduce the reader into agreement. Phrases such as "would that..." or "none but an insensitive..." signal its presence. The aim of this kind of thinking is the establishment of links of agreement that lead to an unqualified acquiescence in the general movement of thought being presented. It sees the human person as the agent of truth.

The theory of normative measure weaves its way between these established cultural ways of seeking the truth. It seeks a wider theoretical vision that allows for a middle region that can accomodate the basic insights of both sides. It does so by tying its theory of knowing to a systematic metaphysics. I have already sketched the main lines of such a theory of reality. The environmental cosmology speculates that the world is constituted through entwined events that achieve their respective determinate identities by integrating environmental conditions. Each such event is an achievement of value. Therefore, to speak the truth about an environmental condition is to express the value achieved by that special set of events. These achievements of value come about by way of structuring the world in certain ways. Each of these structures measures the possibilities provided by environmental conditions and thereby achieves for itself the identity deemed feasible for that set of circumstances.

To return to the opening example, a house can express qualities of durability, efficiency, and beauty because its builder uses measures appropriate for the realization of such qualities within the limits set by its environmental situation. A house built by Frank Lloyd Wright can express one dimension of beauty while one built by Christopher Alexander can express yet another dimension. But both are still beautiful. Normative measure allows for a rich array of realizations. It is not the indifferent application of a rigid set of standards. Rather, it is the selection of appropriately proportionate measures to concrete sets of events so that qualities of beauty, endurance, and efficiency express themselves throughout a structure.

This is how normative thinking can take advantage of the vagueness associated with its metaphysical hypotheses. Again, vague here does not mean fuzzy or ambiguous. It means that the concrete realization of the norm in question awaits its actual instantiation in the set of events making up the specific environmental locale. The measure is the way in which a specific type of possibility is to be realized. The built house is the actual value made real through the environmental integration made possible by the norm selected for the construction of the house—prairie style, bauhaus, or Cape Cod. These are not just styles but relatively appropriate ways to measure out normatively the values to be realized in concretely specific environments.

What gives the doctrine of normative measure its great power as a revitalizing source for environmental thinking is the intimate way in which it connects metaphysics, value, identity, and thinking. It makes it impossible to indulge in either of the two other culturally dominant ways of thinking. The facts that are so important to objective thinking are preserved but placed in their proper context. It is necessary to understand the objective conditions that define the parameters of environmental possibility. The world is not a fantasy. And the values appropriate to subjective thinking are also preserved but kept in their right place.

Values are truly expressed in the interactions of the world. But they are actualized within the real limits set by environmental conditions. It is within the zone established by the interplay of facts and values that normative measures are to be found.

I call the kind of thinking necessary for this work "Normative Thinking." It is prior to both objective and subjective thinking. In fact, it makes possible both those kinds of thinking. How else does the term "objective" acquire meaning but through the selection and application of some kind of normative measure that identifies its presence? How would one know the subjective unless some normative measure for its presence were employed? To practice normative thinking is simply to put Plato's "Forms" to work at the level of environmental experience. To discover and apply appropriate normative measures to natural environmental events is the goal of this book.[3]

It should now be clearer why this work can be read as an an exercise in Platonic naturalism. This type of philosophy is best understood when seen at work. Indeed, the sections of this book devoted to environmental spacetime regions are concrete examples of this form of philosophic speculation. When effectively employed, the normative description of environments exhibits great strength in terms describing the qualities embodied by those same environments. Also, it loses some of its oddness as it becomes a familiar tool with which to identify types of environmental worth. It is not an inappropriate attempt to describe environmental situations in anthropormorphic terms. Still less is it lacking any objective rigor. Rather, it involves a speculative and systematic attempt to identify, express, and relate the actual values achieved by structures in their concrete environmental locations. Normative thinking does this by discovering the measures employed to achieve the values actually and really present in the environment. The powerful grace of the lion is really present and so is the massive energy bound into a boulder. Platonic naturalism says these values are there by reason of the way in which sets of events participate in them through the norms exhibited in their various structural integrities.

Three Levels of Participation

Structures differ among themselves by reason of the norms selected to achieve their respective values. In environmental terms, it is important to differentiate between three levels of participation.

Types of Environmental Participation
Physical
Living (Biological)
Cultural

Figure 2

Each level embodies a unique form of participatory activity. These levels are: The physical, the living, and the cultural (see figure 2). The distinguishing characteristics of these forms of participation are to be found in the special ways in which they configure space-time regions. As the category of transmission maintains, the experiences of space and time are central to the values achieved in concrete environmental regions.

Likewise, these levels of environmental experience integrate the metaphysically ultimate realms of the actual and the possible in distinct ways. In so doing they establish contrasts and patterns of being and becoming such that different normative measures governing the relation between the actual and the possible come into play. Taken together, the physical, the living, and the cultural form the main lines of environmental existence in the present cosmic epoch.

Application of the categoreal scheme sketched in the preceding chapter provides a deeper understanding of the special values established by each of these levels of environmental experience. These categories are: Inscape, contrast, pattern, and transmission. Each provides an insight into the ways in which structural systems express, sustain, and alter environmental values.

The Physical

The effort to dissolve the prejudices resulting from scientific materialism requires a recasting of the concept of matter. By physical, I mean those sets of events that make up the large-scale physical presences that dominate environmental regions. I mean mountains, deserts, and plains along with those elements that make up their respective patterns of becoming. The outstanding characteristic of these physical environmental beings is a certain massive averageness that culminates in an overwhelming sense of endurance. Thus, this environmental cosmology demands that we forego the usual characterization of matter as that which simply takes up space. Rather than defining the physical as that which is characterized by extension, stress is here laid on the temporal dimension of the physical.

The category of inscape explains this achievement in the following way. What happens most especially in physical beings is repetition. Their inscape is that of a sheer, almost unending repetition of the past. In fact, the very inscape of matter is that of the overwhelming presence of the past as it pushes relentlessly and endlessly into the present. It is the heavy hand of the past that constrains the rocks, boulders, and stones that make up the massiveness of stolid physical environments. Matter is that set of events that repeats the past in tightly configured reiterative patterns. It is not solely the occupation of space that is the major feature of the physical. Rather, time builds up a massive thickness through the presence of temporal cycles that reflect only the slightest variations in their rhythmic rounds. The physical is the past endlessly repeated.

The category of contrast concerns itself with the way in which the actual and possible are harmonized within environmental regions. In the realm of the physical, the harmony between the actual and the possible is decidedly one-sided in favor of the actual. The possible as the sense of what might or could be is reduced to a non-effective level. It is there, but only in a recessive and constrained manner. The past and its achievements dominates. Therefore, what change there is, is minimal and takes a long period of time to accomplish. It is this sense of the actualized past that gives weight and prominence to physical landmarks. Mountains endure, the hills remain, and the desert stretches on.

On a superficial level, it appears that the category of pattern reveals the dominance of the spatial over the temporal. This is due to the fact that the normative measures governing the structure of physical beings emphasize occupation of space. Viewed from the mesocosmic scale, physical things jam up the regions they occupy with their presence. We see them as full and also as filling up the locales that are their environmental sites. But such density is more the result of time's piling up in heaps of repetitive past patterns than it is the outcome of matter defined in terms of extension. (Chapter Four accounts for the human body's perceptual tendency to notice spatial display rather than the workings of time.)

Finally, the physical tends to influence environmental sites largely through constraining possibilities rather than promoting them. Phrases such as "the heavy hand of the past" and "the iron rod of physical necessity" capture this sense of an overwhelming causal presence at work in the land. The physical exhibits the category of transmission through the felt presence of a powerful regularity. This is the origin of that sense of everlastingness that human beings frequently feel as an important quality suffusing their environmental experience. It is the transmission of reassuring rhythms of being. As a source of solidity the physical can offer security and strength. It is the firm ground on which we walk. Without such an anchor, a mood of futility would invade human consciousness. The precariousness of human existence needs to be balanced by the depth residing within the massive physical presences that make up the world.

The Living

The line between the living and the dead is notoriously difficult to draw. There are even entities, like viruses, that seem to inhabit both worlds. Whitehead's characterization of life as "the clutch at vivid immediacy" provides the most helpful insight into the realm of the living.[4] By living I mean that which exists for its own sake. What distinguishes life is the fact that it remains inexplicable in terms of physical explanation. This amounts to saying that life dwells in the present. It is the sheer joy of being alive that tells us most about life. Life in this sense is always self-justifying. It is its own exuberance. Indeed, there is a dependence upon the physical and especially the security derived from the reiterative presence of the past. But life is lived in the "Now." Its most direct experience is bound to the present moment and its enjoyment. The four basic environmental categories make this evident in a variety of ways.

The category of inscape shows that, paradoxically, life is a kind of emptiness that fills itself up through interactions with its environment. This is surely what Whitehead means by calling life a form of "robbery." At its most elemental level, this emptiness shows itself in the need for food. Life is a spendthrift and in some ways a wastrel, for it gives no thought to tomorrow. It dwells entirely in the present.[5] Originality, spontaneity, novelty, and freedom name the essential character of life. Its inscape is dominated by the present for it moves through its environment as though it were an empty form ingesting all that it encounters. This sense of living openness and creativity will be met again and again as we examine environmental regions of experience.

When applied to living beings, the category of contrast shows a decided reversal of the formula for the physical. There, it was the actual that was dominant. Here, it is the possible that assumes equal importance with the actual. In fact, in living beings we witness a superb integration of the possible with the actual. A harmony exists such that the possible is felt in the present and actualized as such. This is the source of the extraordinary intensity that characterizes the world of the living. The feeling that results from the union of what is and what could be is the essential dimension of life. It speaks of the actual and the possible as dynamic partners. It marries expectation to accomplishment. The vivid and the immediate are the twin feelings that dominate life and its workings.

Life is inherently unstable. This is occasioned by the real presence of possibility within the realm of the living. It is not merely actuality that guides the living. What might be is directly felt as a real dimension of what is. As such, life tends to fluctuate and turn in any number of unexpected directions. The watchfulness observable in all living beings is a sign of this intimate bond between the possible and the actual. In life alertness is an indispensable attribute. Life is called "the quick" because of the high contrast maintained between the actual and possible. The physical is grounded in a stimulus/response network of influences. Reaction tends to dominate. The past is the major factor in environmental processes. When life arrives, originality and novelty emerge as effective environmental presences.

The category of pattern provides reasons for both the joy and the inherent insecurity experienced by living beings. The spatiotemporal pattern exemplified by living organisms exhibits a complex cosmological contrast between various modes of time and types, of spatial configuration. In spatial terms life always finds itself bound back into physical, nonliving patterns. We never find life "alone"; it is always harmonized within some type of nonliving environment. The fragility of life—that which is its chief joy—finds rest in the massive security provided by the physical. Life serves the body and the physical returns the favor by harboring life within its reassuring endurances. Life in its temporal patterns exhibits a quality of wandering in the present moment. It dwells in immediacies and finds expression in any number of body points. At one moment it is in a taste bud and at another in the sexual organs. Sometimes it is the eye that is "alive"; other times see our hands expressing life's presence in the present.

Life moves in, through, and about the physical because it "lives" in the present and at the same time requires the shelter and stability provided by the physical and its reiterative past. The great value achieved by life is the utilization of the past for the sake of enjoyment in the present. The harmony spun by life displays an astoundingly delicate balance between dependence on the past and zest in the present moment. The bid for freedom that characterizes life at its best is only made possible by the security derived from the physical. Through its insistence on the importance of past achievements, the physical saves life from its own tendency to squander its resources. Life is nature's solution to the never-ending quarrel between the past and the present.

In terms of pattern, life is much more like a poet than a mechanic. It moves about the body seeking both intensity and security. It turns itself now this way and now that as it establishes "vital zones" within which to enjoy its being. The balance achieved by life represents an extraordinary union of the spatial and the temporal. Both openness and density are reflected in life's pattern.[6] The diaphanous spatiotemporal patterns characteristic of some forms of life make possible exceptional depth of experience. Surfaces that are open to life need not only harbor the superficial. When deepening layers of the physical are involved, life can and often does register immense experiential depths.[7]

The art of life lies in its power to bring together stability and excitement. When fully "alive," the category of transmission asserts itself through the active presence of originality and spontaneity within environmental systems. Life transforms its environment to suit its needs. Life adapts in order to have more life. Thus, change and flexibility are the hallmarks of life. The dead stiffen. The living change. What cannot bend will be broken. What can alter its stance has the best chance of success. With the emergence of the real presence of possibility, living environments exhibit adventure, zest, movement, joy, and intensity. The vague cosmological concept of "possibility" takes on concrete specificity when it is understood as the effective presence of life in select environmental regions.

When life achieves a consistent and steady level of influence, a sense of expectancy and excitement is transmitted throughout the environment. A sense of the presence of the possible becomes palpable. The present moment becomes charged with a sudden intensity. This is the essential meaning of life: The felt experience of intensity in the present. Just how this sense of life is expressed within specific environments is the concern of a later chapter. For now it is important to note the vague but cosmologically important meaning attributed to life: The possible is felt as really present within the actual. Life is lived when the possible is actualized in the spatiotemporal present. It is this presence of the present that is caught in the expression "the gift of life." The mystery of life resides in the fact that it is not bound to the past. Neither is it explicable solely in terms of physical inheritance. Somehow the contrast between the possible and the actual is held in a rhythmic balance such that intensity of experience and its self-enjoyment emerge as a driving environmental force.

But life is anarchic and contains the seeds of its self-destruction. Something more is required for the stabilization of life than its canalization within the physical realm. Participation has to reach a more attentive level, one associated with plans and the conscious pursuit of normative measures. We call this level, culture.

The Cultural

The inscape of the cultural is far more complex than the other two levels of normative participation. This complexity is largely due to the active and forceful presence of the imagined future in cultural dealings. When we speak of the cultural, we are generally speaking of the ways in which human beings sort through their sense of what is important and select appropriate perspectives aimed at gaining its realization. The first step in the process of sorting is by means of active imagination. Through cultural imagery we form worlds of value whose significance is to establish a primary mode of entry into environmental experience. Thus a nomadic culture sees the plains as the home of a roving food supply; another sees it as an opportunity to farm. When culture rises to effective prominence, then images are used to excite plans. Simple enjoyment is replaced by depths of experience that call forth new environmental dimensions.

Culture's inscape is imaginative because humans need some set of primary images with which to organize their worlds. Cultural participation means for the most part living through those images and testing their worth in the light of experience. Life turns in the direction of aims, measures, and goals. Its spontaneity gives way to self-conscious deliberation and planning. Choice becomes an active presence replacing impulse as the dominant environmental agency. Images organize experience so that a world of meaning emerges from the physical and living levels of the environment. By selecting out certain values these images provide perspectives on what is important and at the same time yield up degrees of understanding that are unavailable on the other two levels. In place of the massive presence of the past, the future comes into the foreground as a region of primary concern. Likewise, life's absorption in the present moment gives way to thoughts about life's meaning and its ultimate value. In this way the contours of a human world loom into view. We are now on the threshold of civilization and its triumphs and failures.

The cultural images that structure human interactions with the environment are not empty, vain imaginings. They are very important interpretive schemata. It is through their lenses that we view the world. Much of this study will be given over to a recasting of these images especially as they effect how we view the spatial and temporal dimensions of our environments. In fact, my chapter on "Foundational Ecology" concerns precisely such a cultural task. Such images represent the first cut whereby we organize our sense of environmental values. When they are mistaken, great and sometimes irreparable harm results. When they are true to the values being experienced, surprising depth and nuance can arise within our environmental perceptions. In sum, the cultural level of participation constitutes the way in which we learn to read our environment and assess its significance and value. Its inscape is a complex harmony of the future as we imagine it to be.

The contrast between the actual and the possible that emerges at the cultural level exhibits a decided stress on the future as mediated through the symbols and signs adopted by the culture. Unlike the physical, the cultural responds to the future in an active way. It anticipates and even in some ways creates the future. Projections and plans rise to the forefront and become wrapped in symbolic cultural structures. It is not just the building that is erected. It is, rather, "our city hall," symbol of our community's life and ideals. Cultures hold the environmental world together in such a way as to make available its possibilities. The future is always on the doorstep of the present. What makes the future so open a possibility are the images used to describe it. These images fill in the future's emptiness and become actual lures spurring on further environmental interaction. The human cultural level changes the world so that life and its exuberant enjoyments take on more and more determinate identities. Great satisfaction and great disappointment now can be experienced. The vague cosmological contrast between the actual and the possible now becomes specified through desire and its human companion, conscious effort. By the time the contrast between the actual and the possible is felt on the cultural level, we are already for the most part equipped with the means and ends to work out the specifics of our desires. Without cultural participation we would probably be deprived of the ability to experience anything.

If such is the importance of cultural participation, how does its pattern make its presence felt within spatiotemporal experience? On the cultural level, space and time are almost utterly transformed. Rather than being dense, impacted physical fields or modes of transmission felt almost entirely in the living present, they become regions of experience rooted in meaning.[8] As such they take on a decidedly semiotic character. Within cultural domains it is the sign character of space and time that matters most. Interpretation comes to the forefront as an important cultural activity because the transformation of space and time is so utterly radical.

What happens on a cosmological plane is that space becomes laden with propositional lures that beckon deep interpretive participation. And time takes on a qualitative density due to the layering of past, present, and future within dense, ever-thickening regions. Both the city and nature are transformed into environmental organisms charged with symbolic resonance. The images of natural and urban life directly shape physical and living modes of participation. In fact, in human civilization cultural images become inseparable from physical and biological being. Our symbolic sense of the natural and the urban often overtakes in importance the two other modes of environmental participation. City and nature live in our head and our physical experience is transmuted by their symbolic resonance in our body.

More specifically, space is experienced as a set of lures for feelings. Due to the images of future reality embedded in the inscape and contrasts of the cultural realm, a distinct transparency invades spatial experience. Buildings and landscapes are no longer material entities. Neither are they simply objects for use. Rather, the experience of "place" is born. Entire regions of the physical and the living are transformed into spaces where meaning can and does emerge. The opening of space through cultural participation is a great paradox. For even as a certain emptiness emerges within spatial experience, it is just as quickly filled with meaning.

Time is similarly transformed. In cultural participation, the norms governing temporal experience are so loosened that the past, the present, and the future flow together in densely impacted strands of experience. Sometimes it is the past that dominates, as in the cultural recognition of ancient forests or historic urban regions. Other times it is the present that appears to assert itself, as in the business that circulates within the markets and commercial districts of city life. Likewise, a looming storm drives home the importance of seeking refuge in the present in natural settings. Finally, time as the future continually asserts itself in the building activity that is the very hallmark of urban reality. In actual fact, the past, the present, and the future converge in the cultural experience of cities. But that does not put it strongly enough. Urban experience is marked by temporal collision. What this means for a true appreciation of its achievements of value is the subject of a later study. Suffice it to say that spatiotemporal experience on the cultural level is one of the supreme achievements of the human race.

Cultural participation demands that the category of transmission move radically in the direction of semiotic and purposive activity.

This is because the human animal feels its world as charged with emotional significance. The values inherent in environmental experience transmit themselves as more than the physical weight of the past constraining present experience. Neither is the present overwhelmingly felt as the sphere where life is lived in the present moment. Rather, the reality of cultural participation is more often than not felt on the level of symbolic activity. The values transmitted on the cultural level are carried on networks of meaning.

These interpretive sets are initially created through imaginative activity. Thus, cultural participation is transmitted through the complex relationship connecting the imaginative and the interpretive. This is the reason truth becomes so central an issue in cultural experience. Truth is felt with a directness and immediacy in natural regions. It has a blunt and direct quality to it. The physical transmits itself with undeniable energy and force. The living is always a matter of life and death. But the cultural is another matter entirely. Here, we encounter the twists and turns characteristic of creativity become conscious of itself and its powers. When the city in its full symbolic transmissions emerges as a cultural reality demanding participation, then all the human powers of interpretations are called into play. This is a central reason why James Joyce set *Ulysses* in Dublin.[9] The values experienced on the plane of the physical and the living are emotionally transformed in urban environments. The city is the space and time where the symbol comes fully into play as a semiotic force.

This concludes the analysis of the three levels of participation that dominate the environmental mesocosm. It was for the purpose of analysis that they were abstracted from each other. In the concrete world they are never found separated from each other. The living demands a physical base and is itself a form of the cultural. What is encountered in environmental experience are regions dominated by levels layered with these forms of participation. It is for this reason that I spoke earlier of a need for a science of normative description capable of discerning the various ways in which values are expressions of varying environmental structures. It is only through the cultivation of such an aesthetic sensibility that the real achievements of the structures of environmental passage can gain adequate recognition.

Measuring the Environment

In concluding this chapter on the basic structures to be found in environmental regions, it is helpful to look once again at Plato's insight into the importance of participation. In the *Philebus,* Plato distinguishes between four different elements that make up reality.[10] There is, he maintains, the unlimited, the limited, the mixture resulting from the interaction of the unlimited and the limited, and the cause of that mixture. In terms of the four basic ideas guiding this study, we can say that the unlimited is the equivalent of the sphere of importance—that region of possible value always coming into play whenever we speak of environments and their achievements. Similarly, the limited is the functional equivalent of the concept of expression, for it is through the interplay between identity and normative measure that modes of determinate expression suffuse themselves throughout the environment. The mixture of the unlimited and the limited is the result of the presence of effective perspectives that create the values dominating particular dimensions of the mesocosm. Finally, through identifying the measure used to mix these four elements, a true understanding of the environment comes into being.

Importance is to the unlimited as expression is to the limited. Perspective is to the mixture as understanding is to the cause of the mixture. In bringing together these ideas, the radical consequences of this environmental philosophy come into sharp relief. There is no longer any place on the planet where human beings can escape their environmental responsibility. The reason for this claim lies in the essential connection between knowing and ruling. In Plato's philosophy, to know something is to know what is good about it. Responsibility for caring for that achieved good goes hand in hand with such knowledge. Just as previously the gap between the aesthetic and the ethical narrowed, so also in this particular instance what separates the ethical and the epistemological disappears.

In this environmental cosmology, value and existence are now synonymous. The sheer falseness of the separation between fact and value becomes more and more evident. When speaking of environmental reality, it is philosophically irresponsible to think of these two realms as ontologically different. Environmental cosmology makes manifest the vicious abstractions at work in all such ways of thinking and talking. Such distinctions derive from inadequate assumptions about what is really going on in environmental domains. To the extent that our culture remains wedded to these abstractions, to that same extent the ability to say true things about our environmental being is fundamentally weakened.

To know an environment is therefore to be able to appreciate its achievements. The primary way in which an environment expresses its being is through the feelings it generates in its inhabitants. In turn, these feelings are the result of the various types of order dominating the environment in question. All forms of environmental goodness are dependent upon endurance. Without the temporal and spatial spread provided by modes of order no sense of lasting importance could ever emerge from the ever-changing passage that marks environmental reality. The mesocosm is marked by enduring structures that rise up and cast forth important environmental perspectives that eventually come to express the values characterizing particular ecological domains. Thus we can speak in a true fashion about mountainous deserts, for we are identifying what is and what is not important within a specific environmental area. To tell the truth about an environment is to identify the values expressed within its perspective. In this way, the unity between the good and the true is preserved as the central feature of environmental philosophy.

Similarly, the real presence of the beautiful in the environment is also preserved as an actual environmental dimension. If to be is always to be a harmony, then the many modes of the beautiful are intrinsically present in all environmental regions. Once again, the sharp distinction drawn between between fact and value must surrender its philosophical preeminence. What can take its place as an important analytical tool is the concept of the environment as an aesthetic field. Once this reconstruction takes firm hold, then environmental achievements can be identified through modes of aesthetic discourse. The great advantage of such an environmental reformation lies in its power to bring to the fore the place of "feelings" in our environmental being.

If this cosmology is true to the workings of the environment, then what is at play in such a region are ways of fitting the world together. Each way has its own peculiar "feel." It is toward this realm of feeling that environmental philosophy ought to devote its attention when it seeks to say true things. To view the environment as a place where feelings connect so as to create the regions of value that we experience is to move far closer to its concrete reality than any description dependent on the mechanical theories favored by scientific materialism.

To speak systematically of feelings requires measures whereby their actual presence in environmental regions can be effectively gauged. Through such an aesthetic hypothesis a conceptual scheme as well as a vocabulary well qualified for naming environmental achievements becomes available. The terms required for carrying out this project include concepts such as intensity, narrowness, vagueness, and depth. In addition, categories of simplicity and complexity must also be added to our cosmological scheme. Above all, what is needed is the development of a philosophically nuanced sense of the varieties of feelings available for experience within the regions of city and nature. Providing such intellectual resources is the task of the next chapter.

Chapter Three

A World of Feelings

Good aesthetic apprehension consists in the capacity to do certain things at the same time. First, one must sense how an entity expresses itself in its uniqueness. Then one must understand how that expression is really a perspective holding together the many things of an environment in a novel unity. In terms of our earlier discussions, the essential features of an environmental being mold its conditional features so that an expression combining both complexity and simplicity results. Thus, every environmental being is itself an order and at the same time exists within an order. The many become one within the wider one of the environmental setting.

This chapter discusses the fundamental ways in which these modes of aesthetic attainment are carried out. It begins with an analysis of the formal dynamics of environmental value. From there it discusses four levels of environmental order. These in turn establish important environmental moods or feeling tones. The chapter concludes with an analysis of certain ideal environmental values. By the end of this analysis, a good grasp of how to speak about and give an account of the environment as a world of feelings should have been made available.

The Dynamics of Environmental Value

Up to now, this study has concentrated on the formal side of environmental cosmology. Structures, composition, and categoreal analysis have been a major concern. But an environment is far more than a bare formula. It is an active and dynamic process. A major aim of this chapter is to put some flesh and blood on what up to now has been a largely skeletal analysis. When environments are at work, they achieve units of value. These achieved values are the outcome of the interplay of two dynamic forces at play in every ecological situation. One force is the drive toward simplicity which is allied with the fundamental sense of identity that makes up the reality of particular things.

The other is complexity, which recognizes the richness of being available in the workings of the environment in question. Simplicity is the achievement of the one; complexity is the reward of the many. The dynamism at work in an ecological setting is the outcome of the tension spanning these different dimensions of environmental expression. Just how these different but not opposed qualities work together is the miracle of order that is at the base of all forms of environmental beauty. If we are to understand how harmony is tensile expression and not saccharine compromise, a clear analysis of each partner to this cosmological dance must be provided.

Simplicity

To be this rather than that is to express a difference. In the final analysis all such expressions of identity come down to the adoption of a form of simplicity whereby the uniqueness of a specific perspective on the universe is established. This must be simple in the sense that no other being can occupy exactly that portion of the universe at that particular space and time. Simplicity here means the elimination of confusion. It is the assertion of a special stance in the face of the plenitude of the universe.

This is the ground of pluralism as a metaphysical position. It says that the world is simple because its many "ones" are what they are and no other. Comparisons are possible and so are estimations of the value achieved by the members of environmental niches. But this does not say that all members of the universe are the same.

Each is what it is in the way that it is. To claim otherwise is to fall into the fallacy that besets all forms of monism—the denial of the real value achieved by the members of the universe. Such denigration of the particulars of the world is a denial of the real presence of simplicity as a force in environmental workings.

Simplicity works through elimination. Its aim is to streamline options such that a single elemental presence is felt in reality. It chooses the direct over the indirect, the straightforward instead of the oblique. Its perspective focuses acutely on the sense of the essential. Authentic identity pays the price of exclusion. Simplicity prefers clarity to ambiguous twists and turns. It decides in favor of the clear. It despises the obscure. It determines the world to be strictly such and so and no other.

Simplicity expresses itself without excuses. Its presence is felt directly and with an astonishing clarity. It can be so simple as to prevent further analysis. It is in this sense that simplicity is often compared with the self-evident; which is to say, to be simple is to carry your own proof with you. Each time the simple is present, it can be recognized as such. It is its own warrant of being what it is. Being requires simplicity for its being.

In terms of the previously discussed four basic ideas, the understanding of simplicity requires the establishment of a perspective that, above all else, yields up a direct expression of importance. The self-declaration of the achievement of a level of value is the very signature of simplicity. When simplicity achieves appropriate expression, there can be no doubt about the real presence of an entity. It is simply there in its simple reality. The vague infinitude of importance is narrowed down to this particular spot of being. What bursts forth is directly important. Compromise is eliminated.

The perspective adopted so that importance can be disclosed is characterized by an extreme directness. Simplicity's point of view is singular. Uniqueness is therefore the gift of simplicity. Sharp lines can be drawn between domains of being because simplicity does not deal well with a set of mixed levels of reality. It is because of simplicity's indifference to the potential riches of reality that it is often equated with poverty.

Similarly, the understanding of simplicity has a certain poverty associated with it. There is only so much one can say about the simple. Then words fail or even cover up the directness of simplicity. This is one reason why feelings are so often associated with simplicity. One feels a certain way and that is all that can be said. Just as an emotion claims our being with an undeniable directness, so also simplicity stares us directly in the face foreclosing further comment. To understand simplicity is to reach a certain state of attentive silence within which the simple gives itself in an immediate expression of its own importance.

When all is said and done, the simple cannot be understood as anything except itself. This is why the simple and the essential form a dyad of metaphysical concepts bearing directly upon the question of identity and truth. Reality is simple in the sense that there are real things that simply are what they are. To recall Aristotle, to speak the truth about them is to say what they are. To speak falsely is to say what they are not. On the level of simplicity, reality and truth are as simple as that. But reality is not only simple. It is also complex.

Complexity

It is the plurality of the world that demands the acknowledgement of complexity as an ingredient equally primordial in the functioning of the world. Complexity takes account of the differences in the world. It recognizes that elimination for the sake of simplicity is not always the way of strength. Sometimes, incorporation of the world's multiform richness is equally important. To embrace otherness is to make room for it within the essential structure of being. Complexity, therefore, works on a wider level than that of simplicity. It endorses the conditions that surround the essential simplicity of environmental beings. Complexity is to the conditional features of an environmental being what simplicity is to its essential features. Where simplicity is the sign of "the one," complexity is the sign of "the many." Complexity has a central place in this environmental cosmology because of its commitment to metaphysical pluralism. Simplicity brings about a universe of many things, each simple in its essential being. In its turn, this cosmological character demands an equal development of appropriate complexity so that the singularity of individuals can be respected within the simplicity of being. The paradox of simplicity is that it generates the necessary presence of its opposite, complexity. As in the case of simplicity, here also complexity is different but not opposed. Once again, order is the miracle by which these strands are woven into the particular integrity of particular environments.

Developed through the four concepts of importance, expression, perspective, and understanding, complexity reveals itself to be that quality of being whereby plurality and its consequent interrelations are recognized and lifted into prominence. When complexity registers importance, it does so by bringing a democratic sensibility to the realm of value. It acknowledges that there are many forms of importance. Furthermore, it respects the differences between values by refusing to collapse them into an undifferentiated sameness. It is the potential unity of values that is complexity's concern. How values relate to each other and how they stand together is the major question faced by complexity. Its responses drive the realm of environmental value away from the concerns of simplicity. In place of an insistence on uniqueness and particularity, complexity fosters the connections between values. It asserts that what environmental beings hold in common is as important as what separates them. Complexity alters the mixture of values so that simplicity does not have the entire say in determining environmental quality.

The expression of complexity is the result of its perspective. Rather than narrowness, complexity's perspective emphasizes width. It is this open point of view that gives complex, expression its characteristic density. It takes time to comprehend the complex for there are many layers to its disclosure. Complexity organizes itself around respect and tolerance for difference. It seeks room for what is not the same. Complexity is therefore the sworn enemy of uniformity. The narrowness essential to simplicity needs the width of perspective associated with complexity if simplicity is to avoid an unhappy thinness of expression. At the same time, complexity can easily slide into an unneccessary indulgence in variety that leads to a trivializing of experience. As should be expected, it is the appropriate harmony of the two factors, complexity and simplicity, that yields up the right balance.

Patience is the primary virtue required for understanding complexity. The ambiguous and the indirect, the relational and the involved are the proper subject matter of complex understanding. To know complexity is to know the various ways in which environmental events can relate to each other. Complexity requires a deft understanding sensitive to the nuances that emerge when simple things are thrown into new and fresh combinations. Complex expression demands a wide perspective such that levels of importance and their possible combinations can be concretely understood.

What must not be lost sight of in this analysis of the simple and the complex is the intimate way in which they generate and require each other's presence. The simple and the complex belong together because they are coherent notions. The simple coheres to the complex because it brings into being the need to account for difference. The simple creates itself by being different from its neighbor in a simple way. But this achievement crowds the field of being and makes necessary some way of accounting for all these differences. Complexity provides this service by connecting the very different beings whose identity results from the quality of simplicity. In fact, simplicity can only be understood through its relation to complexity. Likewise, complexity must be understood through a necessary reference to simplicity. This is the meaning of "coherence" that was developed in the construction of the cosmological scheme.

What happens when simplicity and complexity are understood together? The answer lies in the experience of dynamics. Simplicity and complexity constrain each other by placing a burden on each other. What is simple strains to be itself by eliminating complexity; what is complex strains to be itself by rejecting simplicity. The resultant struggle tests the value of each quality. In this test what emerges is some measure of simplicity and some measure of complexity. When either one eliminates the other, environmental being disappears.

The tensile strength established between these qualities sets up an environmental tone, one that courses through an entire region of being. When deftly felt, a pervasive rhythm of being can be sensed throughout an ecological region. These rhythms of being are dependent upon the levels of order that come to dominate these various environmental regions. Furthermore, insofar as these rhythms reside within environmental structures, we can identify these tones with the effective presence of specific normative measures. Recall that to have a structure is to uphold a normative measure. Granting, then, the equivalence of tone and structure, we can say that those environments dominated by simplicity will express a high degree of economy in organizing their members. When well organized, they will necessarily subordinate their constituents such that an extraordinary depth tends to suffuse itself throughout the environment. But another outcome is equally possible. Too much simplicity creates an environment woefully deficient in flexibility. In so losing its resilience, it will also tend to collapse when faced with change.

Turning to complexity, a well-organized complex environment will express an extraordinary relevance throughout its contours. This will be due to the effective presence of many diverse forms throughout the environment. But it is equally possible that an over-reliance on complexity can lead to a loss of a sense of what is important. When there are too many important things, importance tends to disappear.

All this leads to the conclusion that simplicity and complexity require each other if strong and effective environmental harmonies are to emerge. Simplicity joined to complexity balances complexity's tendency to overindulge in importances. Complexity joined to simplicity corrects simplicity's drive toward excessive narrowness. The value that environments achieve is therefore the outcome of the dynamics of complexity and simplicity as measured out by the respective forces at work. This foregoing analysis is important in three ways. First, we have secured a way around the fact/value dichotomy that paralyzes so much of contemporary environmental philosophy. Second, a concrete understanding of this way of thinking depends upon the utilization of aesthetic theory and concepts. Third, all the previous work in establishing a cosmological scheme and detailing the normative dimensions of environmental structures has pointed toward the steady convergence of the ethical and the asethetic. Here, finally, these two philosophical disciplines meet by reason of the emergence of a third discipline, axiology. For if this analysis is correct, the most meaningful way to describe, analyze, and coordinate environmental thinking is through the values actually produced within ecological regions.

Four Levels of Environmental Order

The dynamics of environmental value take place through the achievement of form in ecological regions. This dynamic does not occur in a vacuum. Rather, as category four indicates, transmission takes place across a sweep of experiences that are already ordered by reason of past environmental transactions. In what follows I will be following Whitehead's hypothesis that the number of fundamental

Levels of Environmental Order
Trivial
Vague
Narrow
Width

Figure 3

types of order in environmental regions can be reduced to four basic types. Of course, these types are themselves expandable through compounds and contrasts into an indefinite range of orders.

I therefore use the term "level" to suggest potential heights and depths of order (see figure 3). To feel the value of these heights and depths as well as the regions in between is the aim of this analysis. It must be remembered that each of these orders can combine with the others to create a dizzying array of values. Also, each resultant order will have its own balance of simplicity and complexity, adding to the particular value structures emergent throughout the environment.

What we are about to discuss is a hypothetical application of the "logically vague" as a starting point for organizing a cosmological understanding of environments. Even though four are noted, it is not my intent to narrow down environments to a single set of possible orders. Rather, these are the basic types of order that by hypothesis function throughout environments. Their permutations are indefinite in number, even as their origins can be identified as consisting in this quartet of fundamental levels of order. The advantages of this hypotheses will become evident when we analyze the feelings that are experienced through the types of existence maintained within these levels of order.

Whitehead suggests that environmental order is the result of the mixture of some four different levels of ecological organization.[1] These orders are: The trivial, the vague, the narrow, and the wide. Each represents a way of expressing a certain type of value and each elicits a certain type of response from the creatures that inhabit its domain. Furthermore, each can combine with the others in order to create further environmental responses. In this analysis we begin by examining each level separately. Then we turn to the question of combining their various attributes so as to account for a rich array of possible environmental regions.

Triviality

This environmental quality results from a lack of order such that no aspect of an environment is reinforced by another. This is due to a lack of coordination within the environment. Things stand apart in isolated novelty. The members of the environment are without any theme, structure, or sense of belonging. There may be great difference present but it is of the sort that prevents any community of action. No one aspect of an environment stands out with vigor, clarity, or strength. In Whitehead's words: "Incompatibility has triumphed over contrast."[2]

It is not true that chaos is interesting. Rather, it induces the most extraordinary boredom, since no one thing stands out with a decisive importance. Nevertheless, triviality is the first emergence of a sense of order, since its lack of order calls attention to the beginning edges of order. What is noticed is the tenuous claims to attention set forth by the beings arranged within the order of triviality. None claim attention and by that fact they announce the absence of important forms of order.

The paradox of triviality lies in the fact that an extreme complexity is achieved by reducing everything to the least common denominator. That is to say, what counts in a trivial order is the simple fact of existence. How and why something exists is pushed aside for the sake of an uncoordinated mass of entities. At the trivial level, organization is obtained by assigning equality to all things. Thus, trivial orders pay a huge price: They make everything important and thereby secure an order within which nothing is important.

Just as it is wrong to identify the chaotic with the surprising, so also it is a fallacy to equate the trivial with the simple. Triviality is brought about by embracing complexity with a vengeance. Triviality is therefore an order that is made up of contradictions. Faced with the enormous complexity of the universe, trivial orders express massive indifference and thereby exhibit a superficiality that masks the staggering complexity that makes up its formal structure. What triviality needs is not less simplicity but more. It is precisely recognition of this unbounded complexity that induces a sense of paralysis in those who would seek to understand the trivial.

In sum, trivial orders do not handle complexity in a good way. They succumb to the easy solution of placing everything on the same level even though everything is existentially different. Through a lack of simplicity, trivial orders create an environment within which anything can gain admittance. A radical complexity usurps the place of selective simplicity and no decisive criterion of value emerges as an effective normative measure.

Now, the positive side of this type of order lies in its openness to experience. Because difference is the only measure for order, anything at all may enter the field of being. But what looks like acceptance turns out to be a vicious form of rejection. Triviality must locate difference along such a severe line of uncoordinated equality that it flattens the very difference that it is supposed to welcome.

What this analysis of trivial order reveals is that all forms of order are also forms of discrimination. Each order utilizes a measure (often unacknowledged) to organize its field of being. And as is often the case in environmental cosmology, what begins as a virtue turns out, in the wrong hands, to be a vice. As a true understanding of harmony ought to tell us, it is always a question of hitting the mark just right. By now, the need for developing a good aesthetic sensibility should be quite clear. It is a matter of gaining the right "feel" for an environment. It is never a case of the mechanical application of rigid formulas. Environmental cosmology is more an art form than a scientific investigation. It requires much experience and deft understanding to sense just what is at play in a particular ecological region.

Vagueness

The conjoint quality of these levels of order becomes even clearer when we analyze the realm of the vague. Where triviality stresses the loosest of orders—a type of bare conjunction—vagueness asserts itself through the highlighting of similarities between the members of the environment. Vagueness appears when, in Whitehead's words, there is an "excess of identification."[3] Simplicity displaces radically uncoordinated complexity through the selection of certain features as representative of the region as a whole. What occurs is the reduction of the world to a level of manageable proportions. In place of the dizzying "manyness" of the trivial, we are given the mild unity of the vague. It is called "mild" because it does not do full justice to the radical pluralism residing at the base of environmental activity. Still, the possibility of doing justice to that ever-emerging creativity exists since, again in Whitehead's words, "by reason of vagueness, many count as one, and are subject to indefinite possibilities of division into multifold unities."[4]

What is experienced in the domain of vagueness is unity in its most rudimentary form. Vague environmental structures tie together regions of activity by identifying elements that represent major dimensions of the environmental field. As such, what is held in common tends to come to the forefront, and triviality and its chaotic dissonance is pushed into the background. The world becomes more interesting because more of it can be grasped.

The vague is not to be confused with the ambiguous or the fuzzy. An order is there to be sensed and grasped, but it is order in a most elemental manner. Left to itself, vagueness quickly evaporates because it lacks the strength that can be gained through strong forms of unity. In effect, this means that vagueness awaits narrowness for its proper completion. But that is getting ahead of the story.

What is needed here is clear recognition of the value of vagueness in an environmental cosmology. Most forms of environmental value come into serious play when vagueness makes its presence felt as an important environmental quality. By establishing the beginnings of order it makes room for the kind of creativity that can make important differences.

So far we have concentrated on the complex side of the environmental situation. Both triviality and vagueness are special ways of handling complexity. Triviality surrenders to complexity. Vagueness seeks to make some sense of the plenitude of possibilities breeding in the interstices of environmental reality. This is why Whitehead notes that both triviality and vagueness suffer from excess. In the case of triviality it is an excess of differentiation; on the other hand, vagueness gives into an excess of identification. It is simplicity that is most effective in reining in excess. But that brings the discussion to the question of narrowness.

Narrowness

Earlier, simplicity was described as the power to eliminate what is irrelevant. Narrowness shares some of that power. Narrowness is achieved by reason of emphasizing certain components at the expense of others. Narrowness engages the world and its complexity with a certain directness that lifts dimensions of experience into great clarity even as others are dismissed into darkness.

Narrowness appears to know what it wants. It asserts the primacy of its aims over that of other claims. It is insistent, powerful, and self-assured. The narrow will brook no opposition. Rather, it intends to force everything it encounters in the direction of its wishes. It is therefore best understood as a precursor of individuality. When experience is tightened to a level of streamlined efficiency, then great strength of presence is made possible. In terms of environmental influence, narrowness sets the stage for the kind of variety that makes for rich diversity.

At this point, what begins to emerge from these analyses is the great paradox of the grounds of environmental stability. An enduring environment must be sought through the active presence of diversity. Furthermore, such diversity must be grounded in the reality of strong individuals. This only appears paradoxical to a mind accustomed to thinking of stability in terms of sameness. Regarding difference as a threat is the trademark of the logical order. Here, as we have increasingly seen, it is the aesthetic order that makes environments function well. The aesthetic order does not just tolerate difference. For its full effectiveness it requires the steady presence of difference.

Strong and consistent difference is the result of individuality. Narrowness is the first step toward the achievement of individuality. An environment without the real presence of narrowness is an environment condemned to shifting excesses. In the order of the trivial, an absence of unity results in a sense of sameness due to an overabundance of difference. Vagueness is produced when normative measures insufficiently sensitive to difference are put into play. Neither the trivial nor the vague have in their environmental structures normative measures suitable for taming their excesses. What each requires is the kind of radical emphasis that narrowness can supply. The narrow is to the trivial and the vague as the simple is to the complex. It supplies what the other lacks and cannot contribute within its own structural form. Narrowness is essential if environments are to be capable of creating the kind of individual presences that give them both diversity and stability.

Still: The narrow, in itself, is incapable of bringing about a healthy environmental order. Left to its own devices narrowness will eliminate itself. Its own intolerance of difference will work against its fruitfulness as an environmental force. That which is unwilling to cooperate, dies a quick death. Its lack of flexibility makes it snap under environmental pressures of various sorts. Persistence by itself is not a virtue. Where the vague and the trivial reveal a weakness by reason of a certain diffusion of interests, the narrow compromises its own relevance through an inability to accommodate difference through the adoption of an alternative point of view. What narrowness does provide is emphasis. It therefore remains the primary way in which expression enters upon the environmental scene. Through its insistence upon a singular perspective, narrowness stresses only certain modes of importance. In drawing such a line narrowness contributes definiteness and precision, but it also can lead toward an inevitable thinness of experience. The chief danger of narrowness is that it produces a brittleness in its creatures that frequently prevents the growth of a supple and generous sense of order. Narrowness suffers from a defect in complexity.

Width

This last tier of environmental order is the outcome of the fortunate fusion of two other orders. When narrowness can be woven onto a fabric of vagueness, then great width is achieved. In the experience of width, simplicity and complexity gain appropriate placement. In an authentically wide environment, the narrow features compose the vague features in such a manner as to highlight an overall harmony that expresses great unity. The major sign of width is flexibility—a responsiveness that is able to take account of numerous dimensions of experience without compromising its own integrity or diluting the individuality of its parts. In many ways, width is the supreme environmental achievement. As the next chapter demonstrates, the human body is the most excellent example of environmental width in action.

In a wide environment, simplicity cooperates with complexity to bring about an extraordinary deftness. Two modes of being receive simultaneous expression. On the one hand, individuality gains significant expression. On the other, room is made for more than one type of environmental narrowness. Narrow perspectives signal a gain in forceful expressions throughout the environment, while the vague dimensions serve to pull them together into a strong environmental unity. Width is to be understood as the triumph of importance as expressed through significant simplicity and complexity. Vague environmental forces supply complexity and narrow components contribute strong individuals. The result is that an important harmony receives massive reinforcement and generous distribution throughout the field of being.

The union of the vague and the narrow that produces width is a supreme example of the category of contrast. This category describes the formal structure whereby a rich and stable environmental unity is achieved. In this environmental cosmology to contrast is always "to put into a unity with..." When an environment expresses width as a major value structure, it is always the result of the dynamic unity provided by the category of contrast. Now, there are degrees of contrast just as there are degrees of simplicity and complexity as well as degrees of triviality, vagueness, and width. The levels of order mentioned here are ideal types seldom fully realized in natural or urban regions. What is to be remembered is that all environmental orders have some elements of these four levels of organization. The precise environmental character is to be determined by the special arts and sciences dedicated to such aims.

We can see here one more confirmation of the usefulness of environmental cosmology as a philosophical discipline. It produces important knowledge in a vague way that can be concretely specified by other cultural arts and sciences. What is gained is a synoptic vision that can guide overall cultural aims even as particular projects are pursued. Such global sensibility is required if the fallacy of simple location is to be avoided. Further, a synoptic vision grants great powers of appreciation. This is precisely the strength needed if environmental philosophy is to develop in directions that can move it away from excessive legalisms and positivistic mimicking of the sciences. We have in this fourfold sense of environmental order the roots of a philosophically valid way of understanding the important dimensions of environmental experience. The potential fruitfulness of this set of cosmological norms will be disclosed as this study develops its implications for understanding the concrete dynamics of various environmental regions.

A general understanding of the importance of the aesthetic order involves gaining a concrete grasp of what is at work in environments. It is always a question of togetherness of certain sorts. It is never a simple case of exclusion. For in environmental reality such tactics spell doom for the members of the community in question. The major achievement of environmental orders is the way in which events elaborate structures that allow for entwined existences without compromising individual identities. This is the great secret of nature.

Finally, it must be remembered that these orders are always dynamic. Their ebb and flow is what guarantees environmental creativity. Still, in the present age a certain fundamental stability of rhythm and structure can always be discerned. It affects all environmental realities and therefore will be of great import when we study the precise dimensions of natural experience.

There are two sources for creativity. The first is the workings of the immediate environment itself. Within that region vagueness, triviality, narrowness, and width sort themselves out so as to establish dominant environmental patterns. Here is where we encounter material, living, and conscious environmental beings. But it is to be remembered that these dominant actual creatures are themselves the fortunate results of prior levels of order. In fact, all beings carry in themselves the mark of the four levels of environmental order. Each has a trivial dimension such that excess of difference can be detected. Each has a vague dimension such that variety coalesces to form identifiable communities of interest. Each has narrow regions exhibiting simplicity and high selectivity. Each also has a certain width such that their unity exhibits a high degree of integrity together with a high degree of harmonized individuality. It is the rhythmic presence of these levels of environmental order that makes nature such an astonishing work of art.

Environmental Moods

When felt with aesthetic sensitivity, each of these environmental levels sends out a certain "feel." It is the presence of these feelings that justifies the title of this chapter, "A World of Feelings." Once again, as we develop an analysis of these feelings, it must be remembered that these are vague, ideal types which in actual environmental settings are encountered in mixed and jumbled forms. These are the building blocks out of which an almost indefinite array of environmental feelings can emerge. Again, the important function of this analysis lies in its capacity to speak meaningfully about the real presence of normative measures within environmental experience. As correlates of the levels of environmental order, these feelings are four in number: Indifference, expectation, intensity, and involvement (see figure 4).

Indifference

The mood that settles over a trivial environment is one of indifference. Nothing gains prominence and therefore nothing moves to the forefront of experience. Due to the presence of unorganized complexity, a mood of unimportance pervades the region. Indifference registers its presence even though there is enormous variety present in the region. How can this be so? What eliminates the sense of interest and even excitement that should be the common reaction to massive variety and difference? Faced with such an extraordinary array of possibilities, one searches for a measure whereby lines of continuity and discrimination can be drawn. Finding none, the tendency is to

Levels of Environmental Order	Environmental Moods
Trivial	Indifference
Vague	Expectation
Narrow	Intensity
Width	Involvement

Figure 4. Environmental Moods

feel overwhelmed. But there is nothing of importance to be overwhelmed by. The next best solution is to gather the trivial together and acknowledge what it really is—unimportant.

This is the truth of the trivial: It expresses a quality of indifference to matters of importance. Without a measure for importance, nothing can stand out as significant either in itself or as related to others. The mood that settles over such an environment is what its perspective grants: An utter indifference to difference itself. The trivial contradicts the destiny of all environments. As the environmental thesis suggests, an environment that does not give birth to value ceases to be an environment. Trivial orders contradict the aims of environmental creativity: The expression of value from novel perspectives such that importance can be understood in many different ways. The mood of indifference infecting trivial environments easily slides into a kind of slack openness that paves the way for that order's dissolution.

The indifference that marks trivial orders is a sign of their potential malleabilty. The trivial awaits importance so that it can be rescued from its own complexity. It is this tone of expectation running about the edges of trivial orders that moves such orders up the grade toward deeper values. The trivial is not simply the trivial and to be dismissed as such. In point of fact the trivial is the environment's reservoir of value. It is the treasure house wherein sources of value take up their possibilities. Without the room for importance provided by triviality, it is doubtful that importance could ever find a perspective for its appropriate expression. The next step in that move toward expression is the order of vagueness.

Expectation

Vagueness provides a sense of opportunity that diffuses itself throughout an environment as a mood of expectation. The lure for feeling in a vague environment becomes compelling because of the hints and suggestions contained in the rudimentary forms of order defining that region. Order is the ground of identity and enduring goodness. Therefore, the slightest suggestion as to its potential realization as an ingredient in the environmental mix lends an atmosphere of oppportunity to the region in question. A sense of imminent possibility replaces the tedium associated with triviality. Some degree of real possibility lessens the boredom infecting environmental activity.

It is by reason of this sense of expectation that temporality becomes a real factor in the environment. Spatial inertia is disturbed and the feel of a future suggestive of real possibility begins to emerge. Without the sense of expectation afforded by vagueness, little or no dynamism could be detected in environmental patterns.

In particular, vagueness makes narrowness possible. The slight shift toward order renders the ecological niche workable. It makes selection for the sake of emphasis a ready and efficient way of dealing with environmental choices. The excess of identification that characterizes vagueness promotes a simplification of environmental activity. Insofar as the many can now act as a loose one, then narrowness can go about its business of replacing simplicity with complexity. Expectation is therefore the first mood that settles over environments ready for creative change. In vague orders what is possible becomes tangible. This palpable readiness for the achievement of value can be felt within the activities dominating the region in question. The stage is set for the emergence of the kind of solid identities that accompany the achievement of intense values.

The opportunity to express clear values suggests the importance of vagueness as an environmental feeling. What is preeminently felt in vague environmental regions is the presence of signs ripe for future determination. In place of the chaotic feelings associated with trivial regions, there is experienced a sense of looming importances awaiting realizations. "What might be" takes on an increasing presence as the region pushes toward further definition. This mood is what fills the region with temporal feelings of expectation. A later chapter will point out just how crucial this burgeoning sense of an alternative is for understanding the origins of consciousness.

Similarly, the spatial configuration of a region steeped in vague feelings takes on a transparency unlike the spatial qualities felt in trivial domains. Here the region is ordered so as to undo the generic sense of obstruction that clogs up trivial domains with feelings of indifference. Space opens up and an expression of possible values comes to the fore. Within the real presence of expectation, spatial contours shape themselves in deeply suggestive ways. Spatial and temporal dimensions join together to reinforce a concrete mood of definite possibility. The tensile strength of spacetime inscapes, patterns, and contrasts transmit a sense of expectation throughout vague environmental orders. The difference between the trivial and the vague is grounded in the moods separating indifference from expectation. In the realm of the vague, real possibilities are tangibly felt. They offer opportunities for the environmental expression of important ways of being valuable. In the mood of expectation felt in vague orders, a sense of the immense potential that lurks in the womb of a process universe comes to expression. These possibilities are brought to intense expression through narrowness.

Intensity

Feelings of intensity depend upon elimination of irrelevant factors within an environment. To eliminate is to select out what will be important and to emphasize it with a certain ruthlessness. This capacity to remove obstacles is what is meant by narrowness. As Whitehead put it: "Intensity is the reward of narrowness."[5] Triviality is the result of an uncritical acceptance of difference. Narrowness, on the other hand, severely restricts such complexity. It is threatened by difference and must develop strategies of width to make up for its bias toward the simple.

Intensity displays itself whenever similar patterns of inscape are reinforced and repeated throughout an environment. By narrowing down the possibilities of environmental expression, a mood of intensity is lifted into prominence. This is caused by the simultaneous presence of two modes of environmental activity. There is the simple fact of repetition, which builds up a reserve of energetic quality that serves to establish a continuing backdrop to environmental activities. This resource spills over into the ecological region so that a certain mode of identity receives a continual emphasis. Within this repetition of a narrow selection of ecological characteristics, only a few types of identity gain full expression. As these types establish environmental relevance, they tend to drown out alternative values.

The upshot of this narrowness is the reinforced repetition of select values to the exclusion of others. Narrowness means dominance. It is a sign of great environmental force. But that intensity easily cracks because it lacks inherent flexibility. Like all modes of being emphasizing simplicity, there is a built-in tendency to reduce the variety of the world to a few modalities. While strength is found in such orders of being, its lack of resilience is not to be overlooked. Something very much like this obviously occurs in nature when entire forests are destroyed by single organisms. For all their majesty, spruce trees fall before the persistent presence of the budworm that is its enemy. New England's gracious elm trees were wiped out by the Dutch elm disease. Narrowness has its own forms of weakness despite the obvious intensity of its forceful environmental expression. Exclusion for the wrong reasons spells environmental doom.

The experience of environmental intensity usually signals the imminent presence of individuality. When some event is able to take on a consistent character, then its environmental presence assumes greater and greater importance. In fact, given the metaphysical assumptions underlying this environmental cosmology, it is the achievement of individual expression that is at the heart of all environmental values. The less there is of individuality in an ecological region, the more there is of triviality and its accompanying indifference. Narrowness marks the beginnings of a gradient in environmental intensity.

With the growth of such importance, there is an increase in perspectival focus such that genuine modes of individualized expression become possible. Of course, there always remains the question of the relevance of such individualized expressions of value. Will the environment tolerate such perspectives? The answer to this question lies in the domain of the fourth environmental level—the order of width and the feeling of involvement that accompanies its active presence.

Involvement

The experience of environmental width is the outcome of the right weaving together of the orders of narrowness and vagueness. When such a harmony is achieved, the relevant environmental field expresses the character of involvement. Events lock together so as to provide a perspective that takes into account both individual achievements and significant environmental relationships. This weaving together takes advantage of the sense of opportunity afforded by vague environmental orders and the intense value experience brought about by narrow environmental expressions. The resultant width felt throughout the region welcomes both the diversity inherent in individual intensities of value and the sense of opportune connectedness brought about through the presence of orders of vagueness. Narrowness weds vagueness. Intensity embraces opportunity. A sense of real involvement is felt throughout such wide ecological regions.

When such a feeling of involvement floods an environment, there emerges the possibility of great depth and great breadth. The environment loosens up to the extent that layers of value can come to expression; hence, an intense depth of value becomes a real possibility. At the same time, the continuity chracterizing the region does not dissolve under the pressure of individuality. Rather, its flexibility is such that hidden modes of appropriate togetherness are brought to the fore. It is the simultaneous expression of oneness and manyness that is the crowning achievement of great environmental regions. The felt sign of this maximization of intensity and opportunity is the feeling of overwhelming involvement at every level of environmental activity.

Such involvement is the height of effective contrast. It marks the successful emergence of patterns of inscape that literally involve each other by reason of wide lines of environmental transmission. In effect, the categories of physical, conceptual, and propositional transmission come to full expression. The past as felt through the transmission of physical being is fully represented. Similarly, the future as felt through lines of conceptual transmission receives its full measure of expression. The intense sense of the lure of real possibility is experienced through the presence of propositional lures felt through the region. And lastly, these modes of environmental being conspire together to spread a mood of expectant stillness across the rhythm of the environment's feeling tones. Later, this mood of integrated width, depth, and stillness will be seen to be at the heart of the experience of the beauty of nature. The goodness of nature resides in this integration of the fair and the fitting. To gain a level of contemporary effectiveness environmental ethics needs to develop and articulate precisely this sense of the value of nature. The aesthetic order must replace the logical order as the ground of environmental thinking.

Furthermore, moods of involvement are realized in both urban and natural environments. Here it is important to note that, even though this study is confined to nature, this environmental cosmology can point also toward the continuity of value present in both natural and urban environments. In this way a fundamental aim of this study receives an important confirmation—to demonstrate that the difference between the natural and the built is one of degree, not kind.

To summarize this analysis of the feeling tones that accompany the four fundamental levels of environmental order:

- The order of triviality invokes a feeling tone of indifference.
- The order of vagueness invokes a feeling tone of expectation.
- The order of narrowness invokes a feeling tone of intensity.
- The order of width invokes a feeling tone of involvement.

Within the inscapes, contrasts, and patterns transmitted by these orders lie the relevant possibilities for understanding environmental regions of value and experience.

A Schema of Ideal Environmental Values

In this attempt to forge a new way to think and speak about the environment, there is always the possibility of missing the forest for the trees. In concluding this chapter on the environment as a world of feelings, it is therefore quite important to sum up in as clear a manner as possible the major lines of argument so far developed. This can be done by using the four basic environmental categories of inscape, contrast, pattern, and transmission to examine a proposed set of ideal environmental values. It will bring together in a summary fashion the central concerns of this study—the use of cosmological categories to express important environmental values.

Remember: This study seeks to replace the outworn categories of scientific materialism with a set of cosmological hypotheses that demand that we look upon the environment as a vast reservoir of feelings. It is for the sake of understanding this world of feelings that a novel set of categories as well as analyses of various environmental structures have been put forth. Two theses are central to this attempt to replace the materialistic doctrines of the contemporary world view. The first is the concept of environmental participation through normative measure. The second is that these levels of participation establish feeling tones that vibrate throughout specific environmental fields. Be it on the level of environmental matrices spreading themselves along horizontal spatiotemporal lines or in the inscape of individual environmental events rising up to challenge and even reconstruct entire environmental orders, the essential meaning of these environmental happenings remains the same: The expression of feelings. Sometimes these feelings represent the conditional features of environmental activity and sometimes they represent the essential features. That determination results from the specific use of these vague categories. Whatever the case may be, any environment is always a structure of feelings.

This effort to translate the language of materialism into the language of aesthetics must take into account the extreme vagueness of such categories as well as the indefinite range of contrasted feelings that are possible in any given environment. Such an effort is fraught with difficulties. Indeed, the dizzying array of possible combinations makes the development of a scheme of ideal normative environmental measures a methodological necessity. Without some such ideal environmental schema the possibility of organizing a comprehensive, nuanced understanding fades from view.

What follows is a speculative attempt to provide such a model for organizing environmental feelings in terms of their respective importances and perspectives. Insofar as it results from speculation, this cosmological model, together with its environmental norms, is

Ideal Environmental Values
Intensity
Integrity
Wholeness
Depth

Figure 5.

entirely ideal. Its application to actual environmental situations will always be fallible and subject to correction. However, the pragmatic gain achieved by its use should not be overlooked. At the very least, these ideal modes of environmental participation offer a conceptual structure and vocabulary that emphasize value as well as fact and quality as well as quantity. The leading premise of this environmental cosmology is that the interweaving of these axiological dimensions is the heart and soul of any environment whatsoever. Within these normative measures we find the philosophic resources with which to understand the environment as one, true, good, and beautiful. It is the thesis of this study that every environment whatsoever expresses these ideals to some degree (see figure 5).

The schema for ideal environmental participation has four dimensions: Wholeness, depth, intensity, and integrity. Each quality represents a normative measure whereby we can estimate in a vague but important manner the values achieved in environmental settings. This would be true for both the diachronic and the synchronic domains. That is to say, the ideals can measure an environment in its width of conditions as well as an individual environmental event in its unique essential suchness. The correspondence between these two domains would be a matter of actual environmental study to be carried out by the ecological disciplines through their special methodologies. Just as a vector is a physical force generating material configurations in the the physical world, so also the feeling tones dominant in an environment spread through its domain making possible or impossible various forms of wholeness, depth, intensity, and integrity. Equally so, the scalar element in the physical world expresses itself by overcoming the dominant vector forms. Expressed in the language of environmental cosmology, we can say that individual environmental events can invade and sometimes upset the regularity of vectoral fields. Thus real novelty enters the environmental field.

The point is that we have established a correspondence between the language of the physical sciences and the axiological terminology of this environmental cosmology. What was previously termed "the horizontal domain of conditional features" and "the diachronic dimension" is now the cosmological equivalent of the vector dimension in physics. Similarly, the scalar domain is the physical equivalent of the "vertical domain of essential features" and "the synchronic dimension" of environmental activities. Keeping this translation in mind, we now proceed to an analysis of the schema for ideal environmental participation.

Wholeness

The experience of wholeness is grounded in the presence of real unity. This is because in its rise to individuality an event must weave many things into its being without losing its identity. Thus, the one triumphs over the many. Wholeness means the special way in which an event can take into its own reality a maximum of the conditional features in its environment. Wholeness also suggests the presence of a kind of completeness. It is not the completeness meant by absolute perfection, for that would signify the achievement of the ideal. Once the ideal is achieved, it ceases to be the ideal and becomes the actual. Perfection is not possible in a process world. There are, however, degrees of perfection that emphasize completeness without stopping the onward movement of time. They can be understood as "modes of completeness according to their own kind." Wholeness implies balance, symmetry, and openness to difference and diversity. Wholeness is therefore that mode of completeness whereby maximum levels of inclusiveness are expressed without the loss of essential unity.

We can employ the four basic environmental categories to situate the status of wholeness among the ideal environmental values. In terms of the category of inscape, wholeness provides a dimension of openness whereby each entity can find its proper place. Likewise, as exemplified within the category of contrast, wholeness is expressed when perspectives powerful enough to transmute incompatibles take hold of environmental processes. Human consciousness is a dramatic example of such a perspective. Wholeness is itself a unique pattern, one that fuses the world into unities respectful of diversities. Finally, within the category of transmission, wholeness expresses itself environmentally as a feeling of exceptional stillness. This is because in wholeness all things are given their proper place. And to the extent possible in a process universe, such stillness is experienced as a sense of restful completeness.

Depth

This value marks the effective presence of layers of order such that the environment displays an extraordinary thickness in terms of its diachronic and synchronic textures. Repeated conformations of the past to the present build up layers of felt values such that a seamless unity infuses the environment. Depth permits levels of order to stack up so as to provide voluminous space and time. Within these environmental volumes great room for contrasted types of horizontal and vertical experience is made available. The type of order most useful for depth experience is vagueness, for within its loose networks opportunity for increased intensity of experience can be directly felt. This explains why triviality is the opposite of depth. It allows no opportunity for the growth of the right combination of forces. Depth signals real opportunity.

The categories of inscape and contrast are strongly conjoined in depth values. In fact the inscape of achieved depth values is precisely that of intense contrast. Without the expansiveness that results from contrasted unity, no depth could be made realistically available. Similarly, the category of pattern is essential to depth experience. Interlocking events must tie together in richly articulated patterns in order to make available the volume ideally characteristic of depth. Finally, the transmission of depth is carried out through the dominant presence of propositional lures. Whenever depth is experienced, the real possibility of great novelty enters into environmental experience.[6] As such, depth presages the advent of beauty and is therefore a key to founding environmental ethics on an aesthetic basis.

Intensity

To the extent that a region expresses significant degrees of intensity, to that same extent it has succeeded in incorporating relevant features of the past into its perspective. Through conformation to its past it secures a repetition of energetic value such that a particular presence comes to dominate a particular spacetime region. Such conformation provides effective expression by building up reserves of feeling that overwhelm contrary perspectives. This explains why intensity is the reward of narrowness. By excluding difference, strong lines of conformity are introduced into the environmental field. At the same time, such narrow intensity serves to reinforce the status quo. What can result from bad forms of intensity is a rigidity that prevents cooperation. This will eventually spell environmental doom.

A more fortunate way to enhance intensity is by taking advantage of the category of contrast. By bringing together into a unity different environmental aspects, the inscape of the environmental event is narrowed at a more expansive level of inclusiveness. Through achieving a wider expression, more of the environment's riches are poured into the event. The new perspective provides a more inclusive focus which, in turn, pushes the event toward a more intense level of value. In strongly effective contrasts, identity and diversity combine to forge new levels of environmental novelty. One way of understanding evolutionary "advance" is by seeing it as the story of the success and failure of new forms of contrasts. Of course, the category of pattern also comes into important play whenever intensity is experienced. A contrast is itself a form of pattern and, therefore, its power to express intensity within an appropriate scale is all-important. As regions of value and experience, environments are the result of exceptional patterns of contrasts. The category of transmission is experienced in different ways in different regions. But in any region intensity is always transmitted as "physical," "conceptual," or "propositional." And sometimes, at exceptional moments, as "stillness." The actual differences of transmission marking different environmental settings are the subject of later chapters. For now, it is sufficient to remark that the ideal value of environmental intensity is achieved either by the reiterative conformation of the past to the present or through the emergence of contrasts that bring environmental activity to richer levels of unity. A wider one includes a richer many, and great intensity flows through the environment.

Integrity

What happens in a well-integrated environmental event is the successful fusion of otherness and identity. Integrity is the outcome of flexibility and coordination. The event in question must bring into itself what it is not and at the same time not lose what is unique to its own being. Flexibility names this ability to harmonize difference. Coordination, on the other hand, is necessary if due balance is to be achieved. This is the reason why integrity is always associated with some degree of symmetry. Integrity, therefore, is the summation of the other environmental ideals. Wholeness, depth, and intensity receive multiple layers of expression within well-integrated environments. Width of perspective grants a certain wholeness and intense expression brings importance to the forefront. The act of understanding the integrity of an environment is the ultimate exercise of normative thinking.

In terms of the environmental categories, integrity's inscape is characterized by a unity that produces a maximum coordination of diversity. This is the outcome of the special way in which the many are integrated in the unity of the one. It is evident that integrity demands the active use of contrast and pattern. The former brings about the intensity and depth that authentic integrity requires, while the latter establishes the room necessary for the proper placement characteristic of wholeness. Because it is a summation of the other ideals, integrity's transmission is always environmentally powerful. Its significance—be it physical, conceptual, or propositional—is felt throughout the entire environment. And of course, integrity by its very nature displays a certain stillness insofar as it sums up and completes the schema of ideal environmental values. As will become evident later, this is because integrity is another name for beauty and the goodness of nature is grounded in its beauty.[7]

This chapter has attempted to hold up a new picture of the environment—one that presents it as a vast panorama of shifting interrelations and feelings that express certain normative values. Four levels of environmental order were discussed and along with them their corresponding moods. Finally, ideal environmental values were put forth as pivots around which an understanding of actual environments can be measured out.

What makes such an environmental vision possible is the the human body. In its own way, it is both the ultimate expression of environmental integrity as well as the way in which we feel the environment in all its richness. Just how it performs such prodigious feats of understanding is the subject of the final chapter of this first part of our environmental cosmology.

Chapter Four

The Human Body and Its Environmental Field

The human body is the way in which the environment at large enters human experience. It is itself a complex environment requiring sophisticated understanding. The special way in which the body interprets its environmental field is called perception. But this deeply human act is far richer than the mere reception of sense data. Neither is the complexity of perception exhausted by examining the physiology of the human sense organs. Rather, the human body registers the meaning of its environmental situation (which is to say it perceives environments) in an act that is a mixture of feelings of both causal efficacy and presentational immediacy. Furthermore, these two pure modes of participating in environmental processes are for the most part experienced as mediated by a third mixed mode of perception, symbolic reference.

What we generally experience is perception in the mode of symbolic reference. This is the mode of environmental experience discussed earlier under the theme of cultural participation. But the semiotic field that constitutes our way of negotiating the stream of events making up a process world is also built out of layers of physical experience that are dramatically spatial and temporal in texture; that is to say, there are primitive forms of perception that are essentially non-sensuous. To be alive in a human way is to take the information derived from these more primitive forms of perception and refer it to the objects of our daily experience.

It is crucial for the argument of this book that the dynamics at play on each perceptual level—causal, presentational, and symbolic—be understood. Each has its special powers and merits as well as its deficiencies. No account of environmental experience can afford to ignore these decidedly different modes of moving toward the otherness of the environmental field and making it part of the human domain. In this chapter, we replay some of the major metaphysical themes already discussed. Once again, it is a question of the relation between the one and the many, identity and difference, and participation theory. But with this difference—now it is a matter of how we perceive the world by reason of our bodily environmental field.

I therefore conclude Part One—An Environmental Cosmology—with a restatement of the issues with which this study was introduced. For even in a postmodern age clamorous in its scorn for classical modes of reasoning, the need for maintaining the appropriate relation between metaphysics, civilization, and the environment remains evident. Perception is itself a process of unifying and making use of the four basic ideas with which this study began. Perception is a process of understanding that expresses matters of importance from a particular perspective.

Causal Efficacy and the Legacy of the Past

Fundamental to this study is insistence on the fact that we are always already in a world of actual feelings. What makes this premise so fundamental and yet so easy to forget and so difficult to grasp is the presence of our bodies. It is remarkable that we are for the most part largely unaware of the presence of our bodies. In fact, one sign of a well-functioning body is the fact that we are seldom aware of its presence. It is usually in sickness and in pain that the body becomes visible to us. Thus, an injured thumb upsets to an extraordinary degree the seamless unity of our world. This intimate union with the environment is brought about by what Whitehead calls the "withness" of the body. By this term, he means the concrete manner in which the body functions as an amplifier funneling the richness of environmental experience into our consciousness.

This mode of participating in environmental processes is called perception in the mode of causal efficacy. As a mode of establishing a perspective on the environment, it has profound influences. It is non-sensuous, purely dependent upon the inheritance of immediate past states, and it brings in its train deeply important information about the status of the neighboring environment.

Why does Whitehead call perception in the mode of causal efficacy a "non-sensuous" perception? How can one experience something without the senses? And why would a philosopher as astute as Whitehead take such trouble to argue such a claim? To answer these questions we have to return to the previous discussion of empiricism. There we saw that a rigid adherence to Hume's fact/value distinction, *viz.*, that only sensed facts are objective and all value statements are rooted in subjective experience, was the point around which much of the present discussion of environmental ethics foundered. Whitehead, along with other philosophers like James, Peirce, and Dewey, also chafed under this epistemological iron rod. For within sense experience only the immediate present can be experienced. (We shall see this directly when presentational immediacy is discussed.) We cannot in other words sense what we take to be an ordinary, well-founded dimension of our lives. I am referring to the fact of continuity and the way in which it plays so vital a part in our experience. We inherit from the past. We expect the future. We assume continuity along the lines of causal efficacy. Yet all of this—the very cement that holds our environmental life together—cannot be experienced through our senses.

The response of the British Empiricists and the Idealist tradition descendent from Kant to this lack of evidence regarding the continuity that undergirds our everyday experience is sheer bluff. They claim we make up the story through associations, habits of perception, or innate forms of sensibilities that organize the raw data of our sense perceptions.

As a committed naturalist, Whitehead rejects such elaborate explanatory schemata. He insists that we feel directly the presence of the past as it seeps into the present. Further, he claims that this is the very experience of causality itself. This non-sensuous experience is rarely felt in any pure manner, but we do have hints and suggestions as to its continuing influence in our lives. He provides a number of examples. The experience of sitting in a darkened room and sensing the presences of surrounding objects. Or the experience of heavy pressure felt at the height of an August afternoon in the woodlands. Or the sense of anticipation that infects the pronunciation of a polysyllabic phrase like "United Fruit Company."[1] In all these moments, we feel the pressure of the past as it edges into the present moment of experience.

Thus, this form of non-sensuous perception is called "perception in the mode of causal efficacy" because what we in reality are perceiving is the causal efficacy of the past—the immediately experienced past—as it slides up to and into the domain of its successor. These experiences, Whitehead insists, are as real and as important as our more immediately perceived sensory perceptions. In fact, their very vagueness is a sign of their significance, for they are freighted with the weight of the past. They convey into us the reality of our continuity with the world of environmental experience. These are the feelings that are at the base of what I termed, in Chapter Three, "A World of Feelings."

Causal efficacy witnesses our situatedness within the environmental world. It carries us through succeeding environmental domains. But the way in which it does so accounts for its lack of precision. For what we feel is not the environment itself but rather the environment as experienced through the antecedent states of our bodily being. What we finally feel has survived a long journey through various routes of our body. But at each stage what has actually happened is a handing over of past experience to the present moment. This occurs through the body and throughout the body. Thus: We see with our eyes; we touch with our skin; we smell with our nose; we hear with our ears; we taste with our tongue. It is really the antecedent states of our body—that is to say—the pressure of the past that we feel. What we preeminently feel in this non-sensuous experience is the weight of the past as it constrains our being in the present. Again, it is this experience that Whitehead terms, "the withness of the body."[2]

Causal efficacy lays the heavy hand of the past upon our environmental being. It lays bare one of the central but forgotten meanings of time: Constraint. When dealing with environmental matters we are often most apt to emphasize the future when we speak of threats to ecological integrity. There is, however, a forgotten temporal dimension equal in importance to the future. In many different ways, sometimes hidden and sometimes quite clearly out in the open, the past is profoundly present in environmental settings. It is the human body that registers this impact.

Much of the fear of alienation and the homogenization of experience brought about by contemporary uses of technology revolves about a loss of this concretely felt bodily presence. We forget the past and its importances because the body so effortlessly lets us use the past for our own advantage. But deeply hidden in the body's tissues are the messages of the past. We forget them at our peril.

Without the human body and its act of perceiving in the mode of causal efficacy, we would be bodiless subjects floating aimlessly throughout space. Such rootlessness brings in its train recognition of the human need for place, a major theme of this work. Through its feelings of causal efficacy the human body settles us down and serves as an existential anchor in a sea of swarming environmental processes. The somatic dimension of environmental behavior begins within this sense of the felt impact of time. I say "within" because the body through the power of its "withness" really does act as a temple that houses all sorts of environmental riches. It is a remarkably deft instrument that plays time's tune in a special way.

Perception in the mode of causal efficacy is essentially an experience of inheritance and derivation. It marks out the lines of continuity between ourselves in the present and in the past. It also establishes the lines of continuity between our bodily being and our environmental fields. What it tells us about is the immediate past, that aspect of reality out of which our present experience is arising.[3]

These words are at the heart of the argument of this study. We have an essential and direct relation to environmental presences by reason of the reality of our bodies. This connection, while direct, is also vague, dim, fleeting, and very difficult to fix with any degree of accuracy. We are like blind beings absorbed in the flux and buzz of a process universe. Nevertheless, causal efficacy is there in our lives. It is the ground of all environmental knowing. It is also the source of common sense. Without causal efficacy we would not be able to negotiate our world in any effective manner.

Earlier I spoke of the category of transmission. Perception in the mode of causal efficacy is a marked example of this environmental category. Through it, physical feelings are transmitted throughout environmental processes. Causal efficacy is at the heart of the feeling of environmental solidarity. Through it, the tone of environmental values is felt with an insistent immediacy. Though its origins are often difficult to trace, its rich presence is there with an emphasis that cannot be denied. Causal efficacy involves the settling in of massive reiterative forces that are best understood as the felt impact of time. Through causal efficacy we sense the achievements of the past and the human obligation to acknowledge their ineluctable presences. Without causal efficacy, environmental ethics would lack all reference to a concretely particular world.

In sum, perception in the mode of causal efficacy involves the remarking of the reality of time. Through it, time wraps itself environmentally around a place, a situation, or an object. We feel time's real presence as it compels our conformal attention to its achievements. Causal efficacy makes known in a non-sensuous manner the way in which value has spread through an environment. Humans feel the achievements of value as temporal monuments. The attention and respect granted the physical world expresses the value inherent in the legacy of the past. Perception in the mode of causal efficacy directly registers the reality of environmental worth. This is the gift of the human body in its activity as an environmental field.

Sense Perception and the Dazzle of the Senses

There is yet another mode of perception available to human beings. Whitehead calls it "perception in the mode of presentational immediacy." This type of perception is what we usually term sense perception. Whitehead employs the admittedly awkward term "presentational immediacy" to convey the basic character of all knowledge derived from the five senses; *viz.,* it is a mode of dwelling entirely in the present moment. As such, this way of reaching toward the otherness of the environment tells us very little about the past or the future. Yet it is on our sense perception that we characteristically rely whenever we wish to navigate our world. Indeed, it is sense knowledge that informs us about the important events in our environment. And as we have seen, it is to the senses that empiricism as well as all other forms of scientific materialism appeal whenever there is need of corroboration or evidence. But brilliant and compelling as this sense knowledge may be, Whitehead warns us that such knowledge is a potentially delusive abstraction.

It would be difficult to underestimate the importance of presentational immediacy for a study of the environment. In the first place, the rendition of nature provided by our five senses is incomplete. Further, this rendition omits what is most crucial for any appreciation of nature—the emotions that arise from value achieved by the events of nature. Thus, despite its brilliance and its clarity, the act of sense perception freezes the world of process, robbing it of that very flow of value that throbs through its many manifestations.

Also, what we derive from sense perception is a world that is straight-away, over there, in that direction. It therefore omits the essential connection between things that is so much a part of the ecological understanding of nature. It is a world of objects, objectively given and objectively present. Its claim on our attention is incontestable. It is in fact "immediate" because it is a "presentation" of what is sensibly present. But it tells no tales about its past. Neither does it suggest its future. It is arresting but barren, deprived of the axiological weight that is the hallmark of causal efficacy.

Nevertheless, its importance for human environmental interactions is undeniable. It provides us with a spatial matrix upon which we can build our directional maps. It clarifies our situation and renders up a sense of the environment remarkable for its approximate accuracy. And it does so with a force that gains our attention. Indeed, that is what "presentational immediacy" means: Here is the present, spatially spread out before us, in clear-cut fashion, and decorated with sounds, textures, colors, and tastes.

But the dangers inherent in taking such a picture as a complete portrait of the environmental situation should also be evident. It is an abstraction and the result of a selective emphasis that stresses spatial characteristics at the expense of temporal ones. The environment tends to get locked in place and we become used to seeing isolated scenes and simply located landscapes in place of environmental activities entwined in patterns of effective process. What gets shunted aside in the dazzle of the senses is precisely what is most important about the environment—its connections and relations. How one event enters into the essential makeup of another is replaced by the preeminence of "things"—in place of events we are given substances that appear static and self-contained. Isolated entities prevail where process once was. We take the immediate and forget the past from which it arose as well as the rich activities that underlie its display.

Built into the knowledge derived from the five senses is the important feeling of clarity and vividness with which much of our environmental participation is clothed. The sense of a sharp-cut difference between things, as well as their respective modes of spatial coordination as part of the landscape "out there," is the gift of presentational immediacy. We see the world as contemporaneous with ourselves. We hear its sounds as causally independent of the past. We feel its textures as they are in the present and quite obviously "there in that place." We taste and smell its presence as it presents itself in seeming openness and sharpness. But all the while we are enmeshed in its processes and subject to the throbbing dynamics of its causal efficacy.

In many ways these two modes of perception—causal efficacy and presentational immediacy—can be viewed as the converse sides of the same coin. Causal efficacy is dim and vague as to its origins and significance. Presentational immediacy is sharp, arresting, and clear-cut. It is the world as vividly decorated by the sense qualities we see, feel, hear, smell, and touch. Where the world of causal efficacy is heavy with importance and laden with the achievements of past activities, the world of presentational immediacy is dazzling in its self-manifestation, but shallow and impoverished when we attempt to look beneath its surface display. "Deep but vague" and "shallow but sharp": How do we put these two opposed deliverances of the human bodily environmental field together? The third mode of perception, symbolic reference, is what performs that task.

Symbolic Reference

What is needed is a common ground wherein these two original modes can mix. This ground is the region established by the proximity between the human body and its environmental field. Call such a field the region of symbolic reference. Then each such region shall have in it the data and information supplied by the modes of causal efficacy and presentational immediacy. These regions will be interpreted by the human body along the lines of symbolic reference, which it has inherited from its own somatic habits as well as its cultural heritage. A stone age man will cringe as an airplane flies over head. A citizen of the contemporary age pays it no mind. Each response is due to the way in which a symbol is recognized as bearing a message from the environment.

The reason for spending so much time on what may seem like an arcane epistemological topic is, as mentioned earlier, the fact that the idea of "place" will later play a crucial role in this study. Perception in its two pure modes and in its mixed mode of symbolic reference establishes a theory that justifies taking "place" seriously as a central environmental act. For if the body does not really intersect with the environment, then all talk of nature is merely imaginary experience having no direct relevance to the field of environmental philosophy.

The theory of symbolic reference argues against such a dismissal of environmental experience. It maintains that the rich and value-laden information derived fom the legacy of the past is handed on symbolically to the human being by reason of its referral to immediately presented contemporary regions of spacetime. Thus, in the one case, the airplane is a terrifying experience; in the other, it is a normal event that is part and parcel of everyday experience. What this means is that in ordinary human experience the objects of our environmental participation take on the status of symbols. They are never mere objects. Rather, they are freighted with value. They convey information important for our survival as well as our enjoyment of life. Colors, shapes, textures, tastes, smells, sounds, movements, places, landscapes, and regions really are there in our experience. And they make a real difference. The essential differences between environmental types reside within these forms of symbolic reference. There is no escape to a world of pure mind or a world of pure physical sensation. For better or worse human beings experience their environmental fields as suffused with symbols bearing the weight of different values. Such value is the gift of our bodies.

It should now be clear that the the earlier discussion of environmental orders and the corresponding ways in which they are felt was not an idle speculative gesture. Rather, the correlation between types of order and types of environmental moods can be seen as the necessary outcome of perception in the mixed mode of symbolic reference. Thus trivial order is felt indifferently. Vague orders do arouse a sense of expectation. Narrow orders are felt intensely. Wide orders do invite involvement. Rather than regarding these feelings as mere subjective responses arbitrarily arising from various environmental scenes, they are to be understood as the consequences of different bodily states. Environmental moods are not a matter of taste; they are rooted in the feelings that emerge from participating in different types of environmental orders.

We live in a world dominated by vivid sense data. These are the pivots around which our immediate present lives revolve. At the same time, we live in a world that is laden with the achieved values of the past. These are the feelings that mark our sense of continuity with the legacy of the past. The former mode of perception alerts us to our life in the present, while the latter registers the sense of continuity and depth that engenders feelings of importance. Both are fused in the act of symbolic reference whereby we enjoy our environmental being. This is the meaning that lies beneath the surface display of environmental forms.

In summary, symbolic reference fuses the two pure modes of perception in such a way that we can have depth without obscurity and clarity without superficiality. The symbol eliminates the obscurity associated with causal efficacy. It also supplements the dazzling but barren quality of sense perception with depth of value. Everyday environmental perception is always a matter of symbolic reference. Without it we would perish, for we would have no clue as to the relative importance of the various objects we encounter. Even with it our success rate is not perfect. Approximate as it is, it remains, however, our one clue to successful environmental adaptation. Through it systems of indication are set up throughout our environment. We get to know weather patterns, the signs of favorable or unfavorable habitats; also, threats can be detected and inviting places to live discerned. Symbolic reference is the natural way in which we habitually navigate our environmental abodes. Of course, the deeper the level of cultural participation in an environment, the deeper the semiotic significance of the symbols. This is a major reason why urban environments are so complex and intricate.

Symbolic Reference and Environmental Ideals

In concluding this chapter on the human body as well as this environmental cosmology, I want to underscore a central theme of my argument. Earlier I spoke of the necessity of a Platonic naturalism if we are to think adequately about the environment. The charge most often levelled against Platonism is that it is too "otherworldly" and relies too heavily on abstract ideals that have no actual bearing on the temporal world of becoming. It is claimed that the transcendental features of Platonic metaphysics force all modes of immanence to take a back seat. Furthermore, it is argued that by privileging the mind Plato's concept of the ideal realm makes any adequate recognition of the importance of the body impossible. In large measure, Plato's thought has been judged by the tradition to be anti-body and inimical to all forms of thinking that would seek to root thought in somatic being.

This analysis of the role of the human body in environmental philosophy directly contradicts such a shallow interpretation of Plato's thought. For the human body through its powers of symbolic reference is seen to be the very factor whereby the ideal, the actual, and the real intersect. Ideals are already immanent in the body structure when it perceives in the mixed mode of symbolic reference. What the body attempts to do is draw together the various dimensions of environmental process so that the vivid but empty display of sense qualities gets filled with the treasures of values felt by causal efficacy. Symbolic reference is therefore that mode of perception that seeks to "actualize" ideals. Of course, it is not always successful, It often falls short of the ideal. That does not mean, however, that the ideal is irrelevant to the process of environmental becoming. Indeed, it is only by reason of the normative measures that discussion of environmental processes can take place.

Recall the four categories of the environmental scheme. Inscape named the unique manner in which environmental events achieved their particular and special contours of value. They did so by reason of the ideals that shaped their manner of achieving value. Contrast named the way in which the event in question sorted out its various possibilities so as to achieve just this sort of value and no other. The ideal and the actual met to form the real. Pattern named the various ways in which these events interlocked to establish dominant environmental structures. Finally, transmission named the ways in which the feelings that make up the value of environmental events were transferred around different regions of the ecosystem.

It will also be remembered that this cosmology isolated four ideal environmental values: Intensity, integrity, wholeness, and depth. My argument demonstrates that these ideal values are the result of the existential conditions laid down by the environmental categories themselves. They are not speculations idly dreamt up. Rather, they spring from the very structure of a process universe. The logic of environmental systems demands the effective presence of these ideals as normative measures causally present in the makeup of environmental orders. Therefore, in terms of the construction of a Platonic naturalism, these four environmental ideals function as natural referential symbols for the assessment of various forms of environmental worth. The reason these ideals can so function lies in the somatic fact of the human body itself. For when it is functioning perceptually in the mixed mode of symbolic reference, it necessarily compares and contrasts the environmental data derived from the two pure modes of presentational immediacy and causal efficacy. And as should be evident, all forms of comparison and contrast depend upon the use of normative measures. There is no way around acknowledging the real presence of ideals as active agents in the coming-to-be of environmental processes.

A summary review of the categoreal scheme confirms this judgment. Every event achieves its value by shaping itself according to the possibilities available in its environment. This "inscape" is the outcome of the way in which it "contrasts" what might be with what can be. The ideal intervenes as a normative measure for estimating the worth of what is real. On a mesocosmic level, its "pattern" results from the mutual determining factors dominant within its special environmental niche. It receives these possibilities by reason of the "transmission" of feelings that take place within that niche. When these feelings are predominantly "physical," the past repeats itself with an insistent rhythm so as to secure a set level of physical responses. On the other hand, when "conceptual" feelings dominate, possibilities begin to overflow and make for an environment alive with chance and spontaneity. Now, when symbolic reference intervenes on the level of human cultural participation, propositional feelings tailored to the ways in which actual environments can possibly structure themselves take on greater and greater specificity. Distinct building styles begin to emerge and cultural environmental forms can be identified. The Greeks sort out their possibilities one way and present-day Boston does it another way. Both rely on normative measures to carry out this environmental creativity.

What is most important at this level of environmental participation is that human beings have at their disposal sets of ideals or appropriate normative measures whereby they can estimate the worth of environments. It is in this sense that ideal environmental values embedded in the human body's structure become all-important. By their being there through symbolic reference, they can guide the assessment of environmental activities and achievements in a way that combines physically felt values with ideal conceptual feelings. The resultant mix is a proposition that lures human judgment toward entertaining particular environmental situations as embodying to a greater or lesser degree certain ideal values. In this way, Plato's form of the good is naturalized within civilized expressions.

Environments can be experienced as intense or lacking in intensity. They can also be judged as whole or lacking in wholeness. Similarly, an environment can exhibit depth or shallowness. Finally, an environment can manifest great integrity or an utter lack of coordination. The point is, these ways of assessing environmental values are not the outcome of a "spectator" view of knowledge that sees the human knower as merely "out there" viewing a scene in pure neutral objectivity. Neither are such assessments merely subjective reactions to supremely indifferent physical scenes. This environmental cosmology maintains that the values experienced in actual empirical situations are really there in both the knower and the environment. The accuracy and truth of assessment depends, on the one hand, upon the the knower's embodied sense of the ideal and, on the other, upon the the environment's capacity to embody and express certain ideal presences. As will be seen later, it is this conflux of presences —the body and the environment—that forms the basis of a needed new discipline of foundational ecology. For it is through a regained sense of the richness of our body acts that the environment most forcefully expresses its enduring achievements of value.

Part One—an Environmental Cosmology—is now complete. From this vantage point the four basic ideas examined in the introduction take on even greater concreteness. *Perspective* is the the lens which an event, human or natural, uses to shape its view of what is possible and what is actual. Perspective, therefore, always entails the active use of ideals to shape the kinds of and types of value environmentally available. *Importance* is the gift of perspective insofar as particular ideals are actualized in concrete environmental situations. *Expression* is the way in which any event functions in an environment so as to display its value. *Understanding* begins and ends with the proper coordination of an event's perspective, expression, and importance.

Part Two

Nature

Chapter Five

Natural Space

The central character of natural space is its shy openness to form.[1] Space is both the most prominent and the most reserved dimension of nature. Its public quality is shown by the way it appears before our very eyes. Its hidden and private character is revealed by the fact that we cannot touch or feel it. In fact if we do, we know that what we have felt is not space but rather that which is taking up space. Space slips through our hands even as we try to grasp it. At the same time, it is quite misleading to think of space as empty. Space does give room but emptiness is not its primary characteristic.

Furthermore, space is pliable. When pushed, it yields, and when contained, it stays. Also, space seems to be indefinitely malleable, for it can assume any number of shapes and still remain space. Again, space separates but it can also join things together. It is both barrier and entrance. Space can welcome and space can forbid. Space is open and space is also closed. What is needed is a grasp of the inscape of space.

The Inscape of Natural Space

It is a cultural fact that we are conditioned to think of space as empty. This is a hangover from the age of thinking about space in

Newtonian terms as an absolute container. It is also one of the chief cultural obstacles standing in the way of a reformed environmental vision. Scientific materialism would have us regard this fundamental axis of experience as a type of empty vessel within which experience takes place. Nothing could be further from the truth. (A similar difficulty will be encountered when we deal with the inscape of time.)

The doctrine of process as the fundamental reality directly opposes this idea. Rather this study maintains—in line with the tenets of modern relativity theory as well as quantum physics—that space and time arise out of the activities of environmental entities. Thus, everything that comes to be expresses itself through an essential spatiotemporal spread. This means that all environments express certain spatial and temporal textures. It is part of the task of this study to identify and articulate these elementary forms.

For the sake of clarity and consistency, it is assumed throughout this part of the study that space always means natural space; that is to say, space unmarked by human intervention. A similar convention will be adopted when I speak of time. Once again, it is important to restate the fact that the spatial and temporal configurations to be discussed always and everywhere arise from the activities of the creatures embedded within the environments themselves. To think of space and time as separate from the environmental processes within which they occur is to commit yet again the fallacy of misplaced concreteness. Space is concrete. Time is concrete. Space and time—or better, spacetime—is the outcome of environmental activities. Neither space nor time exist independently of the creatures whose spatiotemporal perspective they express. To separate space and time from the environment is to drive a vicious abstraction between beings and the environments they inhabit.

This tendency to separate space and time from the environment is at the root of much ecological disturbance. Tearing apart the fabric of space and time distorts in the most fundamental way possible the integrity of environmental domains. The categories of this environmental cosmology are framed to make evident the absolute importance of fitting together essential and conditional environmental features in appropriate patterns. What could be more disruptive than a distortion of spatiotemporal relations?

What then is space? It is the very first expression of creativity in nature.[2] (Time, of course, is equiprimordial with space in expressing this elemental creative power in the natural world.) As soon as any instance of creativity appears on the scene, space is always already there. This is what it means to say that each event spreads itself in a spatial manner. There can be no creativity in the actual world without there also being an accompanying spatial mark. These marks are in fact the regions of space and time that environmental activities express in their process of coming to be.

It is important to underline this fusion of space and creativity. Precisely because of its unobtrusive quality, we are most likely to overlook spatial creativity. Its pliability and generosity of accommodation works against taking account of its real presence in the environment. It could be the case that in other cosmic epochs space does not play so fundamental a role but here in this world, space (along with time) is the primary initial emergence of novelty and value. Every environmental event, no matter how small or how large, occupies a region as its first instance of coming to be. When it does so, it at the same time establishes an extensive standpoint which is its own unique position. This act of registering both spatial location and spatial spread is what is meant by the primal act of creativity in nature.

In its inscape space displays two central aspects. It is "extensive" and it is "continuous." The extensive dimension of space signifies that power whereby space renders itself indefinitely plastic. Space extends itself according to the demands placed upon it by the events that make up its contours. In the *Timaeus,* Plato faces the question, what is space? How does one speak of that which seemingly has no content? Such an entity would be akin to nothing, and as Parmenides has told us, "of nothing, nothing can be said." The solution adopted by Plato is to understand space as primarily the capacity to accept extension. He calls it "The Receptacle."[3] Thus in one of its dimensions space is extensiveness itself. It is in Plato's evocative words: "The foster mother of all becoming." In its character as sheer extensiveness, natural space takes on the shape and form of that which comes to be within its precincts. If it is occluded entities that rise up, space shows itself as dense and occupied. If the environment is open and empty, space shows itself in like manner. Space in its mode of extensiveness exhibits an essential generosity toward environmental activities. Like the rainbow stretching across the sky, space allows what comes to be to extend itself to its respective determinate limits.

The second primary dimension of space is its "continuous" character. This can best be understood as its capacity for indefinite divisibility. For along with its extensive quality, space also has within it the real presence of potentiality. It is this potentiality that renders space divisible. Without this divisibility, space would, as it were, run out of space. But were that to occur, the universe as we know it would cease to be. Such is the importance of the primary and elemental inscape of space. Without the continuum provided by space, there could be no process of emergent environmental activities. Space in its inscape as continuous joins with extensiveness to register the primary expression of creativity. Whitehead calls this inscape of space the "extensive continuum".[4]

It is by reason of both the extensive and continuous character of this receptacle that distinct spatial patterns emerge. Because of its inscape, natural space can exhibit both directionality and solidarity. Spatial forms express a potential for direction because they display themselves according to the essential and conditional features laid out by the events marking actual positions in the extensive continuum. Spatial solidarity is achieved through the interlocking of events as they rise up and come to be at the edges of each other's respective domains. Space "spatializes" when a sufficient measure of layering characterizes the inscape of events. The first outcome of such spatial interplay is the recurrent cycle of building up and decaying that marks the rise and fall of events and entities in the natural world. In its inscape as an extensive continuum space makes all such creativity possible. The environmental processes situated at each locale atomize the extensive continuum and thereby form the bodies, shapes, directions, and contours of the natural world. This is to repeat what was insisted upon earlier: It is always the case that space is the initial concrete emergence of creativity in nature.

As this environmental cosmology demonstrates, every event expresses certain essential and conditional features as part of its own reality. In terms of the inscape of natural space, all such environmental events have as an essential feature a spatial presence that marks its first moment of environmental creativity. This establishment of a certain spatial region becomes in its turn a condition for future environmental events. Likewise, the newly emergent event must also take into consideration the spatial values of its predecessors. Space is therefore both an essential and a conditional feature of every environmental event. It is through and through perspectival. It is essential when it expresses the actual position of the event in question. It is conditional when newly emergent events must take into account the already achieved locations of other environmental events. When woven together into large-scale environmental regions, the active presence of the category of pattern manifests itself in a variety of important ways.

The Patterns of Natural Space

It is impossible to name all the spatial patterns of nature. As part of the extensive continuum there are by definition an indefinite number of such patterns. They are as many as there are forms of geometry to detail their characteristics. Therefore, in what follows there will be no attempt to list spatial types. Rather, the important point for this study is establishing an understanding of the essential characteristics of the natural spatial patterns experienced on this planet.

Thus, whenever space is encountered, it is always felt as over there in that direction. This is to say that space is experienced as objectified. Furthermore, this objectification is experienced as directional. Space has within it the potential for orientations such as up and down, inside and outside. Also, when appropriate conventions are employed, the spatial textures of objectified directionality can take on such characteristics as north and south, east and west, and so forth. In other words, space presents itself as ready for various types of coordinate division.

In addition to objectified directionality, the category of pattern reveals that natural space exhibits a threefold character of separativeness, integration, and continuity.[5] By separativeness is meant the fact that each region of space has its own unique determinateness. This follows from the category of inscape, which demands that every event express its own unique essential features. Integration, on the other hand, signifies the way in which each region of space pulls together into a unique harmony all the features, both essential and conditional, that make up its environmental niche. Thus, along with determinateness natural space also exhibits togetherness. Continuity is the third characteristic of natural space. Through it is created the sense of seamless flow that is the hallmark of natural space. Borders and edges run up to each other and there are no gaps. Nature displays itself as belonging to a common continuum of extension. In cosmological terms, the extensive continuum exhibits extensive connection. All three features are derivative from natural space understood as the extensive continuum.

In its own special way natural space also expresses the fundamental metaphysical theme of the one and the many. The patterns of natural space are one because they integrate their components so as to always express a harmony of unique determinateness that grasps within its spatial spread all the essential and conditional features of its spatial position. These same harmonies are also many because each expresses its own unique perspective of importance that spreads itself throughout the environment in question. Finally, each region of natural space is again also one because of the continuity that spreads through and among the separated regions. In natural space one never runs out of space. The initial creativity emergent from the extensive continuum is always available. As separate, integrated, and continuous, natural space expresses in its essential and conditional features the signs "farther" and "further." It unites fact, form, and value.

From this there follow two qualities of natural space. Natural space is both interruptive and bounded. As interruptive it is always full of surprises. Just when we think we have mastered the contour of a hillside, we fall into a hole. The sea smashes into a cliff. And a sparrow lands on a branch that we failed to notice. Surprise is the general reaction of the attentive walker in nature. Natural space alternates between the highly different and the tediously similar. This sense of irregularity results from the second quality of natural space, the way in which it is always tied to concrete natural objects. Call such a characteristic its boundedness. The contours and dimensions of natural space are always the outcome of the events that inhabit its domain. Since these creaturely events are always to some degree novel and creative, the interruptive and bounded qualities of natural space lay the groundwork for an important axiom that governs all forms of natural space: ***Natural space is always "found."*** Thus, the great natural landmarks identified by human beings in the course of history are always distinguished by the way in which their uniqueness both interrupts and bounds an environment. They can be large or even minutely small. They stand out because in some fundamental way or other they are different and this difference is not the result of human action. They therefore embody the creative urge of nature to a high degree. They are unmistakable, peculiar, and special. This "found" character of natural space will receive significant expansion and development in the last section of this chapter.

This environmental cosmology defined the category of pattern as a type of order and also identified some four levels of environmental order: The trivial, the vague, the narrow, and the wide. Use of these levels of order can deepen the understanding of natural space. Every pattern is already a type of order and every order achieves its aim by arranging in a special way the simple and complex components that make up its spatial region. Just as the inscape of space was marked by the emergence of essential and conditional features, so also the patterns of space display different variations of simplicity and complexity. A look at each level of environmental order shows just how powerful such patterns of space can be in determining the value of environmental regions.

A trivial spatial pattern is one marked by an excess of incompatible elements. There is a general failure in contrast, for nothing stands out as more important than anything else. As was said earlier, trivial environments prevent the emergence of importance because paradoxically everything is important in a trivial spatial region. An extreme complexity overtakes the environment and nothing simple can emerge. Due to the absence of any level of coordination, trivial space can achieve no community of action within its borders. The creatures dwelling in trivial space are infected by an extreme passivity. By succumbing to the demands of an excessive complexity, trivial spatial regions move toward a collapse into nonentity.

It has already been seen that nature as we presently experience it on this planet has no trivial orders. In the emergence of nature over past aeons of time, nature has already built up here on earth levels of vague order that stand as backdrops for more specialized forms of order. To find examples of trivial space it would be necessary to travel far out into galactic space, where, some scientists estimate, one encounters a single hydrogen atom every five yards or so. Or metaphorically speaking, one might imagine a slag heap outside an iron mine as representing trivial order. But even here vagueness would be a more precise term, since the slag granules form orders within orders of specialized spatial patterns. As an example such an image is only a metaphor, not a reality. Also, it must be remembered that the act of coordinate division whereby levels of order can be determined is dependent upon the interests of the ordering agent. What is vague to one can be intensely narrow to another. For the regions selected fall into the orders selected by the interests of the observers. A geologist might find a slag heap intensely interesting. And the lion ant dwelling in it regards each trivial grain of sand as a potential food source.

A vague spatial pattern is one that exists on the edge between the chaotic and the orderly. As stated previously, vagueness is not fuzziness. Rather, it is a very special form of order that allows certain objects to stand in as representative of other objects. A rudimentary form of unity takes the place of the lack of coordination present in the spatially trivial. Vagueness supplants the complexity of triviality by bringing into play some modes of importance that can assume defining roles within the spatial region. Vagueness shares with triviality the character of excess. For triviality, excess lay in the direction of incompatibility. The excess that affects vagueness is an excess of identification. As has been seen, it is by reason of this defect that vagueness can allow the many to count as one.

When a spatial order displays a fundamental vagueness, its component features exhibit simplicity as a guiding trait. Within vague patterns of spatial order an overall uniformity rises up to assert itself. Thus, one can "vaguely" speak of an environment as being arid or fertile or boggy and all the while make room for opposite conditions within its domain. A good concrete example of a vague spatial order would be a mountain range as seen from a distance. Undoubtedly, there are rivers, ravines, lakes, and valleys running all through such a spatial display, but from a distance, the many count as one and we see the mountain range in all its vague majesty.

A narrow spatial pattern is characterized by an extreme simplicity such that little or no distractions are allowed within its domain. Narrowness marks out a particular channel for space to follow and what cannot "fit in" gets very short shrift. Its lack of generosity has been noted before and when narrowness characterizes a spatial domain, it most often is accompanied by a feeling of incompleteness. This comes about because narrowness contradicts an essential trait of natural space, its generosity or openness. An intolerantly narrow space trenches on the very essence of spatial being. It thwarts both the extensive and the continuous features that are essential to the inscape of natural space. The very word, narrow, conjures up the specter of the potential disappearance of space.

One of the more obvious examples of a narrow spatial pattern is a dense impacted material object. A stone lets nothing in and isolates itself spatially from the rest of the surrounding environment. Narrow environments specialize in separation. Unlike the trivial, which lets any kind of space into its domain, the narrow reacts against complex additions even if by itself it may be quite complex. Similarly, the narrow stands opposed to the vague. Where vagueness eschews clarity, narrowness endorses it. An environment steeped in narrowness presents great presence and individuality. It is impossible to overlook a narrow environment, for it demands attention through the collective strength of its individual moments of self-assertion. Clear perspectives and a high degree of individual character are common marks of narrow spatial environmental patterns.

A wide spatial pattern is the outcome of a fortunate blending of the vague and the narrow. Natural spatial width is distinguished by its capacity to surround and embrace without eliminating distinctive individual features. Both simplicity and complexity are attuned to each other. The resultant harmony is such that individuality which is the gift of narrowness and unity which is the gift of vagueness are brought into fruitful contrast. From one side a complex simplicity reigns which is then seen from the other side as a form of simple complexity. Width lets both the narrow and the vague assert their full weight and in so doing elevates the environment to a totally new level of importance and value.

Consider a hillside in the Connemara district of Western Ireland. It sits back and through its width it embraces numerous stones, boulders, and rocky outcroppings such that they all appear to belong quite naturally to the hillside. Such is the width of this special environmental embrace that even the sheep that pasture on it are accepted. They appear to belong in the most natural way to the hillside itself. All such spatially wide natural landscapes are correctly judged to be beautiful for they do two things quite well. First of all, they "fit" into their settings the strong individuality of their members. In this way they embrace the narrow. Second, they "harmonize" their components in such a way as to pull together differences and thereby preserve the unity that is the hallmark of strong modes of beauty. Experienced spatially, width creates appropriate room for the right amount of simplicity and complexity. Such observations bring the discussion quite naturally to the question of the perception of spatial patterns.

The Symbolic Perception of Natural Space

Human beings experience the spatial patterns of nature through perception in the mixed mode of symbolic reference. These perceptual experiences culminate in the environmental moods discussed in Part One of this environmental cosmology. It will be recalled that perception in the mode of symbolic reference has its roots in two more primordial modes of perception, that of causal efficacy and that of presentational immediacy. Causal efficacy signals that mode of experiencing that is grounded in a non-sensuous perception of the environment. This causal efficacy is felt by reason of the "withness" of the body, which produces feelings of continuity with various environmental regions. These lines of continuity establish the push of the past as a real factor within the present moment. Causal efficacy, therefore, makes available the legacy of the past. As such, it gives knowledge that is heavy with value but quite dim as to origins. Shrouded in human flesh, causal efficacy senses the immense importance of the past but cannot locate it with any high degree of accuracy. Pinpointing presences within the contemporary world is the result of perception in the mode of presentational immediacy. The five senses carry out this task within a generally accurate schema of relations. What presentational immediacy grants is a sharp but shallow understanding of the processes emergent within a contemporary region of space and time. Each mode of perception has its merits and its defects. It is up to the act of perception in the mixed mode of symbolic reference to seize the value of environmental processes.

In what follows, I argue that the environmental moods felt by human beings caught up in the spatial patterns just discussed are precisely the outcome of such mixed symbolic perception. In fact, I argue that the environmental moods discussed in Part One of this environmental cosmology result from the way in which the environment in question participates in such normative measures as are required to stir such feelings. Thus when a trivial environment is encountered in the mixed mode of symbolic reference, it is experienced with indifference. This is due to the lack of important values distributed throughout the spatial patterns of the environment. Similarly, a vague environment is symbolically perceived with expectation. This is caused by the presence of suggestive values that are felt as insinuated throughout the spatial region. Narrow spatial patterns evoke in turn an intensity of feeling due to the strong presence of certain types of value. Lastly, an environment characterized by spatial width will be symbolized by a feeling of involvement as genuinely present within the spatial region in question.

In all this I am simply drawing out the consequences of following in a rigorous manner the tenets of a Platonic naturalism. It is not the case that the environmental moods are merely felt in some imaginary manner. To maintain such a doctrine would be to reassert a form of dualism already discredited. This study retains its commitment to a view of the environment as primarily a world of feelings. What is felt is really there in the environment, because what is felt is the way in which the environment participates in the ideals that it seeks to actualize. The human being feels these values as the ways in which the environment more or less measures up to certain ideals. I call such perceptions moods because they are somewhat dim and for the most part difficult to speak of. But such difficulties ought not to be used to denigrate environmental achievements for the sake of adhering to some scientific dogma that refuses to acknowledge the real presence of normative measures in nature. Indeed, we are in need of an educational process that will sharpen our skills in detecting such natural spatial patterns and their attendant normative measures. That skill seems to have eroded when the city came to be our prominent mode of dwelling. Think of the way in which Native Americans are able to find their way by scouting the signs that nature leaves about. It is but a short step from recognizing their talents for such activities to seeing its possibilities in our modern urban way of life. Humans need to be encouraged to recover this sense of the normative measures embedded in their spatial surroundings. Without it they are truly without symbolic reference. They are effectively lost in space and without a clue as to its value.

Perception in the mixed mode of symbolic reference takes place whenever information derived from one of the pure modes (causal efficacy and presentational immediacy) is transferred symbolically to some environmental presence. This presence could be a weather pattern, a hillside, a stream, or any other significant region. So, in my example of the Connemara hillside, what is transferred to the spatial region contemporary with my body are previous experiences of involvement with which I have had some familiarity. Of course what is immediately evident is the fact that if I have had no such experience, then no such symbolic reference can ever take place. This is similar to Eliot's important insight into the loss of an objective correlative for direct natural experiences suffered by English culture in the time of the metaphysical poets.[6] I wish to extend Eliot's point and suggest that we are now in danger of losing such "objective correlatives" in our natural environmental experience. Under the pressures applied by a culturally dominant scientific materialism, we lose confidence in our felt reactions to the environment. We doubt their "truth" and suspect their validity. But in terms of the cosmology developed in this study, there is every reason to rely upon our intuitions in these matters. What is more, we need to sharpen and expand these powers of feeling spatial patterns. Without them our sense of the natural and its value diminishes drastically and we tend to fall back on a false rationalism that leaves to science the last judgment on what is of value in natural processes. Again, the importance of aesthetic training for preserving a sense of the beauty, wholeness, and value of nature suggests itself.

There is yet another concrete way to experience the symbolic presence of normative measures as active determinants in the spatial configurations of nature. Consider the well known phenomenon of liminal spatial experience.[7] It is a felt fact that one senses when one region of space has been left and another has been entered upon. There are spatial corridors entwined in natural processes. We travel across these thresholds and notice that now we are in a valley lush with life whereas before we were isolated in some lifeless mountain pass. Our body senses the different spatial patterns that it passes through. In fact when such modes of spatial differentiation are absent or unfelt, the tedium associated with trivial spatial patterns begins very quickly to assert itself. We become bored or fatigued when in fact there is no physiological reason for such a sense of spent energy. What we are feeling is the indifference of space to our presence. Feelings of boredom or fatigue register our immersion in unimportance. Liminal spatial transitions signal the effective presence of normative measures affecting our sense of place.

Similarly, we ride the rising curve of expectation when we enter upon an environment haunted by vague presences. We sense the presences of things unseen and unheard. Our body alerts us to potential values lurking in the spatial contours of a mountain glen. We feel the urge to explore. Our body knows we are on the edge of symbolically rich terrain. Such vague environments can actually lead us into them by reason of their hints and clues. Expectation emerges when the threshold of vagueness is crossed. Perhaps it is youth that feels this mood most keenly, but it can be noted in every stage of human growth and development if we pay attention to our bodily feelings.

Passages that lead into narrow spatial regions impress us with their seriousness. We feel there is no way out, for options are being closed off even as we move forward. This is precisely the normative dimension of narrowness. It produces great feelings of intensity by compressing our experience into ever more tightly wound spatial channels. In entering upon narrow spatial patterns we instinctively feel pushed to focus intently on the matters at hand.

Finally, the liminal feel of a wide environment presents itself as inviting generous exploration. We feel involved and at home because an ambience of welcome surrounds us. We feel the embrace of the land as it involves us in its process of becoming. We participate in its full diversity because our bodies sense at the same time the presence of a measure of unity that pulls together difference in a most powerful way. Part of the appeal of great landscape painting is precisely this undoubted sense of stepping into a wide scene of great beauty. For aesthetically educated eyes, sight provides touch at a distance. We move through the painting with our eyes, and our bodies symbolically involve themselves with the presence of great beauty.

In sum, the symbolic perception of natural space is a process determined by the body's capacity to discern the effective presence of those normative measures that are at work shaping the various spatial patterns of the environment. Such perception never reaches a point of exactness, for it is not a matter of quantitative reckoning. In these matters of environmental sensibility what counts most is a certain deft attention to the ways in which space plays its way through natural environmental fields. The symbolic perception of natural spatial patterns is always a matter of moods and measures.

The Value of Natural Space

Space is no empty container. Neither is it a region devoid of value. It is in fact the very first evidence of creativity at work in nature. For as nature sculpts its extensive continuum by means of the events that make up its various environmental fields, what comes to be are expressions of value displayed in spatial forms. It is time to assess the character of those values. Given our analysis, there would appear to be four fundamental qualities to the values inscribed in nature by space. Natural space is essential, creative, spontaneous, and embedded. An understanding of these four qualities helps eliminate the more egregious examples of the fallacy of misplaced concreteness that presently infect environmental discourse.

In the first place, natural space can no longer be taken as some accidental condition. It is riven into the very heart of nature. It is neither neutral nor value free. Rather, it marks out the space of value as it emerges from environmental processes. To ignore the essential reality and value of natural space is to put the entire environment at risk. The spatial patterns that play across a landscape are as much a part of its value as the creatures that inhabit it.

Neither is natural space a dead zone wherein nothing occurs. On the contrary, there is no such thing as "empty space," for all regions of space have patterns in them even if they only be trivial ones. This is to say that natural space is a creative event that is happening even as we encounter it. Natural space is always "doing something" because every event in a process environment is spreading itself spatially (as well as temporally). There is no environmental event, region, or creature that is not existentially spread out in space. And as has been repeatedly said, each such moment of existential spread is a creative act unique to both the creature and the ecological niche it inhabits. It can never be repeated, for its ***haeccitas***—its special uniqueness as just this event and no other—can never be repeated. It is precious in its spatial reality because its position (and its date) is inscribed just once in the universe. Such is the radical creativity expressed by the natural acts of spatial activity.

Now, it follows from this radical spatial creativity that natural space is also spontaneous and grows up, out, and into the environment in its own special way. True enough, it must take account of the conditional features that surround its coming to be. Nevertheless, each act of spatial spread has its measure of spontaneity. This is the ground of the irregularity of natural space that was discussed in the previous section. Natural space does not come ready-formed in straight planes and angles. Neither is it homogenized so that all spaces are the same, being bound together in a common straitjacket. Rather, the very possibility of conceiving liminal spaces, as well as the differentiation of natural space into types of patterns, depends upon a direct recognition of the vital spontaneity inherent in the character of natural space. Natural space is fresh, new, and different every time we encounter it.[8]

Finally, there is the embedded character of natural space. This is the most direct evidence of space's concrete character. For natural space is always tied to the objects that spatialize themselves within the environment. To say that natural space is embedded is to say that it arises simultaneously with the objects and events that make up an environmental region. This is simply a more concrete way of saying that space is an essential dimension of environmental structures.

Given these four aspects of natural space, it is now possible to understand just why natural space is always "found." When natural space is encountered, nothing can be added to it. It is what it is and is just so in this particular spatial way. We can be surprised by it. We can be stunned by it. We can merely notice it. We can discover it. We can identify it. We can locate it. We can even preserve it. But we cannot make it!

This is the great truth that nature conservation movements uphold. Therefore, the primary way in which we acknowledge the values of natural space is through respect. In acknowledging the presence of natural space we also recognize something that is not ourselves. This act of respect for what is other than human is the initial gesture that is at the base of all appropriate systems of environmental ethics. Without the capacity to recognize what is other and different from ourselves, we degenerate into deeper and deeper pools of narcissistic disorder.[9] In respecting natural space we initiate an important movement toward reclaiming for nature its proper sphere as a place where significant value emerges for its own sake. The careful cosmological analysis of natural space demonstrates the real existence of non-instrumental value in nature. Natural space concretely expresses intrinsic natural values.

But it is not enough merely to respect natural space. We must also know just what we are respecting. It is important to recognize the structural patterns of natural space. But even if such an act of aesthetic sensitivity is accomplished, there is something more required. Mere knowledge of the presence of trivial, vague, narrow, and wide orders of natural space will not suffice to improve environmental sensitivity. We also need some measures whereby we can judge the presence of significant spatial achievement. Some set of normative measures for estimating the value of natural space must be granted significant cultural recognition.

I suggest that to participate in a good way in the assessment of natural space requires the active use of the ideal environmental values developed in Part One of this environmental cosmology. Recall that a set of ideal environmental values was worked out from the general metaphysics of the speculative scheme. These were intensity, integrity, wholeness, and depth. These ideal values form a framework for good cultural participation in natural environments. Used properly, they allow us to find, understand, and protect the achievements of nature, especially in regard to its spatial configurations. If they become widespread throughout a culture, they can serve to anchor that culture's sense of respect for nature. When it is known why something is respected, the chances of preserving it are doubled. For without knowledge of the values inscribed in natural space, we are reduced to the status of worshippers. And one person's religion is another's sign of ignorance. Environmental preservation based on ill-understood respect is guaranteed to fail.

The four ideal values about to be discussed are never found in a perfected state. If they were, they would cease to be ideals. But they do present themselves in varying degrees in natural environments. What is needed is the insight to estimate just how well or how poorly they are upheld in regions of natural space. More especially in terms of this study, there is an important axiomatic gradient to be used in measuring the expression and development of these ideal values in natural space. That gradient is as follows: The more a spatial region tends toward the development of an increasing individuality, the more value that spatial region has achieved. There are two very important reasons for this rule. Individuality is a mark of great intensity and intensity of experience is the fundamental measure marked out by this cosmology for assessing all environmental worth. Indeed, individuality is the sign of creativity itself.[10] The second reason concerns two themes to be developed in later chapters: The arrival of life, and the central role of beauty in determining an ethical vision for nature. Suffice it to say here that life without some mode of individuality is as unthinkable as beauty without some measure of uniqueness.

What is the mark of intensity when achieved in natural space? All events in nature exhibit a certain tensile strength. This is due to the way in which they arrange their conditional features so as to express their essential features. This effort at self-creation results in a harmony. But harmony, to remind ourselves once again, is not about niceness or smoothness. Rather, the effort to create a harmony often requires a certain jolt. In the jostling about that marks a natural environment, some elements win out and others are lost. There is a point to the doctrine of nature as a war of antagonists. What wins out is that which has the level of intensity required to take part in that particular spatial region. Intensity is the sign of an identity in formation.[11] This is one reason that narrowness always grants intensity. Through the centering process made available by forms of narrowness, strong spatial configurations emerge and assert themselves. When spatial intensity dissipates, we are on the verge of so-called "empty space." The reason for the importance of intensity as an ideal spatial environmental value is the rather obvious fact that without it, space does not come to be in any environmentally significant manner.[12]

Integrity is the ideal environmental value that balances intensity. By reason of integrity, a maximum degree of diversity is allowed into a natural spatial region. Integrity allows for the difference which intensity in its narrowness tends to experience as a mere obstruction. Integrity does not merely tolerate difference. If it did, then a real potential for triviality would loom for the region in question. Diversity can always overtake a spatial region and render it trivial through excess of incompatibility. Rather, what integrity brings to a spatial region is the coordination of diversity. Integrity is a mode of order that arranges diversity without eliminating intensity.

It carries out this role by reason of building up contrasts upon contrasts so that the spatial region exhibits marked individuality. This gain in individual value is the outcome of allowing difference to play a real part in the spatial composition of the environment.[13]

Wholeness is the third ideal environmental value to be discussed. It confers upon a spatial region a special sense of completeness such that everything that should be included in that space finds its proper place. The feeling most often associated with the presence of wholeness in a natural spatial environment is satisfaction. A sense of contentment is achieved because the content of the spatial environment is filled with what is appropriate to it. Now, the word "filled" must be used with some caution. Otherwise, we fall back into the trap of thinking of space as some sort of empty container. Filled here indicates the special way in which the unity of the spatial region has been able to include a maximum set of conditional features into its contours. When achieved, we have what Whitehead called "perfection in its own kind."[14] Spatial regions express their wholeness by breathing forth a certain stillness. This stillness results from the way in which each feature has managed to gain access to spatial expression in a manner most in accord with its way of being. It is within such spatial regions that the transmission of stillness as a definite environmental quality can be symbolically perceived by humans. Simplicity has coordinated complexity without eliminating difference. It should be evident that in such a special spatial setting great individuality has been achieved.[15]

Depth is the final ideal value, and it expresses itself when layers on layers of spatial process unite to form a great volume of space. Room is made for the individuality residing within each layer of existence. Spatial events interlock so as to expand the levels of possibility available within the region. One senses the real presence of novelty, but depth does not detail beforehand what specific values lurk within the spatial region. The depths of space are therefore experienced as initially vague, but once engaged, an extraordinary sense of importance and worth can be summoned out of such depths. When an environment displays spatially deep configurations, it appears to offer itself as an unending source of potential creativity. The phrase "fathomless depths" partially expresses the power depth has to invite our unceasing exploration. Depth arises from fortunate contrasts that allow diversities to play off each other so that ever new levels of process reveal themselves. Of all the ideal environmental values, it is spatial depth that best portrays the sense of bottomless creativity that lies at the heart of a process universe. When "depth cries out to depth," natural spatial experience has reached a certain creative climax.[16] In the depths of space are to be found those inexhaustible resources that call forth a sense of the freshness of nature.[17]

If respect for natural space is informed by the normative measures of intensity, integrity, wholeness, and depth, then the effort to protect environmental places will be grounded in an intelligent understanding of their importances. Without such knowledge environmentalists wind up either preaching to the choir or being taken for fools indulging in primitive forms of nature worship. Natural space is too charged with value to hand it over to those who are ignorant of its worth. At the very least, measuring the environment by using appropriate normative standards moves the debate in the direction of intelligent cultural participation. At this point in the history of environmentalism, such a development would bring some welcome relief. For the most part recent debate has too often consisted of slogans slung back and forth between the "treehuggers" and the "rednecks." Aesthetic discourse informed by normative modes of thinking would transform the debate to an entirely different level.

As essential, creative, spontaneous, and embedded, natural space still stands in need of being found. And once found it still needs to be defended. Understanding its worth in terms of the cosmology developed so far is one step in the direction of securing its value for ourselves and those who come after us.

By way of concluding this presentation on the value of natural space, let us take a trip on "The Sky Road." It is some five miles long and runs from Clifden to Derreen, Streamstown, County Galway, Ireland. It winds across the hills of Connemara, dipping and rising with the contours of the land. Its track passes extremely close to the very edge of the West Coast of Ireland. The Islands of Inisboffin, Inisshark, Inisturk, and Turbot hove in and out of view as the road banks, turns in upon itself, and then plunges forward to the Northwest. Sheep, cattle, and Connemara ponies graze on the hillsides. Enormous boulders rise out of the green ground and cling to the edges of the surrounding heights. The fields are scattered with rocks of the most extraordinary colors and shapes. Occasionally, deep brown bogland presents itself. The light changes with a stunning suddenness. In the background the mountainous shapes of the Twelve Bens loom forward. The rocks begin to sing. In the misty air a rainbow is thrown up. It is altogether an astonishing vista of intense beauty.

Had I skill enough I could describe in greater concrete detail the beauty I am witnessing. But would that serve to inscribe the natural space in a more effective way than the abstract ideals I have just listed and discussed? I think not. All the concreteness of detail would not present the hidden standards by which I judged this scene as "astonishing." By what am I stunned? Indeed, it is the actual natural space of The Sky Road that takes my breath away. But in the retelling of the scene must I not make use of the normative measures of intensity, integrity, wholeness, and depth in order to share what it is that compels me to stop and gape astonished at this most marvellous space of beauty?

It is the intensity of the space that fills my body's eyes. It is the integrity of the landscape that holds forth to me all its different features. I am embraced by the wholeness of The Sky Road that pulls together in all its completeness the islands, the sea, the hills, and the animals. It is the depth of the vista that makes me come back for more and more. And every time I do, more of its importance and value is revealed to me. This is the proper use of the abstractions I have been presenting. Used as signposts, they signal to us the real presence of beauty, importance, unity, and goodness.

What is genuinely mysterious about natural space is the sudden and surprising act of emergence. One minute we are facing a level plain and the next we encounter looming mountains rising from that same plain. This is what is meant by the found dimension of natural space. Given this quality, it is essential that respect be the mode of comportment adopted toward nature. Without such an attitude what is most central to natural space—its creative spontaneous presence—will be missed altogether. One way to safeguard the dimension of mystery in our encounter with nature is insistence upon this "found" quality. But respect without thematic understanding will quickly lose its edge. A respect for the mysterious spatial spontaneity of nature is not an invitation to stop thinking. What is needed is better and better abstractions. At the very least, I would hope that the ideal environmental values of intensity, integrity, wholeness, and depth point the way toward such an aesthetically rich encounter with the concrete presence of natural space.

And yet for all their suggestiveness the abstractions deployed in this chapter to get a hold on the concrete remain just that—"abstractions." There hovers over the descriptions of natural space developed in this chapter an undeniable idyllic scenic quality. The analysis is short on what Plato called "life and motion." In one sense that is inevitable, for we fail in the face of so elastic a modality as space. It ever eludes our grasp despite its concrete embeddedness in the landscape. But there is a more fundamental cause for the abstractness clinging to these discussions. We have not yet dealt with time—the coequal partner of space in the primal creative moments of nature. It is there that "life and motion" begin to express themselves.

Chapter Six

Natural Time

Time takes time! A full understanding of this remark depends upon an analysis of the inscape, patterns, symbolic perception, and value of time. Time, like space, is an essential feature of every event that comes to be and perishes in the environment. That which rises up naturally and falls away naturally always does so within a temporal dimension of its own making. Of course, just as in spatial environments, each event must take into account the temporal conditions that surround it. Still, what is essential about natural time is the self-creativity by which it expresses its own unique temporal perspective. This inscape of time derives from "the epochal character of the process of becoming," and a discussion of it forms the first part of this chapter. After that, the patterns of time—the past, the present, and the future—are analyzed. Each of these temporal modalities has its own characteristics and nature has special ways of expressing these temporal perspectives. The third section deals with the symbolic perception of time and concerns the ways in which humans grasp the significance of these varying dimensions of natural time. A discussion of the value of natural time in terms of environmental processes forms the conclusion of this chapter.

As in the previous chapter, major emphasis will be given here to the the categories of inscape and pattern. But with our discussion of time, the processive activities of nature gain more environmental importance. For all its dynamic creativity, space remains a relatively static dimension of environmental events. This is decidely not the case with time. The expansion and deepening of time's process involves the rise to prominence of the category of contrast. Indeed, it is precisely ever-increasing sets of contrasts spanning the actual and the possible domains that deepen time's developmental inscape. Also, along with this stress on budding modes of contrast, the category of transmission begins to emerge as an important natural factor. Time hurls itself forward. And out of that process arise the forms of life that express nature's most profound creative act. Just as the most important gradient in space was the emergence of individuality, so also the emergence of types and kinds of "full time" depends upon a qualitative increase in the individualized contrast of actuality and possibility maintained by natural events. Eventually, when these contrasts have taken on the character of "temporal acts with genuine individuality," then the natural environment through the patterning of such temporal acts takes on the qualities that humans generally associate with the natural domain. Beings with aims and interests start to populate the environment. In addition, each of these temporal acts will begin to take on the role of providing significant normative measures for the environments in question. Out of these temporal acts will grow trivial, vague, narrow, and wide levels of environmental order as well as such actualized ideal values as intensity, integrity, wholeness, and depth.

In beginning this discusssion of time it is again important to keep in mind the fallacy of misplaced concreteness. For once again, the temptation will be to regard time as some form of empty container that gets filled up with natural activities. But this is to mistake the abstract for the concrete and once again allow scientific materialism to overtake our habits of thought. Time is no abstraction. It is as primal in its concreteness as space. Time grows with the events that make up the natural environment. The inscape of time makes clear the character of its concreteness.

The Inscape of Natural Time

The inscape of natural time is grounded in the epochal character of process. As such, natural time has two features. As natural, time is in itself either "epochal" or "transitional." Epochal time and transitional time are not to be confused with physical time. I reserve the term physical time for all those kinds of time that depend upon retrospective forms of measurement. Thus, the kind of time derived from clocks, calendars, or any other sort of abstract logically deduced measuring devices is named physical time. All such forms of physical time are derivative from natural time since they rely upon the measurement of already-completed epochal and transitional time. In brief, physical time is another dimension of the thinking we have been calling scientific materialism. Such time is purely quantitative. It only measures the lapses between modes of time that are detected according to predecided standards. As its measures of seconds, minutes, hours, days, months, years, and centuries indicate, physical time is abstract time. Natural time, on the other hand, is qualitative. In both its epochal form and its transitional patterns natural time spreads through dimensions filled with concrete feelings. It is experienced as expressing various levels of environmental order. Also, as qualitatively concrete, natural time is felt through the moods that accompany such levels of order. Like natural space, natural time is an essential dimension of the world of feelings that make up environmental regions.

The subject matter of this section concerns itself solely with epochal time. As stated above, natural time is also characterized by transitional time. It flows out of a past and toward a future. This aspect of time is dealt with in the second section of this chapter, where the patterns of time are discussed. Natural time in its epochal and transitional dimensions is radically different from our culture's customary view of time. That view of time hinges on an acceptance of the tenets of scientific materialism. Once again, what is under challenge is the viewpoint of scientific materialism. What must be understood and underscored at the outset is the fact that concrete natural time, in its epochal character, comes all at once or not at all. Process occurs through the coming-to-be and the perishing of epochs of time, each one of which is a seamless unity including all the felt dimensions of its world. Thus, each occasion or event is a unique drop of experience that forges its own distinct perspective on the universe and at the same time expresses the *haeccitas* of its value.

When these occasions succeed one another in varying types of order, then this succession of occasions is what is meant by the term, transition. It is the succession of such events that bring about the levels of order earlier termed trivial, vague, narrow, and wide. Each event in its utter concreteness is a unique happening of time that brings distinct, particular expressions of values into the environment. Such epochs cannot be divided or torn apart. They happen all at once or not at all. The patterns of time past, present, and future, on the other hand, are experienced as the transition resulting from the becoming and the perishing of these epochal occasions.[1] In the case of either epochal becoming or epochal transition, what is experienced is not what our culture ordinarily means by time. That is why I have reserved the term physical time for this customary sense of time.

In sum, what this environmental cosmology has been calling events of value are also to be understood as epochs of temporality. Time in its concrete inscape is a corruscating ebullience of value. It ramifies outward and converges inward and each time it does so, value is lost and gained, increased and decreased. This doctrine guarantees two qualities to the temporal world of nature and neither of them can be ignored. First, time is discontinuous, for it plunges on in seamless unities. It is always a one. But this truth is to be balanced by another one: Time is also creative transition and passage. It is always a many expressing an essential incompleteness. Each epoch's perishing marks the birth of another. This is the heart and the soul of the doctrine of epochal time.

This doctrine also maintains that time does not flow evenly and at a constant rate. Rather, time is discontinuous. It flows unevenly and is experienced differently in different time zones. This is one fundamental aspect of the term "epochal." Time is not an absolute container within which things happen—this is the thesis of scientific materialism and remains a hangover from the Newtonian world view. Such a concept conceals the primordial sense of natural time. And this creative process is always naturally epochal. It comes in durations whose spans mark out the achievements of value that make up the very texture and fabric of environments. These "quanta," "epochs," "occasions," or "events"—the exact term used is at the moment irrelevant—are the real concrete togethernesses that make up the temporal patterns we experience in nature. These epochs of becoming are the reason why ***time takes time.***

Let us try to understand this theory better. What is it saying? The epochal theory of time says that time comes as drops of experience. When something comes to be, it emerges with its own temporal duration already intact and complete. When an event comes to be, it floods the world with its temporality. It cannot be divided and still be the same event. To be able to divide epochal time would be the same as saying it was not epochal time. Therefore, the most concrete aspect of time—in its essential feature as a temporal event—is the fact that time is given all at once. Epochal time is time spilling forth in chunks. Time indivisible, time without parts, time simultaneous with itself—these are the ways in which epochal time comes to be. Epochal time is completely concrete temporal being and is nothing but itself. It is completely itself having no parts. Epochal time is time *simpliciter,* time unalloyed and unadulterated. Epochal time does not change. Epochal time does not grow. Epochal time does not develop. It is time by itself pure and simple.

But a time that does not change, grow, or develop appears to be the very opposite of the kind of time needed to undergird the process cosmology that has been constructed. Where do change, growth, and development fit into this picture of epochal time? The answer lies in making a distinction between time in its inscape as epochal and the temporal patterns of transition. Epochal time is the concrete inscape of natural time. It is time in its essential feature as concrete. The patterns of growth and decay that are also the hallmarks of natural time arise out of the transitions betwen various streams of epochal time. The next section, on the patterns of natural time, will detail these structures.

Epochal time is here and now, indivisible, given all at once and completely concrete. It is the temporal partner of space in its character as the extensive continuum. Just as space is to be understood as an infinitely divisible continuum (being a form of immediate potentiality), so also the inscape of epochal time is purely atomic (being a form of immediate actuality). Epochal time atomizes the natural world with drops of temporal experience. Space localizes the extensive continuum. Equally archaic is time's epochal coming-to-be. Each event in the natural world has its own date and time even as it has its own position and location. Space develops regions and time develops durations. These regional durations lock together to form a variety of spatiotemporal structures. Depending upon the spatiotemporal patterns dominating the events in question, certain forms and types of entities emerge. It is therefore just as valid to call our environment timespace as it is to call it spacetime.

This is one key to understanding the qualitatively intense depth and width of the material world. For material objects are not just spatially extended, they also have temporal contours and dimensions. Some are thick with time; others are quite slight. Each, however, is born out of a process different from physical time. Each emerges from and continues to be governed by a succession of temporal epochs. It is these epochs that form the creative advance of the temporal processes that make up natural environments. Through its epochal character time provides for the emergence of value as a real fact in the natural world.

Now, if all this sounds fantastical, to some degree it is. But then by the same token, so also are contemporary particle physics and relativity theory, not to mention more recent speculations in the philosophy of mind. Why bother with so difficult a theory as that of epochal time? The reason lies in its role as guarantor of the concreteness of value. Without epochal time we are thrown back into the Newtonian cosmos of absolute but vacuous time. Time becomes once again that empty container wherein material events simply take place. The theory of epochal time saves us from making time this kind of an abstraction. It therefore warns us away from committing yet one more time the fallacy of misplaced concreteness. With the doctrine of epochal time we are assured of viewing time as concretely valuable. In terms of this study, what the theory of epochal time really says is: Every seemingly material object in the natural world is made up of drops of time and these epochs are themselves the emergence of value.

Nature is through and through temporal. No matter where you cut it, and no matter how deep you dissect it, what you find at the bottom of nature is time in its epochal guise. Recall the definition of inscape. It signified the uniqueness of each entity as it emerged into environmental being. What was thus gained was the most radical form of environmental pluralism. Given time's inscape we can see just how radical this pluralism really is. For what the inscape of time reveals is the fact that each event has its own unique temporal epoch (as well as a unique spatial niche). These epochs are its expressions of value. Therefore, understanding the value of nature requires understanding time as consisting of unique temporal perspectives, each of which expresses a level of intense value.

In Part One, it was demanded that this environmental cosmology be applicable to all the other sciences. Here, then, is another domain in which the efficacy of the cosmological scheme demonstrates itself. The findings of contemporary science, especially in the disciplines of quantum physics and relativity theory, demand for the sake of intellectual coherence some form of the theory of epochal time.[2] There are great mysteries here. The mysteries are to be welcomed whether they come from the physical sciences or cosmological theory. By reason of Heisenberg's principle of indeterminacy, quantum physics demands that we see matter as either wave or particle but never both at the same time. Such indeterminacy would violate nature's epochal processes. Relativity theory demands that we accept the possibility of different spatial and temporal zones—in effect, this means recognizing the real possibility of other worlds.[3]

Relativity theory and particle physics are very difficult to understand. Nevertheless, most people accept the main consequences of these theories as they affect their understanding of nature. As regards the epochal theory of time, I would ask the same tolerance. Time's great mystery is made even more mysterious through its epochal inscape. In fact, given what we have discussed concerning space and time, it would not be incorrect to say that these two seemingly abstract notions are by far the most archaic and primal mysteries in nature (though we have not yet touched on life).

If we contrast space and time, the mystery deepens. Space is continuous and extensive; time is epochal and intensive. Yet we know that each event at the very moment of its birth is both spatial and temporal. It has only been for the sake of analysis that I have separated these two essential features. An environmental event is always a spacetime event. It is also always a timespace event. "Why is there something rather than nothing?" Leibniz's question becomes even more compelling when the miracle of the interwoven patterns of time is investigated.

The Patterns of Natural Time

The transitional character of natural time exhibits itself through the patterns of the past, the present, and the future. But the patterns of time past and time future are only experienced in the present. This is another reason for insisting on the epochal theory of time. The present must have the capacity to experience both past time and future time in the present. If we experience the future, it is no longer the future but the present. Likewise, if we experience the past it must also be experienced in the present. To experience the past in the past is to be in the past. But in the present cosmic epoch time is irreversible. Therefore when we experience the past and the future, it must be the experience of the past and the future as experienced in the present. Now, this makes for the possibility of highly textured epochs of time. Also, each moment of time can harmonize its experience of past and future in different ways. Sometimes, more weight can be given to the future; other times, it may be the past that receives dominant stress. The patterns of time have as much flexibility as those of space. Multilayered, densely structured, and polyvalent dimensions of time spread naturally around the environment. What is required is an understanding of the different ways in which time past, time present, and time future exhibit themselves in the environment.

Time Past

When time repeats itself , we are in the presence of time past as a dominant feature of the natural environment. Now, given the premises of this process cosmology, there is no way for time to perfectly repeat itself. Novelty, no matter how slight, remains the norm for all natural environments. Still, there are forms of time that are so similar that we can speak of them as indefinitely repetitive. This is the basic structure of large-scale material objects. A boulder, for example, is largely identical with itself over the vast stretches of time it has been in being. (Of course, I am now speaking in mesocosmic perspective; in quantum perspective, the boulder is a storm of active novelty.) When material objects heap themselves up in a temporal way, they exhibit an extraordinary conformal quality. Each new set of events repeats the structures and patterns of the earlier ones. This is what is implied by a phrase such as "the everlasting hills."

Parallel to this conformal character is time past's manifestation of density. Time past expresses a solidity that is unmistakable. To run one's hand over a stone is to feel the massive repetition of time built up over its lifetime. Since time past can only be experienced in the present, we feel the presence of time past as a type of pressure ever edging into the future. A sense of profound and undeniable conformity affects time present when it is in the grip of time past. The massiveness of the past tends to squeeze out all sense of room. Options for novelty die out, for the past "is too much with us." The patterns of time past continually assert themselves as durations having dense temporal and spatial magnitude. In these durations the past all but overcomes the present by stressing the conformation of experience as the key to environmental success. Habits, instinctual responses, the profound age of the earth itself—all these experiences share in time past as a massively conformal and dominant environmental presence.

Time Future

The future is what is not yet. Its very mode of being is an absence of presence. How does the future express itself as present? Of course, if the environment is massively indebted to the presence of the past, the future will be slow to show itself. Such is the case in most stable environments. They achieve their success through slow repetitive conformations of the present to the past. But the future must be present in even so conformal an ecological region as, for example, the Antarctic. There is no place where novelty does not emerge. It may be slight. It may be slow in coming. But sooner or later novelty does arrive to assert itself.

The future's presence in the present is felt as a lure. For the most part, in natural environments the future beckons and shapes the present through an encouragement of slight difference. Such encouragement can be either weak or intense. The presence of the future is signalled through slight variations in the conformal patterns dominating the previous present. This is what Darwin noticed when he examined the Galapagos finches' beaks. Adaptation to an end is a sure sign of the edging of the future into the present. As a mode of the not-yet, the future's presence in nature is very difficult to gauge. Given the deftness with which they detect such subtle changes, this is one reason why the scientific disciplines are so indispensable for contemporary ecological work.

As shall be seen, the presence of the future in nature is not fully perceptible until life arrives. Nevertheless, traces of the future seed themselves throughout the spatiotemporal regions of natural environments.

Time Present

The present is a crowded place. In nature the present accommodates the past by acknowledging its presence in its domain. It also makes room for whatever lures the future casts forth. But the present is still *the present as present.* What the present feels is the intensity of its own being. To the degree that it can house the past and the future, to that same degree it increases its own intensity. This is the outcome of the law of contrast. One reason for making contrast a special category within the categoreal scheme is precisely its omnipresence as an important aspect of present time. Earlier, I spoke of time as harboring the possibility of expressing "temporal acts with genuine individuality." It is when the present can contrast both the achievements of the past with the possibilities of the future that individual intensity emerges as an important dimension in natural environments. Once such individual events emerge with a rhythm of regularity, then the possibility of weaving narrowness onto vagueness so as to achieve width of experience becomes a real possibility.[4] Now, narrowness signifies the presence of intensity just as vagueness signals the presence of loose boundaries between the past and the future. It is the category of contrast that makes possible such rich temporal experience as well as its symbolic perception. It is why I have also termed it "full time." Our experience of the feelings involved in time past, time future, and time present depends upon the human body's symbolic perception of these temporal patterns.

The Symbolic Perception of Natural Time

This analysis of the ways in which natural time is perceived in the mixed mode of symbolic reference rests upon two presuppositions. First, that the measure of time symbolically experienced remains that of the body operating in the mixed mode of symbolic reference. Second, I am assuming that the previous arguments concerning normative thinking retain their validity. For what follows is an effort to identify those normative measures that are at play when past, future, and present modalities of time are in effect in specific environmental regions. When effective levels of contrast have been achieved in temporal events of some magnitude, then time is perceived in nature as deeply contrasted. The past and the future layer themselves into the present and thereby weave an extraordinary tapestry of temporal modalities. The rich individuality of certain types of events is thrown against the vagueness of other temporal orders so as to produce the dazzling array of spatiotemporal shapes that form the natural environment. It spreads out before us in splendid immediacy. But within this immediacy there is also felt the heavy weight of the past as well as the lure of the future. Constraint arising from the felt causal efficacy of the past as well as the sense of possibility latent in the future display themselves as immediately present within the environment. It is the task of symbolic reference to fuse all this information into manageable perceptual experience. A rose, a mountain, and a butterfly are elegant sculptures of time (as well as space).

As in the case of space, it is not possible to enumerate all the potential kinds of temporal experience available in the natural environment. Nevertheless, it is important to sketch out the main features of each pattern of time as they are perceived in the mixed mode of symbolic reference. Once again, it is necessary to underscore the perceptual fact that all these experiences are had in the present. The past is present in the present **as past** and the future is present in the present **as future**. What makes possible their symbolic expression is the room provided **by the present** through the category of contrast.

The past is symbolically experienced as achieved value, as strength and as bound energy. To speak of "the weight of the past" is to symbolize the presence of the past as past in the present. Temporal acts with genuine individuality that privilege the past are heavy with the accomplishments of prior events. They do not yield easily and they demand recognition. The power of the past to achieve its values is a sign of its strength. Strong time is time embedded in the past achievements of natural environments. For example, human willingness to conserve ancient forests depends upon the capacity to symbolically perceive these regions as manifesting awesome temporal value. When past time is felt symbolically as bound energy, then the feel of an environment registers vast and important power. To feel the curve of bound energy in a stone smoothed over by ancient weather patterns is to sense symbolically the presence of forces lurking beneath the surface of a material event. As it was with space so also with time: Temporal presences are embedded in the natural objects that surround us.[5]

As was shown in the case of spatial patterns, the temporal past can be felt as symbolically indifferent, expectant, intense, or involved. The human experience of these moods, of course, are dependent upon the levels of order present in the environment being perceived. In sum, the past is felt in the present as that set of achieved values characterizing the environment in question.

The future is perceived symbolically as that set of expectations suggested by the region's temporal contours. For the most part, the future in natural regions can only be symbolically perceived as a series of propositional lures. The presence of the future is largely dependent upon the category of transmission. Without the sense of dynamic transition derived from strong lines of transmission active throughout an environment, the presence of the future pales before the weight of the past and the intensity of the present moment. (As shall be soon seen, a sense of the future as directly involved in the efficacy of the present is the one of the central themes of life.) But when vagueness together with its accompanying mood of expectation spreads temporally throughout a region, the sense of the immanence of the future in the present is symbolically palpable. Leibniz alluded to this temporal dimension when, in *The Monadology,* he called the present "big with the future." Indeed, the presence of the future in the present is the very meaning of pregnancy. When the future dominates a natural region, it symbolically expresses creativity in important ways.

The imminent emergence of novelty, as felt in the defiles of the present moment, provides an overpowering sense of impending change. Temporally, there is a symbolic sense of buildup such that the very future seems to be upon the environment. Anyone witnessing an oncoming storm knows this feeling of the future as sculpted into the present. The future as concretely symbolized carries with it an urgent sense of sudden transformation. When an environment is on the verge of change, then the future has assumed an overwhelming presence in the present. The harmonic balance between the past as felt in the present and the future as felt in the present has shifted dramatically. Something new is about to happen. Different levels of environmental order yield up different environmental moods.

For the most part, temporal regions dominated by the future are felt as expectant, intense, or involved depending on whether vague, narrow, or wide levels of order are in play. A trivial order by definition would have little sense of the future to offer its constituent members.

The present is the most mysterious dimension of the environment as temporally perceived. By itself the epochal quality of the present moment is enough to guarantee its distinctiveness. But when time present expresses itself in a rich mode of contrast, what is radically different about it is the manner in which it can shelter in itself the two other modes of time. The existential state of contrasted time allows for the symbolic perception of an enormous "temporal fullness." This power of the present to accommodate itself to contrasted feelings of the past and the future while still remaining in the present gives rise to extraordinary feelings of intensity.

In fact, so intense are these feelings of contrast that they really amount to a radical transformation of environmental reality. What occurs is that a new level of experience is reached. What heretofore could be interpreted as rather low-level exchanges of energy has now become the active and intense presence of actuality and possibility as dominant modes of existence. What is actual—the present with its past as present—is put into a unity with what is possible—the present with its future as present. The resultant contrast between the actual and the possible lifts environmental being to a new realm of symbolic interplay.

The environment is now governed by temporal acts with genuine individuality. Full time abounds and the threshold of life and all that implies for environmental integrity has been reached. Strong individuality and heightened contrast are the major ingredients needed to bring about the aesthetic conditions that life requires. Strong individuality provides the narrowness that brings about intensity and heightened contrast makes room for the interfusion of the possible and the actual. Width of experience is now wedded to individual achievement. Something great is at hand in nature. Its temporal field has been altered so as to harbor in itself the possible as a coequal component in the actual environment.

Present time is also subject to the moods consequent upon the four levels of order. Its most likely symbolic mood is that of intensity, for that is what individuality feels like when it is associated with time. But present time can also evoke moods of indifference, expectation, and involvement. Time is as subject to the demands of environmental order as space is. In analyzing the texture of environmental temporality, it is as important to pay attention to the orders within which time occurs as it is to take note of the modalities of time being experienced. Time past, time future, and time present may occur within any of the four levels of environmental order.

In conclusion, the symbolic perception of natural time also includes characteristics similar to those of space. Natural time is so deeply embedded in its environment that one must say that all environmental events display the handiwork of time. Natural time is also concretely rhythmic and concretely cyclical. It is for the most part felt as tied to the presence and absence of light. For example, the concrete natural time experienced during the seasons of the year results from the different levels of light that play throughout nature. Time "begins" at sunrise and "ends" at sunset. But the sun does not naturally rise at an exact hour and minute. Nor does it naturally set at an exact moment. That is to take physical time as more natural than epochal transitional time. Time expressed through varying tones of light "changes" in the spring and "changes" again in the fall. But daylight saving time or eastern standard time do not express natural time's expressive presence. All such concretely natural temporal patterns arise by reason of their own lights. Natural time lingers according to its own "lights."

Like space, natural time is also always **"found."** One cannot make natural time. Humans must respect its precincts. Winter has its own beauty. So does summer, and so do fall and spring. Each is its own temporal value expressing its own symbolic resonances. The perspectives afforded by natural time provide their own unique set of importances. Natural time can be slight and thin. It can also be thick and massive. When it chances to ripen to a requisite fullness, natural time establishes epochs of fundamental contrasts between the actual and the possible. These acts of time with genuine individuality are crucial for the growth of environmental value.

The Value of Natural Time

Each mode of natural time contributes its unique value and thereby shapes, alters, and develops the environment in important directions. Depending on the mode of temporality that achieves dominance in an environment, specifically different values emerge. When **time past** is dominant, the environment is stable and connected. It has a sense of its own rootedness in the past and specific values are held up through dominant processes of conformation.[6] On the other hand, **time future** makes its presence felt through a certain vague openness that often affects the environment in very subtle ways. **Time present** can exhibit a remarkable intensity that brings to the forefront sets of contrasts upon which important environmental changes will be built.

Each modality of time—past, present, and future—can be either thick or thin. Temporal thickness signifies the accumulation of significant value. In terms of the past, this means that massive values have been built through time. These values call for the deepest human respect. Without a sense of the past as active in human lives, the texture of natural being becomes rootless. To be grounded in value is an important natural experience. One of the great concerns of our time is precisely the sense of rootlessness that affects so many human beings as they pass from moment to moment always in search of the new.

But the assemblage of values built up out of the past can also be a hindrance to growth. Nature grows stale and the road to novelty is effectively blocked by too much reliance on past achievements. A full and active sense of the value of the future is indispensable for healthy environmental growth. But here again, a simplistic understanding of "change for change's sake" can spell environmental disaster. It renders what was once thick with opportunity a mere game of diversions. When it comes to the present moment, there is a need for a sense of respect for the fullness of the present moment. In the most profound metaphysical sense the present is all that we really have, since each modality of time must be felt within the present. To lose sight of the present moment is to lose sight of reality. Only in the immediate "now" can something of significance be achieved. A full moment in the present is a treasure not to be dismissed. In my judgment the East's insistence upon the importance of meditation for spiritual growth is precisely an attempt to achieve the fullest possible participation in present reality. However, as is always the case, it is a question of balance, for an obsession with the present spells environmental doom. The present is the great moment of engagement. If the time that is engaged is full and charged with contrasts, then it is indeed a moment of temporality with genuine individuality. How it is used will show the level of respect for value present in the environment.

In the first part of this environmental cosmology the need to create a new sensibility about environmental processes was underscored. The suggestion was made that "feeling" ought to replace "matter" as the fundamental concept for understanding and talking about environmental affairs. There were two major reasons given for this move. In the first place, "feeling" is a term that captures more precisely the dynamic quality of process that is present in every environment. The second reason had to do with the present cultural dominance of scientific materialism. By exchanging event for matter we do more than merely shift metaphors.[7] This move toward an event metaphysics and language forces our consciousness to recognize the centrality of time in all environmental discussions. Nothing, it seems to me, could be more important for reconstructing our vision of environmental goodness. We are not talking about mere "things" strung out in space and time. We are talking about the building up of space and time into moments of great beauty, daring, and value. One way to weaken the grip of the vocabulary of an outmoded scientific materialism is to insist on modes of speech that evoke an appropriate appreciation of the creative process that is at the heart of environmental reality.

Natural time casts a net of organic connection over the environment. It weaves a thread between the past, the present, and the future. This act of temporal transmission seals the environment in a temporal web of unity. This is the fundamental meaning of the category of transmission. Recall the discussion of the four types of transmission: Physical, conceptual, propositional, and stillness. Each mode of transmission can now be seen to represent the dominance of a particular temporal modality. Physical transmission occurs when the past so dominates an environment that material objects of great density come to prominence. Obviously, all natural environments have significant physical transmissions as part of their texture. Conceptual transmission defines that mode of spatiotemporal reality in which the future has dramatically edged up into the present. Conceptual always means a concern for possible forms of definiteness. Conceptual transmission marks the places in an environment where novelty may begin to emerge. Again, it should be obvious that conceptual transmission is rare in natural environments and is confined for the most part to living entities. Propositional transmission occurs when the contrast between the actual and the possible is held up with great emphasis. At such moments a leading edge of change sweeps across the environment and renders the future more dominant than the past. When propositional feelings are at play in an environmental setting, massive switches in its fabric become possible. Good examples would be approaching weather fronts or volcanic eruptions. But again, such propositional feelings are for the most part confined to living beings. The capacity to hold up the future as a region of genuine concern is one of the defining properties of life. Finally, there remains the feelings of stillness that can be transmitted throughout an environmental region. When this occurs, it is the outcome of a fortunate fullness of temporal contrast such that past, present, and future come together in a complete harmony.[8] Environmentally speaking, humans often encounter the transmision of stillness as religious feelings of awe and consummation. Some such feeling is at the root of those forms of environmental philosophy that stress the sacredness of natural processes.

A summary of the many values contributed to the environment through the workings of natural time can be had by looking once again at the schema of ideal environmental values: intensity, integrity, wholeness, and depth. Like space, time works to set up a recessive but massive backdrop against which these ideal environmental values find expressive perspectives. Since it is the epochal inscape of time that holds reality in its grip, the discussion is here confined to the temporal present. Present time has as an ideal environmental value the achievement of maximum intensity. This is carried out through the category of contrast whereby different temporal modalities are held together in varying types of unity. At its epochal best, temporal environments can hold together rich dimensions of the actual and the possible. Ideally, the value of intensity ought to rise proportionately with an increase in simplicity and complexity. Also, since each epoch of time has its own uniqueness, there is an essential narrowness built into present time. This narrowness reenforces the effectiveness of the contrasts and thereby doubles the moment's intensity. Put differently, the more simplicity can embrace complexity, the more an increase in intense feelings will be distributed throughout the environment. Integrity signifies the ways in which unity accommodates diversity. When present time is well-integrated, it distributes in a harmonious fashion the other modalities of time. The past is given its due and so is the future. Both past and future find adequate placement within the unity of epochal time. Thus complexity is also given its due. Again, I would suggest that meditation practices lean on just this sense of temporal integrity to restore balance and health to the inner life of the adept. As an ideal for the present, wholeness signifies a level of completed unity that embraces difference without sacrificing harmonic unity. Finally, present time expresses depth when it sets forth the domains of the past and the future with a requisite clarity. Within the openness of such a clearing, time present expresses layers of temporal thickness that invite exploration. This is epochal time at its fullest.

The manifold values of natural time mark the rise to prominence of the category of transmission. The first two chapters of this study of natural environments placed major emphasis on the categories of inscape and pattern. By a natural progression, the discussions of space and time have culminated in the categories of contrast and transmission. This is as it should be, since the environmental cosmology begins with the most general traits of nature and then is led by its own dynamic into the discussion of more and more specialized levels of environmental functioning. An environment spatially and temporally well-structured is fit for many things, not the least of which is the arrival of life.

Chapter Seven

The Arrival of Life

Life remains obstinately resistant to formal scientific definition.[1] Therefore, this chapter begins not with a definition but rather a description of the characteristics that make up the inscape of life. Even here, difficulties pile up, for no single description captures life in its fullness. Still, certain environmentally important features of the inscape of life can be singled out. Furthermore, as was the case with space and time, the different patterns of life will be also dealt with. Third, the history of the human race testifies to the fact that the spiritual dimension and life are inextricably bound together in our consciousness. So much so that in the present age major aspects of environmental philosophy are given over to its consideration. There is therefore a section devoted to the sacred depths of life. Finally, all these issues raise the most serious questions about the environmental value of life. The practice in this chapter will be the same as that of the others. I will treat each of these themes in turn.

The Inscape of Life

Living beings are characterized by spontaneity and intensity. Furthermore, life always takes place in the present. Life is also an expression of sheer novelty. As its guiding normative measure life forever seeks the different. It searches endlessly for new pathways of growth. Decay is the sign of the end of life. For these reasons the inscape of life is best understood as radical originality. Life therefore has direct contact with possibility as a source of its creativity. It also has self-directing power insofar as final causality comes to play a significant part in its inscape. Because life is not completely shackled by the past, each time it comes to be, it is wholly new. This is the major reason why science has such difficulty defining life in any formal way. Life lacks a defining characteristic because it never repeats itself. Because life is so original, it is not in and of itself self-sustaining. It always requires a supporting subservient physical environment. Thus, life must bind its originality back into sheltering environmental forms. By itself life is an anarchy seeking intensity at any cost. Life is therefore highly erratic, fragile, and rare. It quickly perishes without appropriate environmental support.

Much of what constitutes the inscape of life has already been sketched out in Chapter Two, where the theme of "living participation" was developed. Here, it is important to underscore certain features of life that directly affect the natural environment. In the first place, life is a marauder insistently breaking down the environment in its search for food. It takes from material that is outside itself to repair its extravagant use of energy. That is one major reason why life is never found without some sustaining non-living environment that acts as its support system. Life is therefore not independent of environmental claims. If anything, it is completely dependent upon the spatial and temporal environment for its continued success. While the inorganic world succeeds through a kind of active denial of the pressures of space and time (to a large degree stones, for example, ignore what goes on about them), life must attend to all dimensions of its environmental region. It is an inherently destabilizing force that can, if let alone, wreak havoc in an ecological niche. Therefore, the presence of life raises the most serious moral issues. It is simpleminded to regard life as a wholly benevolent environmental presence, for life is by no means an innocent environmental agent.

Another aspect of life's inscape is that it always comes in individualized forms. There is no such thing as "Life" floating free in the environment. But the line between the living and the non-living is extremely difficult to draw. There are even forms of life, such as viruses, that appear to shuttle back and forth between organic and inorganic levels of being. Likewise, there are degrees of life. Some things can be said to have more life than others. Even our personal lives reveal that there are times when we feel more alive than others. Life's pitch varies with its intensity and originality. To the degree that life ventures into the novel and shows its originality, to that degree it is more alive. At the same time, to the degree that it becomes more original, to that same degree does it venture beyond the environment that gives it safe harbor. Life is the great harmony of creativity thrown up by nature to answer the problem of retaining maximum originality under a wide set of varying environmental circumstances. Life is therefore a kind of natural experiment and is to be measured against other environmental claims in terms of its ultimate importance. The forms of life represent so many demands made on environmental settings. They do not automatically gain the right to existence. This will become more evident when we look at some of the claims made by biocentric forms of environmental ethics.

The inscape of life is a permanent demonstration of the efficacy of the category of contrast. In terms of our environmental categoreal scheme, life is a region of contrast acutely balanced between the realms of the actual and posssible. Life in the present puts into a unity what was (the past in the present) with what can be (the future in the present). It represents an exceptionally delicate balance of temporal and spatial forces such that both the grasp at intense experience as well as adaptability are conjointly realized. Thus, the real mystery of life is how a living event holds together the past and the future so as to act in the fullness of the present moment in an intensely original manner. Given the extreme difficulty of such a feat, the fragility of life becomes understandable. It must gain a measure of security by binding itself back into the environment from which it springs. In natural environments, life is the exception and not the rule.

Insofar as life is the aim at vivid originality, all forms of life take on some level of conceptual feelings. Recall that possibility and its many determinate forms were the object of conceptual feelings. To be alive is to feel the possible as conceptually combined with the actual. In so feeling, the act of being alive always asserts some level of individuality, originality, and creativity. Therefore, every living event has some degree of self-determination. It also has a sense of its own self-enjoyment. Understood in these terms, life can be called its own justification. But life for life's sake is simply an ignorant moral slogan if it means life must be preserved at all costs. Much life can be lost if there is too much life.

It should also be obvious that life is not confined to the form of a person. There are many living things that are not persons. A tree is not a person and neither is a mollusk. Environmental ethics needs to understand these categoreal distinctions if it is to make moral sense of the natural world. To sum up: The inscape of life involves the intense urge toward novelty. Because of this drive, life is to be understood as existing on the precarious edge of the actual and the possible. It is therefore both intense and fragile. It requires significant environmental support and it always comes in individualized forms. Life expresses creativity and struggle, for it does not necessarily survive. All these characteristics drive life to exhibit a multiform environmental presence. It is to these patterns that we now turn.

The Patterns of Life

Because life is itself an act of contrast, the levels of order experienced as life express contrasted patterns of the four primary ordinal levels of triviality, vagueness, narrowness, and width. Of direct interest for this study are contrasts of the vague and the narrow that issue into living patterns of width. It is width that gives life a stable perspective suitable for the acquisition of long-term adaptability. As the clutch at vivid immediacy of experience, life always exhibits an essential feature of narrowness. At the same time, this intensity is bound up with originality. Therefore, the narrowness of life is not confined to the repetitive processes that characterize material objects in the environment. Life breaks open the shackles of the past. Its contrasts take place vividly in the epochal present moment. Intensity, originality, and narrowness drive life forward in search of novel experience.

It is this drive toward originality that makes life enlist vagueness as an essential feature. It must be able to bring together into a flexible common order that which will count as material for the focus of its originality. A good example of a pattern of life expressing narrowness and vagueness is a living animal body. Life wanders through the animal body. Not all its parts are equally alive at the same time. The ears prick up, the nose dilates, the eyes narrow, the stomach growls, and the cat pounces. Life navigates the vague corridors of the body's many systems seeking out those components upon which it can throw a beam of narrowness. A skilled athlete in the accomplished practice of a sport does the same thing. Vague presences illuminated as points of interest by the narrow focus of life's originality are indispensable for a properly functioning living organism. Just as there are degrees of life, so also there are degrees of intensity and originality. Still, the essential features of life remain fundamentally the same: Life expresses exceptionally rich contrasts by reason of bringing together into a unity the vague and the narrow.

As we have already seen, the contrast between the vague and the narrow not only results in the experience of width. It also brings about the environmental mood of involvement. In order to survive, life must experience width as an essential component of its being. When narrowness is too narrow, vagueness is eradicated and the quality of width suffers. A living being established in an environment deficient in width has been handed a death sentence. Conversely, too vague a life fails in the ability to execute life's aims. It is width that strikes the right balance needed for successful life. When effectively present in living environmental events, width expresses degrees of adaptability, a characteristic found in all forms of life. Adaptability allows life to range over a variety of experiences so as to express its individuality. As the inscape of life shows, life is not bound to a past. It is therefore radically original in its quest for novel intensity of experience. Life needs width to satisfy its craving for novelty. Life without the flexibility provided by width grows brittle and dies. A rigid corpse expresses in the most direct way what is lost when life perishes.

The width enjoyed by healthy life forms is the result of a fortunate integration of simplicity and complexity. As ordinal components, these seeming opposites contrast with each other so as to provide for life an openness for novel intensity of experience. At the same time, life accommodates the nascent complexity underlining its vague sense of environmental quest. The resultant novel intensity is therefore an outcome of the adjustment achieved between types of vague environmental probings and the directness associated with life's narrow search for intensity. On the one hand, there is complexity due to vagueness of environmental setting; on the other hand, there is simplicity due to a narrow originality. Life has the capacity to maximize simplicity and complexity at the same time.

The harmony developed by life between the ordinal components of simplicity and complexity is mirrored by a similar harmony between essential and conditional features in living events. It is very difficult to find the exact borderline between a living body and its environment. Is the coffee I just drank me? What is conditional in one set of circumstances can become quite essential in another set. A woman's capacity to be a mother has no essential bearing on her ability to be a scientist. It remains an essential feature, however, if she chooses to bear a child. The tendency of the essential and conditional features of environmental domains to slide back and forth is a manifest expression of life's width.

To sum up: narrowness woven onto vagueness produces in living beings a sense of wide involvement in environmental processes. Events ranging from basic stimulus/response mechanisms up to animal curiosity and even further, to acts of thinking about environmental processes, are signs of the presence of life. The patterns of life are such as always to express the presence of width and its mood of involvement. Life provides a perspective on the importance of intensity as a ruling normative measure. But the discussion of the importance of life must be postponed for now. There remains one more dimension of life that requires discussion. Human beings can experience life as expressing significant depth.

The patterns that establish and maintain human life are exceedingly complex. It is dependent upon a fortunate set of structures that weave and reweave subordinate sets of events into a rich tapestry of original and wide intensity. Life wanders through the human body seeking now here and now there its points of intensity. At times, it responds mechanically, as when the autonomic nervous system alters a peristaltic rhythm. Other times, life centers upon the significance of its surroundings, as when the mixed mode of symbolic perception allows us to avoid an oncoming automobile. Sometimes human life becomes intensely original, as when a new way of interpreting environmental experience emerges. We discover fire. A thorough analysis of human life processes is beyond the aims of this study. Suffice it to say that these and other equally complex sets of events occur throughout the living human body.

One result of this exceptional complexity is the layering of orders throughout the human body. The resultant thickness is experienced within the body as the real and effective presence of depth. In terms of the language of this environmental cosmology, the synchronic and the diachronic orders overlap and reveal the most extraordinary entwining of vertical and horizontal experience. An immense density pervades the human body as these various levels of order stack up. Furthermore, the depth expressed by all these simultaneous functionings of the living human body deepens the sense of overall unity within the human body. The axes of depth throughout the human body express three characteristics. First, wherever depth is, there also is significant contrast. In fact insofar as width is a contrast between the narrow and the vague, depth is a contrast of a contrast. That is to say, depth contrasts the already-contrasted unity of vagueness and narrowness upon which width rests. Therefore, depth puts into unity levels and modes of process previously conceived as incompatible. It is the active presence of depth that provides the sense of volume associated with environmental depth. It must be remembered that patterns of environmental depth are not confined to the human body. There are many forms of environmental process that express depth as an essential feature. Second, when depth occurs it is the result of a fortunate unity of vagueness, narrowness, and width. In the looseness of vagueness is found the opportunity for contrasts that narrowness needs in order to enhance its intensity. Where normally this only produces width, in fortunately constructed patterns like the human body, this width expresses a richly articulated unification. In its turn, this unity provides the final characteristic of depth. Depth is the outcome of sets of interlocking events that tie together complex orders of originality so that an immense reservoir of novelty emerges as a salient environmental fact. Taken together, significant contrast (or the contrasts of contrasts), unity, and intense novelty mark out the boundaries of deep environmental domains. The patterns of life are seemingly inexhaustible. But in concentrating on the human body as an example of the pattern of living depth, one particular dimension of human life is made prominent: The fusion of the sacred and the deep within the domains of life and death.

The Sacred Depths of Life

One has only to witness death in order to realize how special life really is. One minute life is there and the next moment it is gone.

The situation becomes even more palpable when it is human life and death. Matters of life and death are at the extreme end of the continuum of experience. When life has ended, something indefinably precious has been taken away. No price can be put on life. Neither in this life is there any way in which death can be ultimately avoided. When trying to speak about such matters, we are forced into the boundaries of the ultimate: First things...last things... .

Cultures have always formed themselves around the ultimates of life and death. A culture's sense of what is important is revealed in the manner in which it surrounds the facts of life and death. Power over life and death is claimed by the religions of the world and also by civil authorities. *In extremis* marks the beginning of the road leading to the extinction of life. The various masks worn by God in the course of human history bear the same sign: Power over life and death. " I come that you may have life and have it more abundantly"; "In the beginning...was the life of the world... ." Other traditions—East and West, Hindu, Jewish, Moslem, Confucian, Buddhist, or Taoist, native religions and indigenous spiritists cults—all proclaim the same themes. There are ways and means to manage the experiences of life and death. There is another life. There is not another life. There is reincarnation. There is escape from the wheel of death and rebirth. There is bliss. There is punishment. There is nothing to be afraid of and there is everything to fear. Putting aside the specifics of the message or the identity of the messenger, all these cultural attempts to fathom the significance of life agree upon one conclusion: Life has depths.

In terms of the argument sketched in this cosmology there is no need to accept any particular version of the various ways in which cultures have dealt with death. But from the perspective of this study there is an intellectual duty to make sense of the claims about the depths of life. Otherwise, the environmental cosmology would be seriously deficient just where it is needed most. One would expect that serious systematic thought should have something to say about the ultimate moments of environmental existence. After all, it is the phenomenon of life and death that rages through each and every environment. What is at the root of the experience of environmental depth?

As has been just demonstrated, when life has achieved a certain wide dominance through the animal body, the experience of depth becomes possible. Depth signifies the presence of a voluminous reservoir of novel experience. Furthermore, this treasure of originality is built up out of contrasts of contrasts having the capacity to achieve ever greater degrees of unity. One such contrastive experience is had in human consciousness. And it is to human conscious life that we must turn to gain a sense of what is at stake in the experience of depth found at the boundaries of life and death.

Consciousness is by no means an inevitable environmental experience. In fact, it is rarely found, and even when it is present, it does not seem to last very long. In the vastness of nature, consciousness is rare, fleeting, episodic, and fragile. It is by no means basic to the structure of nature. In terms of this environmental cosmology, consciousness is "how we feel the affirmation-negation contrast."[3] Now what can this mean? It means that in the act of consciousness both the actual and the possible are held in novel contrast. "What is" meets "what can be" and results in a feeling for the alternative as a factor in present experience. To affirm the negative is to say: This is not it. We do this when we question something. We do this when we try to discover a new way around a problem. And we also do this when we ask, what is this? Accompanying every act of consciousness is a sense of the alternative. And that is precisely what constitutes the experience of depth. Depth suggests that there is something more. Consciousness has in it a form of depth because it is a contrast of a contrast. It takes the possible—what can be—and contrasts it with the actual—what is. In so doing it draws out reserves of novelty from the depths of process. To be environmentally conscious is therefore to be conscious of the significant presence of depth as an normative measure informing environmental reality. Because a sense of the alternative clings to it, human consciousness also carries with it feelings of loss and incompleteness. This sense of affirmed negation—what is, what was, and what might have been—is what is present in the encounter with death. Human consciousness treads a knife edge between the actual and the ideal. It acknowledges what is. It knows what might have been. And it also senses what might still be. So situated between the actual and the possible, consciousness is responsible for that commerce between the normative and the actual that makes up human culture.

It will be noticed that depth is not listed among the environmental orders selected for this cosmology. Rather, depth is an ideal alongside the other ideal environmental values of wholeness, intensity, and integrity. The reason for this lies in the fact that such high ideals require the active presence of consciousness for their environmental recognition. Ideals are made known through an act of consciousness that affirms the negation of their presence. We do not experience depth per se, but rather events that either approach an ideal or fall short of it. In the land of finite consciousness only asymptotic experience is possible. Ideals are markers and signs. They lay out specific forms of possibility that actuality seeks to make real.

This is also why the other ideal environmental values spring to mind when discussion turns to the ideal of depth. One cannot speak of depth without also mentioning wholeness, intensity, and integrity. The same is true of each of the other ideals for they revolve about each other. Each ideal calls the others into play. The reason for this lies in the fact that all ideals are possibles and therefore share in possibility's major attribute—continuity. We saw in another context how this dimension of possibility affects the inscape of space as an extensive continuum. So also here the discussion of depth demands a necessary reference to the other environmental ideals. Such coherence is a sign of the cosmology's success in adhering to the demands of systematic and speculative philosophy. Thus it is as true to say that depth is felt when there is a wholeness throughout the parts as it is to say that wholeness is present when there is a depth throughout the parts. Similarly, integrity and intensity on the ideal level demand each other's reciprocal presence. This is not a form of doublespeak, but rather a true accounting of the way in which ideal environmental values require each other for their full understanding. Full intensity needs full integrity for its completeness. True depth needs full wholeness and a depth void of intensity or integrity would be no depth at all.

This intimate relationship between wholeness and depth and intensity and integrity is what lies behind those modes of spirituality that find in nature epiphanies and exemplars of growth in holiness. When human life can arrive at the axes of the ideal environmental values, it is in possession of significant power. I prefer to call this power "strength of mind." It will be a significant part of Part Three, An Ethical Vision.

With this gain in an understanding of life and having now travelled a considerable way in this argument, we can glimpse the outline of an effective response to the problems brought about by the cultural supremacy of scientific materialism. I suggest that what is needed is an enrichment of consciousness along the lines laid out in this cosmology. Further, I maintain that such an enrichment must be the outcome of a radical gain in the aesthetic understanding of nature. Now, all this may seem to be a very, very thin reed that is hardly capable of redirecting the course of environmental degradation. But it should be kept in mind that the aesthetics underlying this cosmology is through and through a form of Platonic naturalism. It therefore sees the beautiful and the good as intimately related even as it insists that the one and the true are also firm companions. But that is to get ahead of the story. Nature's goodness is the theme of the next chapter. It is now appropriate to conclude by reflecting on the value of natural life.

The Value of Life

The value of life lies in its originality and intensity which produces depth as its major essential feature. Equally important is the way in which life transmits this intensity, originality, and depth throughout an environment. Because life is a significant transformative force, the ways and means by which life activates the category of transmission are a matter of direct concern for the discipline of environmental ethics. For the theme of the value of life also raises the general question of the goodness of nature.

By life's originality is meant the fact that life's central characteristic lies in the fact that its being cannot be adequately explained by reference to the past. Life strikes a blow for freedom from the dominant line of inheritance that marks material objects. It cannot be totally explained by analyzing past states of being. It signals a break from the past and thereby inserts into the present its own immediacy. Thus, originality is to be taken literally. Life does not owe its existence to some prior event. The whole aim and drive of life is a clutch at vivid immediacy in the present moment. As a creature of profound originality, life looks to its present and its future to determine the limits of its experience. Now, this originality of life has degrees of power. Some living events are more original than others. But life would not be life if it owed its entire being to the past.

Life shows this originality through its grasp of possibility as a major environmental feature. In the higher living organisms, this amounts to the effective presence of conceptual feeling within the organism's structure. The presence of life entails the actualization of novel possibility. Life rises out of a dim past that sets up the conditions for its coming to be, but that past no longer dictates in a totally comprehensive way the conditions of its manner of being. When we reach the level of human beings, of course, this originality takes the form of active thinking about the conditions and features of life itself. Thus, life turns back upon itself and considers what is good for itself both now and in the relevant future. This is the ground of ethical behavior.

In its originality life expresses an exceptional spontaneity. Freshness is the mood and tone of all living things. Of course, the degree and quality of the freshness is dependent on any number of factors. But it is the sense of spontaneous and fresh joy that is characteristic of life in its most original guise. The Chinese call this TAO, and in the ancient classic the *Tao Te Ching* there is recorded a most marvellous description of life in its expression of freshness and spontaneity:

> Great Tao drifts—it can go right or left.
> *The thousands of things depend on it for life,*
> *it rejects nothing.*
> It achieves successes,
> but does not hold tight to the fame.
> *It clothes and feeds the thousands of things*
> *but does not act the ruler.*
> *Always:*
> *Desiring nothing, it can be called of 'no account.'*
> *The thousands of things turn back to it*
> *but it does not act the ruler—*
> *it can be called 'Great.'*
> Because in the end
> it does not insist on its own greatness,
> yet, it is able to achieve its full
> greatness.[4]

These words express the essence of life's originality. Life welcomes the world and embraces it with an unalloyed spontaniety and freshness. Think of the baby at its mother's breast. Consider the five- year-old at play with her friends. Recall the thrill of racing onto the baseball diamond for the beginning of the Little League season. Life is original. Its lack of rootedness to the past is a major reason for its reach toward freshness. A recognition of the marks of spontaneity and freshness makes it impossible to confine the meaning of life to that of mere causal succession. It is the brilliant destiny of all forms of life to be an original.

The intensity of life springs from its character of originality. Life is always to some degree or other marked by zest. In its powerful urge toward becoming, life expresses a level of intensity unmatched by other environmental happenings. It is precisely this drive toward intensity that moves life to make use of the other environmental ideal of integrity. For unless life can balance its intensity through integration of levels of order, it will wither and perish by reason of its own originality. The fragility of life results from its lack of control over its own drive for intensity. Given too much food, a goldfish will eat itself to death. We are warned not to burn the candle at both ends. At the same time, and despite all the difficulties that beset life, what the wise Irish woman said remains true: "Life is sweet."

The zestfulness that attaches itself to life springs from life's need to be involved. Because of the width that is a necessary part of its structural constitution, a mood of involvement hovers over life in its many manifestations. The expression "to lose interest in life" captures in a most distressing way the loss of zest that foretells naturally the onset of depression and even the possible approach of death itself. Zest is worn by youth as a natural garment. Age, too, has its own forms of zest and it is a sign of ebbing life when we lose our enthusiasm for things.

Living thought and zestful living go hand in hand, but such thinking is not always wise nor is such living always justified. It is life's capacity for depth that makes it possible for humans to reflect on the ethical difference between foolish living and bad thinking. Recall that depth meant the power to embrace difference. Further, this power to accept a certain density in life could be employed to enhance the variety of an environment. The achievement of some degree of depth encourages the practice of tolerance. Without the space that depth provides for difference, there would be little to stop the onslaught of life's narrow drive toward intensity of experience.

As intensity needs to acquire integrity in order to preserve its level of value, so also depth needs to enlist the active presence of wholeness if it is to welcome difference. The wisdom characteristic of good environmental living comes from a union of all four ideal environmental values. When intensity and integrity join up with depth and wholeness, there is established a remarkable spiritual strength. It is this strength that marks wise human living. Acquiring the power, both personal and social, to deepen the bonds of intimacy between environmental philosophy, spirituality and life revolves around developing this spiritual strength.

Finally, the wise transmission of life through various environmental pathways constitutes a major challenge to the discipline of environmental ethics. Life can enchant and life can terrify. The measures needed to achieve the right balance concerning the claims of life will not be discovered through the scientific materialism of the present age.

As Robert Neville in *The Puritan Smile* and David Hall and Roger Ames in *Thinking Through Confucius* have pointed out, the dimensions of moral discernment include the capacity to enlarge our imagination so as to bring about new moral options for our dealings with the natural world.[5] A provisional step toward such a growth in moral imagination has been taken in this attempt to provide a theory of the natural environment that resists the value-neutral categories of scientific materialism. By seeing nature as entwined harmonic integrities, aesthetics becomes an important ally of ethics. Its significance for the development of an ethical environmental vision is the subject of the next chapter.

Chapter Eight

The Goodness of Nature

This chapter concludes the second part of this environmental cosmology by bringing together under the theme of goodness the various dimensions of the natural worked out in previous chapters. It presents aesthetics as the foundational discipline underlying the environmental cosmology and sketches the broad outlines of a metaphysical ethics based on the intimate relation between the good, the beautiful, and the important. In so doing it anticipates the major themes of Part Three, An Ethical Vision.

The Primacy of Aesthetics

It was C. S. Peirce who insisted that logic depended upon ethics and in turn ethics was rooted in aesthetics. In saying that "the logic of the normative sciences, of which logic itself is only the third kind, being preceded by Esthetics and Ethics,"[1] he provided an enormously important insight into the future of metaphysics in the tradition of American naturalism. This "guess at the riddle" is at the heart of the environmental cosmology just sketched. Deeply rooted in an aesthetic vision of nature, this version of Platonic naturalism sees all events as harmonies that link up with each other so as to display patterns of varying contrasts and intensities. Furthermore, nature is viewed as transmitting these aesthetic achievements from generation to generation as patterns of time and space are carved out by these essentially aesthetic activities. In addition, the categories chosen and the vocabulary employed are through and through aesthetic in their import and connotation. Finally, this aesthetic orientation provides resources to preserve and uphold the dignity of the particular individual events that make up the plural values of a process environment.[2]

What indications are there to prove the essential correctness of this way of writing about the natural world? There is of course the generally recognized failure of scientific materialism to account for the values in nature. A world of mere fact runs counter to our direct intuitive experience of being alive in nature. The poets have earned their place alongside the scientists. Furthermore, there is the evidence of our senses that nature has a certain "feel" to it. Aesthetics is deeply involved in articulating various levels and degrees of these feelings. There is, too, the sense that order is no arbitrary factor in nature but rather plays an important role in securing the continued and effective presence of the good.

There are, also, deeper historical reasons for adopting aesthetics as the guiding discipline for this study. This study is written out of a commitment to two philosophic traditions, movements of thought that have often been held to be contradictory. I am, of course, referring to American Naturalism and Platonism. There is, I believe, in both traditions a similar drive to invest philosophy with the duty to discover and articulate the types, levels, and degrees of value in the world. This conviction is at the heart of Plato's search for the Good. It is also at the center of American Naturalism's search for a pragmatic method that can identify and underscore the real differences that the various emergences of value in the world bring about. When Emerson writes of "The Oversoul," he is trying to locate the source of value in the temporal world. Thoreau's errand into the wilderness was an adventure on behalf of value. When James wrote *The Varieties of Religious Experience,* he was striving to catalogue the differences made by specific types of value commitments. We have already seen Peirce's deep commitment to the aesthetic base of all the normative sciences. John Dewey's *Art and Experience* is a prolonged effort to get at the aesthetic base of human experience and develop into it an overarching philosophy of culture. Finally, Alfred North Whitehead's *Process and Reality,* the major inspiration for this effort to construct an environmental cosmology, forged a system of thought that unified science, religion, poetry, and speculative metaphysics in a single aesthetic vision. In grounding my work in this tradition, I hope to gain from its accomplishments and at the same time continue and expand its insights.

Of course, the final justification for insisting on the primacy of aesthetics must be a philosophical one. The major advantage gained by using aesthetics as the "Ur" discipline for environmental thinking lies in its essentially normative discourse. Throughout the course of this study I have argued that the primary function of thought is appreciation and not explanation. Aesthetics is par excellence the discipline of appreciation. Its vocabulary and its aims are through and through normative. Its aim is to measure the various expressions of beauty in the world. Also as has been argued, aesthetics provides a type of order that guarantees the rich individuality of the environment even as it does insist on the significance of order for overall environmental functioning. Thus, both rich individual value as well as the intricate natural patterning of events are respected by an aesthetic approach to environmental systems.

But value, and the terms of its achievement, is the soul of this study. The most effective way to speak about value is by orchestrating a world of feelings as the prime examplar of environmental functioning. Feelings are concrete. They also allow for degrees and levels of intensity. Feelings are also central to the discovery and appreciation of beauty. A beauty incapable of being felt is a beauty not born. Within the domain of a world of feelings there is ample room for organizing and developing schemata of values, moods, and ideals. This is precisely what was carried out in detail in Parts One and Two of this study. The categories of inscape, contrast, pattern, and transmission marked out the central feeling processes of the natural environment. Through their interlocking relations the world of felt values that makes up the natural environment received significant articulation. It is for all these reasons that recourse to aesthetics is primary when one begins to talk in a speculative and systematic way about the goodness of nature.

The Principle of Plenitude

The primary meaning of nature is creativity. Historically, this has been defined by metaphysics as the principle of plenitude. Nature is through and through a process of giving birth to novelty. This ever-present creativity has been analyzed in terms of the ways in which it shapes both space and time as well as the inorganic events that make up the natural environment. Also, life has been established as the supreme natural instance of creativity. Plenitude is the natural outcome of the ceaseless striving for novelty that marks the essence of nature.

Arthur Lovejoy's classic *The Great Chain of Being* is a comprehensive presentation of the way in which this principle of plenitude has worked its way through Western metaphysics.[3] When Plato speaks of the Good, it is always of an agency that gives of itself freely and without penalty to those who know it. Plato banishes the old superstitions that one must beg, bribe, or seduce the Good in order to have its gifts. Rather, Plato tells us that it is knowledge that secures for human beings a place in the sunshine of the Good. Similarly, in the East it is *Tao* that freely gives of itself. The plenitude of the *Tao* is there for all who can meet it on its own terms. It is bountiful in its generosity and grants its graces to all who embrace it with sincerity. In the *Tao Te Ching* the three gifts of the *Tao* are simplicity, kindness, and patience. Each of these powers is a mark of fullness.[4] Again and again throughout its history, philosophy has called attention to the fact that the chief attribute of the Good is its non-contentious generosity.

What brings together into an effective intellectual unity the disciplines of metaphysics, ethics, and aesthetics is the principle of plenitude. It provides a pivot around which knowledge of the good, being, and the beautiful can be synthesized. Being is that which overflows creatively throughout the natural world. In its process of becoming, being is marked by a fullness that stretches through all events. The good is that which gives of itself. In nature, value is the outcome of the events that make up the inscapes and patterns of nature. Finally, the beauty of nature is displayed in the ways in which contrasted elements are fitted together so that the environmental ideals of integrity, intensity, wholeness, and depth receive degrees of full expression.

More specifically, metaphysics as a philosophical discipline analyzes the ways in which being spreads itself throughout actual and possible worlds. The principle of plenitude names that aspect of being whereby it pours itself into the various patterns and dimensions of reality. Each and every time humans use the term "is" or any of its cognates, what is being named is the presence of being. This presence is through and through an overflowing act of generosity. When being is, it gives of itself. When being gives of itself, it is. The reciprocity between being and giving is a total one. The principle of plenitude demands that being's "being" and "giving" be thought and expressed together by the same measure and to the same possible extent. Goodness can be lessened by decisions, circumstances, and conditions; being can even be hidden, but all such phenomena point toward an earlier, more primal experience of being's plenitude. How else could being's hiddenness be noted if it did not at some level also reveal its fullness? Metaphysics studies the various domains of being's plenitude and the reasons and causes for its modes of giving and being.

I maintain that the very possibility of constructing such a discipline as ethics rests on the principle of plenitude. For goodness is in the first instance an outcome of the principle of plenitude. To give is to be good. There is no goodness that is not at the same time a mode of giving. If goodness were in principle a scarcity, then the law of fang and claw would be the only possible ethical stance. And ethics would by definition be a mere matter of convenience, an act of agreement drawn up by humans in their self-interest. But an ethics of scarcity is built on the fallacy of misunderstood goodness. There is an innate contradiction between understanding the presence of goodness and at the same time denying its generosity. This is not to say that the distribution of goodness is inevitably filled with plenitude. Humans can stifle goodness. They can also choke it off at the root. Or they can divide it so as to reserve more for themselves and less for others. None of this contradicts the principle of plenitude. It only describes types of unethical human behavior.

At the very beginning of *The Nicomachean Ethics,* Aristotle says that all human beings by nature seek the good.[5] By this he means there is a natural drive in human beings to seek that which satisfies them. For the good is that which brings them happiness. Now they can and do differ on the definition of happiness. Furthermore, they can and do differ on the ways and means of attaining that happiness. They do not, however, differ on the human need to seek the good and thereby experience happiness. The fact that this search is never relinquished, is a direct outcome of the principle of plenitude operating in the sphere of ethical activity. The implacable character of the human search for the good is proof positive of the drawing power of the good. This attractive dimension of the good springs from what has been termed its generosity.[6] The appeal of the good, its attractive character and the ceaseless quality of the human quest for the good together form a dynamic that is only understandable in the light of the principle of plenitude. The good gives and thereby attracts. Humans seek the good and thereby act for the sake of the good even when they are terribly mistaken about its true meaning. This complex of notions—plenitude, the good, and human desire—forms the essential material out of which a contemporary vision for environmental ethics will be constructed in Part Three of this study.

The discipline of aesthetics is rooted in the principle of plenitude. Beauty is the prime instance of the principle of plenitude, for the achievement of beauty rests upon a full expression of completeness and harmony. Understood from the perspective of a process cosmology, beauty is the very sign of the achievement of ideal values in an environmental domain. The attainment of beauty entails the right relation between simplicity and complexity, as well as the appropriate placement of essential and conditional features. It is altogether the exemplar par excellence of both the metaphysics and the ethics underlying this environmental cosmology. In the sense meant by Peirce, aesthetics is the most fundamental discipline because within its contours are to be found all the fundamental principles and elements required for understanding the achievement of value in the natural world as well as its philosophical understanding. It is through the modes of contrast and the types of harmony achieved by nature that the ideal environmental values of intensity, integrity, wholeness, and depth are brought to full expression. Beauty without fullness is not really beauty. It is therefore because beauty is so full that it is the prime expression of the principle of plenitude. Also, since beauty is grounded in contrast (in the special meaning attached to that term in this cosmology), it is the essential avenue through which an inexhaustible novelty enters the environmental world.[7] To sum up: Beauty by its very essence brings to fullness of expression that which lurks in the heart of being as the good.

There is another concept traditionally associated with being, goodness, and beauty. That, of course, is the concept of truth. In

Adventures of Ideas, Whitehead devotes the major part of his discussion of civilization to the many relationships spanning beauty and truth.[8] It is his view that if beauty is to achieve its fullest and most important expression, truth must become an essential part of beauty.[9] Now, in giving such an all-important role to beauty, Whitehead's philosophy of civilization is in danger of falling into an effete aestheticism. He is fully aware of this possibility and therefore assigns a number of important roles to truth in its service to beauty.[10] There is the sense of directness that truth brings to beauty. Furthermore, truth brings strength to beauty for beauty *sans* truth degenerates into a perfume of appearances—which is exactly the postmodern philosophic dénouement Whitehead wishes to avoid. In addition to these important functions, truth provides beauty with another and most vital service. For "the type of Truth required for the final stretch of Beauty is a discovery and not a recapitulation ."[11]

Truthful beauty marks the achievement and summation of all the environmental values and ideals that this cosmology has been at pains to discuss and analyze. At its attainment, integrity and intensity are deeply and wholly present. In fact, the wholeness and the depth of truthful beauty are what brings about such a massive degree of intensity and integrity. Parts are balanced within a whole that respects their individuality. This is because the simplicity of wholeness makes room for the complexity of the parts. The resultant elegance readjusts the parts so as to contribute to the intensity of the whole. In its turn, this essential simplicity wholly contributes to a mutual enhancement of the parts. The conditional and the essential features harmonize to create an even greater truth and an even deeper beauty. Great art does this and so do great environments. Furthermore, in contributing its truth of discovery to beauty, truth strengthens the goodness of beauty in both its whole and its parts. What pours forth from such an amalgam of the good, the true, and the beautiful is the most intense expression of the principle of plenitude. Its intensity is guaranteed by its integrity, which contrasts all the different parts so as to produce a most extraordinary unity of being. Being is seen as both one and many. This is the signature of plenitude itself.

The Harmony of the One and the Many

The goodness of nature receives its most succinct expression in the abstract formula—the One and the Many. When, however, it is joined to the concept of harmony, this abstraction becomes the very standard by which the goodness of nature is most concretely understood. For what is nature if it is not the one and the many locked forever in a process of creative advance?

"The many become one and are increased by one."So wrote Whitehead at his most concrete and at the same time most cryptic.[12] If we were to understand fully this expression, we would understand in general and in particular both the aesthetic dynamics and the ethical destination of this environmental cosmology. What are the many? What is the one? And how are they increased? The many represent the past out of which the present environmental moment rises. The many are the achievements of nature immortalized in their value but no longer actual. The many are the conditions out of which novelty arises. The many are the circumstances that surround the birth of each new environmental event. The many are the levels of order lying in the past and circumscribing the creativity of the present. The many are the spatial inscapes and patterns that bedeck the environment with their sudden irregularities and extraordinary densities. The many are the layers of past time arranged and structured so as to provide a solid base for the present moment. The many are the aeons and aeons of natural effort that have gone into exactly this present moment "N O W" that edges into its time of birth. The many are the lines of continuity stretching out of the far, far distant past and reaching up to this border of novelty called the present. The many are the living creatures whose originality has contributed to the texture of this "N O W." The many are the traditions—physical, living, and cultural—that have donated their values to this particular environment. The many are the environment in the splendor of its disjunctive display of value.

What is the one? The one is the present event in its own uniqueness. It is that moment of *haeccitas* spoken of so eloquently by the philosopher Duns Scotus and the poet Gerard Manley Hopkins.[13] The one is preeminently the moment of unity. In the language of this cosmology it brings together through its own perspective the many importances of the environment and expresses the singular value that results from such a focus. To understand the one is to fathom the very special way in which it compresses the importances of the environment so as to achieve just this value in just this spatiotemporal niche. The one names the event of coming-to-be that marks the emergence of genuine environmental novelty. It is the act of fusing environmental feelings into a single whole never to be exactly reduplicated in terms of position and date. Space and time are forever inscribed with the unique creative energy of the one as it bursts forth into environmental being.

How the one becomes a "one" is the special task of harmony. The way in which the one harmonizes its environment determines the distribution of value in its inscape. If the conditional features of the environment overwhelm the essential features of the newly emergent event, then we have a basic repetition of past inscapes and patterns. This is the dominant harmony running through physical systems. Space and time tend to repeat themselves in large-scale patterns of environmental order. The mountains endure and the sands of the desert stretch onwards. But such uniformity and repetition ought not to be taken too literally for, as has been seen, time is ever new and ever fresh. Novelty emerges even in the bare repetition of physical feelings. It is never the same river twice. On the other hand, when essential features have the capacity to reconstruct environmental conditions, the one is characterized by the emergence of large scale environmental novelty. Such novelty is usually brought about by the strongly effective presence of the category of contrast. For it is through contrast that the actual and the possible are thrown into fresh and effective unities. The resultant novelty alters the environmental conditions and thereby makes possible the emergence of new essential features.

There are three basic ways in which the many are harmonized so as to produce significant novel environmental unities. Large-scale environmental shifts occur through rearrangements of the levels of environmental order. Thus, shifts in triviality, vagueness, narrowness, and width send shock waves through environmental regions. The resultant reconfigurations allow for massive alterations in the physical environment. The Mount St. Helen's volcanic eruption shows how a wide environment characterized by rich variety can be reduced to a region of chaotic triviality. The second way in which the unifying power of the one asserts itself is through the arrival of life. As has been seen, life introduces significant originality and spontaneity into environmental orders. Again, it is a matter of the way in which life manifests the active presence of the category of contrast.

By bringing together into a unity the realms of the actual and the possible, life opens up intense regions of novelty. It is within the depths of life that great and fresh new "ones" are born. The final way in which significant harmonic alteration enters the environment is through the introduction of consciousness as a consistent and important factor in environmental transactions. Once again, it is a matter of the category of contrast making its presence felt. Through its "affirmation of negation," consciousness brings about a strong environmental sense of the alternative. This in its turn can reverse entire environmental orders. The African elephant does this with consistent regularity and so does the spruce budworm. But it is when consciousness assumes the order of a systematic and regular environmental presence that truly massive environmental changes are brought about. Here it is a matter of the rise and fall of civilizations and their systems of importances. Once human thought dominates an environment, the possibilities of new ways in which the many can become one increase exponentially.

In sum, the process whereby the many become a one is the result of the various harmonies wrought by the three different levels of environmental participation. When physical, living, and cultural modes of environmental participation come into play, the normative measures affecting the region in question shift dramatically. New inscapes emerge which in turn force new patterns and contrasts. The category of transmission then asserts itself and the environment shifts dramatically to accommodate new worlds of feelings. If physical feelings are ascendant, then the natural world in its guise of natural space and time dominates the environment. All the values consequent upon the dominance of such a harmony express themselves. Massive endurances, rhythmic temporal cycles, and the conformation of the present to the past are the important ways in which the many become unified in the natural world of physical feelings. On the other hand, if conceptual feelings dominate, then the environment displays a fleeting, evanescent character. For when the conceptual achieves environmental importance, possibility becomes rampant. The upshot of such a condition is usually the large-scale presence of instability. Quick changes occur as spatial and temporal irregularities transmit themselves throughout the environment. When propositional feelings consistently transmit themselves throughout an environment, then for all intents and purposes we are in the presence of a living environment. Originality and spontaneity take on dominance because forms of environmental order arise that can tolerate the radical novelty introduced by life and its power to construct rich contrastive harmonies. The degree to which this living mode of environmental participation can develop into significant cultural participation depends upon the quality of consciousness attained by the members of the environment. Finally, the transmission of feelings of stillness throughout an environment is a special case requiring specially fortunate contrasts that impart successfully realized ideal environmental values throughout the particular region.

The ways in which the many can become a "one" are as various as nature itself. This is another consequence of the principle of plenitude. Therefore: Each such novel one "increases" the many. In this cosmology increase has two different meanings. Increase can mean addition, as in the the sense of arithmetic accumulation. Such a quantitative increase is usually lacking in originality and novelty. But in the case of an event achieving a certain critical mass, then such quantitative increases can result in important qualitative changes. For the most part, increase understood as addition usually results in steady quantitative growth. Such growth results in the spatially reiterative character of the physical world. It is also at the heart of the temporal conformation characteristic of natural physical orders. Such environments display only low-grade novelty. Repetition blocks off the emergence of significant originality. Mere quantitative increase amounts to an accumulation of the past.

It is increase in the sense of enlargement that is of direct concern for this study of nature's goodness. Enlargement occurs when the new event is able to reconstruct the many in such a way as to express a significant difference from the past. Once again, this is due to the power of harmony to work out effective contrasts. It can so happen that the many are thrown into fresh unities of feeling. This new "one" increases the many by enlarging the scope of its realized possibilities. What never was, now is. What could not be, has now happened. Enlargement means that a new scale of values has emerged from the depths of nature's plenitude. It is increase in this sense of the amplification of value that marks the most significant aspect of the harmony of the one and the many. How "the many become one and are increased by one" tells the story of the harmony of the one and the many. The ultimate meaning of the goodness of nature revolves about the type of increase involved in such acts of harmony. So far, the traditional concepts of being, goodness, truth, and beauty have been used to describe the results of the principle of plenitude at work in natural environments. With this discussion of increase as enlargement, the last term usually associated with being is accounted for. It is being in its unity as a "one" that completes the traditional definition of reality as possessing in various degrees the qualities of being One, True, Good, and Beautiful. For this unity is another name for that individuality which was so important for the emergence of life. "Temporal acts with genuine individuality" marked the effective presence of an increasing gradient of creative importance. Taken together, then, these four traits—unity, truth, goodness, and beauty—express the fullness of nature. The harmony of the one and the many makes understandable what would be otherwise quite incomprehensible and a matter of mere chance: The polymorphic fact of the goodness of nature.

The Good, the Fair, and the Fitting

This analysis of the goodness of nature concludes as it began. What is good about nature is best understood in aesthetic terms. The primacy of the aesthetic for grasping the many levels and types of value at work in natural environments has been seriously argued. What remains to be done is to reassert in a summary fashion just how beauty weaves together the essential traits of natural goodness.

The task of converting the good into the beautiful is most directly carried out by identifying the good with both the fair and the fitting. In so doing, I am consciously following Plato's many suggestions that *Agathon and Kalon* always belong together.[14] The fairness of nature has a double meaning. It is most obviously exhibited in nature's openness to the adventures of forms of life. Novelty is given a chance to succeed. But there is a much more important meaning to the fair. It is the fair understood as the beautiful.

Natural goodness is beautifully fair because nature itself is always the outcome of varying types of harmony. When harmony is achieved, there is present a mutual adjustment of parts so as to serve a more expansive whole. Within this enlargement of experience there is the possibility of renewed sources of value. In fact the creativity resident in nature depends directly on the discovery of novel forms of beauty so as to achieve more and more intense values. Called earlier "Truthful Beauty," this type of beauty rests on new forms of contrast that put into a unity elements previously held apart as incompatible. This is nature at its fairest, for what is granted is an opportunity for the expression of real difference. Both senses of fairness come into play here. Nature is fair to that which is different insofar as room is provided for its expression. But this minor form of beauty pales in comparison to the major form of beauty, which not only permits expression of the different but actually endorses it by incorporating it into the general pattern of environmental events.[15] Through nature's fair beauty what once stood out as isolated and alone is given a welcome. When what is by nature different is given a place to come home to, then nature's goodness stamps its presence on an environment. The principle of plenitude is enacted whenever the level of nature's goodness registers such a major degree of fairness.

In all this I am, of course, seeking to expand the meaning of the aesthetic beyond that of the merely "pretty" or "handsome." In calling goodness the "fitting" I am attempting to express another, more functional dimension of the aesthetic. In confining aesthetic experience to the contemplative domain, we neglect the major active role that beauty plays in nature.[16] Beauty fits together that which was once apart. The good is what fits a particular concrete situation. And what fits is what unifies a previously fractured locus of events. Beauty heals these gaps by introducing relevant contrasts where once only conflicts reigned.

To fit events together is to harmonize them in such a manner as to integrate what was previously held apart. Beauty is good when it fits together incompatible environmental dimensions. This is the secret of great environments. They introduce contrasts in place of conflicts. They thereby turn variety into a strength rather than a weakness. A mixed forest is far more ecologically secure than one dominated by a single species. Likewise, an animal endowed with adaptability significantly increases its survival powers. Nature that does not seek to make room for the different is choking off its own wellspring of novelty. Tame natural harmonies can emerge through acts of elimination, but sooner or later what is eliminated comes back to claim its place. This is just another way of saying that an ethics of scarcity will not in the long run work. It may succeed for a time, but its very message—harmony through repressive elimination—runs contrary to the principle of plenitude.

One cannot have it both ways in nature. There is a choice to be made between admitting difference through an enlargement of natural environments and stifling beauty by an insistence on unvarying sameness. The goodness of nature is secured when the fair and the fitting takes environmental precedence. Or what is the same thing: *When the good is also understood as the beautiful.* This is the truth of feeling that rescues nature from the death spiral of repetition and decay.

Part Two, Nature, is now complete. The inscapes and patterns of natural space and time have been laid out and the arrival of life as the advent of intense novelty adapted to a variety of environmental circumstances has been articulated. The goodness of all these natural processes has been seen as one with the beauty it produces. Understanding these intimate relations is the essential contribution that an environmental cosmology can make to the question of the importance of nature. It is only by insisting on the central place of such a cosmological understanding that something like an ethical environmental vision can arise.

Part Three

An Ethical Vision

Chapter Nine

Types of Environmental Ethics
A Dialectical Exchange

The last decade has seen an extraordinary growth of interest in the discipline of environmental ethics. The attention paid to the environment by all sorts of thinkers has resulted in the publication of a number of serious studies. In selecting the works about to be examined there has been no effort to be exhaustive. Rather, I have chosen those books that best represent the major trends and directions in the field.[1] Broadly speaking, there are three schools of thought that presently dominate the field, the deontological, the Utilitarian, and the Aristotelian traditions. By itself each tradition has been unable to address all the difficulties in the field. There is also a strong phenomenological contribution evidenced by the work of Erazim Kohak. In addition to these generally well-known schools of thought, the special problems brought up by a new discipline like environmental ethics has resulted in three differing orientations or points of view. These are the ecocentric, the biocentric, and the natural humanist models of environmental ethics. Finally, the rise to prominence of postmodern philosophy has resulted in a new style of environmental thinking. What follows is a dialectical examination of these ethical traditions and models.

Three Traditions

Moral discourse in the contemporary age is marked by the continuing influence of three decidedly different ethical traditions. There is the deontological tradition with its emphasis upon the rights and duties of rational agents. The Utilitarian tradition, on the other hand, stresses the importance of usefulness as the primary ethical measure. Finally, there is the continuing relevance of the Aristotelian concept of prudential judgment that aims to hit the mean in matters of ethical concern. Each has its strengths and each has its weaknesses. So whether ethical choices are made by reason of the categorical imperative, the utilitarian maxim, or the act of *phronesis,* issues of great environmental concern seem to elude clear moral principles and directives.

The deontological tradition has the great weight of the Kantian moral tradition of universal reason behind it. Only rational agents can be moral agents, for when they make ethical decisions they should do so in the light of a universal rational standard. This Enlightenment tradition moves morality away from religious domains and thereby frees it from arbitrary doctrinal and denominational demands. It is the categorical imperative that enables human beings to extend their moral decisions beyond merely personal concerns and into the sphere of universal moral law. Each moral agent becomes an ethical legislator, for each moral decision must be such as to be allowed to all others in similar situations. Thus the categorical imperative; "So act that your action may become the universal law for mankind," is the rule that extends morality into the universal realm occupied by rationally free and responsible persons. Duty, freedom, and responsibility become an indivisible triad under the bonding force of universal reason.[2]

There are, of course, gains and losses in such a system. The great gain is in the self-justifying width of moral decisions. I must choose not only for myself but also for all others in similar circumstances. The taint of egotistical self-absorption is removed from the sphere of ethical action. I must base my decisions on reason and my reason must pass the standards of a universalizing, non-contradictory rationality. The categorical imperative adds the character of necessity to moral procedures, for it brings into consideration what I should do rather than what I may want to do. My duty comes into play precisely when my reason assumes its traits of universality and necessity. Ethics has stamped on its decisions the signs "always" and "everywhere." As "the moral law within," the deontological tradition is the counterpart of the fixed universal laws of nature that govern "the starry sky above." My station in life and its duties are the concrete expression of the categorical imperative.

As powerful as this Enlightenment ethics is, its application to environmental matters leaves much to be desired. In the first place, the deontological tradition restricts moral considerability to rational persons. As this environmental cosmology has been at pains to point out, there is much more of value in nature than human persons. Their place in the sphere of ethical consideration is not guaranteed by the Kantian tradition. In fact, the Kantian tradition was devised precisely to stand as the ethical counterforce to the scientific materialism that presently dominates our cultural discourse about nature. In the Enlightenment scheme of things there is the Newtonian world of natural fact and the Kantian world of human value-making.

It is an overreliance on this ethical tradition that creates the need for such ethical devices as "moral extensionism" in its many guises. [3] Furthermore, it is also this tradition that leads to the intellectual contortions surrounding animal rights debates. If only human agents are ethical subjects, then the only way to transfer rights to animals is to make them somehow the ethical equivalent of humans. This is done by making certain kind of animals the equivalent of children who suffer from mental disability.[4] Now, this is neither fitting or fair to the animals in question nor the humans to whom they are compared. The need for such rather bizarre comparisons is proof positive that more than the deontological tradition is required if environmental ethics is to meet all the challenges in its field. As Christopher Stone has pointed out in his influential article, "Do Trees Have Standing?," a similar inability to deal with objects in the natural order also affects deontologically inspired ethics.[5] By splitting the world into the separate domains of fact and value, this type of Enlightenment morality only serves to extend into the ethical realm the vicious abstractions that follow from forms of dualism.

The Utilitarian tradition brings about a major revision in ethical considerations. It does this by radically redefining the meaning of the good. The good is now to be understood as the useful. And the useful is that which maximizes each individual's opportunity for the pursuit of pleasure. What is done away with is any formal sense of a universal ethics that applies indifferently to human beings in their role as moral agents. Henceforth, ethics is confined to the individual sphere. What comes to the fore is the importance of individual liberty, and Utilitarianism is at pains to try to render politically and socially feasible such a radical ethical individualism.

The difficulty faced by such an ethical system is obvious. How does one guarantee maximum individual liberty while at the same time protecting the rights of each individual? Although it is at this point that numerous theoretical variations on utilitarian theory begin to emerge, it is fair to say that the major strategy devised to meet with the obvious difficulties to be encountered in a pluralistic society is the famous Utilitarian Maxim: "The greatest good for the greatest number." When faced with sets of competing demands, one counts out the goods and distributes them according to a formula that will maximize goodness and minimize evil. In this way, fairness is achieved by allowing the most usefulness to emerge in situations where individual competition threatens to compromise individual freedom. This means that there is no formal content to utilitarian ethics beyond that of individual freedom to pursue the good.

By so stressing the value of freedom, the utilitarian tradition makes social conflict inevitable. It is at this point of conflict that justice understood as fairness must be given a more functional definition. In the utilitarian tradition justice is redefined as "fairness of procedure." The administration of justice is handed over to the courts and their officers. Litigation takes the place of force, and conflict resolution through legal means becomes a primary social institution. One has received justice when one has received fairness of procedure.

As the literature demonstrates, the positives and the negatives of such a system are legion. My concern is with its appropriateness as a framework for environmental ethics. Now, to a great degree contemporary industrial democracies have adopted just such an ethical framework as the basis of their legal and social policy. How well has it served the environment? In essence, utilitarian ethics attempts to civilize disputes. By ranking individual freedom primary, it sets the stage for an adversarial system of justice. At the end of the day the argument is won by those who have the power to persuade others. I stress "power" because, as Foucault has made so clear, the power to persuade comes in many forms and is not confined to the use of reason alone. In utilitarian legal and political systems the value placed on the environment will be proportionate to the power its defenders have. And in industrialized democracies such power depends upon the legal, political, and educational skills of environmentalists. To someone convinced of the virtues of the North Atlantic democracies, such an ethical system might be viewed as "fair enough."[6]

But the problem with handing environmental concerns over to utilitarian considerations is that the real value of environments only appears when their very existence is threatened. Thus, we get an "Endangered Species Act" just when the flora and the fauna are at the edge of extinction. Similarly, "Wilderness Preservation Acts" are passed only at the most critical times. Consonant with good utilitarian tradition the value of the environment is confined to its use.

Still, there is a major gain to be had from the extension of Utilitarianism into environmental ethics. As Peter Singer has pointed out, the utilitarian tradition can support animal rights.[7] This is due to the Benthamite emphasis on the calculus of pleasure as the only sure guide to the good. For if pleasure is the good, then pain is the bad. Thus, the question to be asked concerning animals is not whether they can think (that is, the deontological question), but rather can they suffer? Animals obviously do feel pain and therefore their welfare also comes under the utilitarian maxim. Insofar as they suffer, they have moral standing. This is indeed a considerable gain, but no such moral standing can be granted large-scale environmental systems like forests, oceans, and mountain ranges. In a utilitarian world, anything inanimate is really just an object for use. The "Things of Nature" are so many instruments for the use of human beings. Now, a wise utilitarianism could do much to point out the importance of environmental conservation and preservation. In the end, however, any value attributed to the environment must come out of its potential usefulness. The actual value of the environment in itself is nonexistent and unknowable. All of the cosmology I have labored to construct is a fairy tale. Confronted with the really difficult questions of environmental ethics, the utilitarian tradition can only answer with a question of its own devising: What is in it for me? This is dividend ecology, not foundational ecology.[8]

Does the Aristotelian tradition fare better when it comes to environmental ethics? Its sense of the importance of a prudential regard for all matters involved in an ethical case brings a refeshing flexibility into ethical discourse. Also, its loyalty to the values inherent in the actual community in which decisions are made is admirable for its expansion of the ethical field. The tradition of civic republicanism owes much to this tradition.[9] And of course, its insistence on the real actuality and importance of the public and the common good is in line with the major concerns of environmental ethics. Finally, its desire to find a balance in all things brings to the discussion a rare sanity and an important sense of balance. By holding that virtue stands in the middle between extremes of every kind, it establishes a guide for wisdom that is most beneficial in environmental discussions.[10]

The Aristotelian tradition regards ethical reasoning as a kind of practical skill. Such reasoning directs attention toward appropriate ends as well as selecting the best means for achieving that end. It is for this reason that Aristotle lists ethics among the practical sciences. What must be acquired by the person who seeks to be happy is a sense of what is appropriate to the demands of human life both in its most private moments as well as in its public and civic forms. This goal does not admit of any precise formulation, and to seek for such an ethical formula is to betray a complete lack of understanding of the nature of the discipline of ethics.

But if exactness is not possible, a measure of what is fitting for concrete and practical life is attainable. Furthermore, given the daily demands made on us by life, such measures must be rather readily available to us. It is here that the concept of virtue as a well-established habit of action comes into ethical play. The Aristotelian tradition of *phronesis* understood as a quasi-habitual prudential reaction to the often conflicting demands of life is exactly what the person serious about living the good life must learn to cultivate.

Thus it is Aristotle who warns us not to make a swallow's appearance into the reality of summer nor to take one good deed as the sign of an ethical person. Ethics is as much a matter of acquiring habits of prudential reasoning as it is a matter of always making the right choices. There is a need for an almost intuitive grasp of what ought to be done or said or decided in certain situations. Unlike the utilitarian tradition, a calculus by which to mark out the good is exactly what is not needed. Nor is a categorical imperative to be invoked when we are in need of ethical guidance. What is required is a more general practical orientation toward the good. And this good is always to be understood as the means between two extremes. To take a stand in the middle of life's conflicting demands and not to move too far in one direction or another is the essence of the ethical life. It is balance and prudence that moves us in the direction of the good. When experienced over a consistent and prolonged course of time, the good brings us happiness because in terms of our most important capacities we are relatively fulfilled.

The central moral virtue is *sophrosune,* that sense of moderation in the midst of extremes which is the living endowment of the virtuous person. Through *sophrosune* the ethical person rules over life and its demands without falling into exaggerated life styles. Balance, moderation, and the sense of what is appropriate for a particular situation are the right measures to be cultivated within this tradition. It is a matter of gaining a training in acquired wisdom. The acquisition comes through experience and through practice. The wisdom results from using reason to select out what is the best possible outcome in each affair having individual and civil import.

As a practical science, the tradition of Aristotelian ethics demands a sense of continual development as well as a civil situation that will assist in and provide such nurturance. Ethics is not confined to the highly personal and private moral sphere, as it has been in modern times. Rather, ethics is the preeminent concern of the Polis, the public sphere of action. It would seem to be the case that precisely when ethics becomes such a highly public matter its attention would turn to the environment. But that is precisely what does not happen in the Aristotelian tradition. This failure to address the genuine significance of the environment in human affairs comes from the confinement of ethics to the realm of human life and conduct. In reserving the sphere of ethical influence to human matters alone, the Aristotelian tradition commits the same error that besets the the other two traditions.

The basic flaw in each of these attempts to direct human conduct toward the good is the assumption that human existence is a self-sufficent structure "requiring nothing but itself in order to exist." In assigning priority to that which is conceived as independent in itself and without a need for any essential connection with the environment, Aristotle provides the prototype for all substance metaphysics and the ethical traditions that follow from this failure to come to grips with the process character of all reality. Once this original version of the fallacy of simple location is made a root concept of the philosophical tradition, the capacity of ethics to deal in a direct straightforward manner with the natural world is altogether diminished. When historically this substance metaphysics is joined to the fact/value dichotomy that is central to the world view of modern scientific materialism, the ability to raise the question of the value of nature is hopelessly compromised. Whether the dominant philosophical motif is the Greek concept of nature as *phusis* and reality as *ousia*, as that which exists in isolated independence, or the Kantian concept of nature as an unknowable *Ding an sich,* or the utilitarian conversion of the natural world into a realm of matter ready for human use, the devaluation of nature is assured. From all three perspectives the question of the value of nature becomes meaningless.

This double reduction of, first, metaphysical reality to that which is an independently existing substance and, second, ethical reality solely to the human sphere is reflected in Aristotle's methodological preference for schemes of classifications built on types of difference. Though they are useful for generating logical tables and a biology built on the differences between genera and species, these analytic tools are far more suited for separating things into distinct spheres than they are for bringing them together into understandable relationships. It is one thing to be able to tell things apart. It is an entirely other matter to see how they interconnect. A substance metaphysics insists on separate and independent existence for its primary categoreal entities. A process metaphysics takes the opposite point of view and insists that what holds things together is far more important than what keeps them apart.

Plato envisioned reason's primary function to lie in the selection and articulation of appropriate normative measures. It was through levels and degrees of participation in these forms that the actual world took on its concrete character of identity and difference. Further, it was through an analysis of these measures and norms and how they precisely functioned in the world that human beings could come to direct themselves and their environment. For Plato, the purpose of philosophy was to rule well. What was to be directed and organized was the pattern of human relations—both individual (as in the case of the tripartite soul) and social (as in the case of the best form of government). Aristotle's philosophy was driven by another goal. He sought to explain the cosmos through causal analysis. To paraphrase Whitehead: When in doubt, Aristotle says, "classify"; Plato says, "relate."[11] Now, this appears to be a small matter of emphasis, but in the field of environmental ethics it makes all the difference.

In concluding this critique of the three major ethical traditions in Western philosophy, I wish to underscore my respect for their achievements. In terms of establishing principles and ways and means for sorting out the difficulties humans encounter in their relations with themselves and others, these traditions have, to varying degrees, stood the test of time. However, their effectiveness for providing a framework for a relevant contemporary environmental ethics is deeply compromised. There are at least three reasons for this negative judgment. First, each of the traditions completely ignores the question of the value of nature in itself. Therefore: whether the tradition be deontological, utilitarian, or Aristotelian we are left without any effective measures for estimating the worth of environmental events, entities, and systems. It was to supply this lack that the labors of Part One: An Environmental Cosmology were carried out. Second, and this doubles the problem, each of the traditions confines ethics to the sphere of human relations. It is, as we have seen, possible to raise certain environmental questions within these traditions, but the intellectual contortions necessary to do so strains credulity. Third, each of these traditions is grounded in a substance metaphysics that makes it highly unlikely they will have at their disposal the kind of ontological flexibility needed to move effectively from the natural to the human sphere and back again. This is another way of saying they lack a doctrine of participation through normative measure.

By confining the ethical realm to human conduct and by denying in both theory and practice the worth of the natural world, these ethical traditions have failed to provide a solid foundation for the newly emerging discipline of environmental ethics. The categorical imperative, the utilitarian maxim, and the Aristotelian virtues can not solve the problem alone.

What is needed more than anything else is developing skills of moral discernment. Now, my argument is that this process cosmology, through its redefiniton of the good as the fair and the fitting as well as its basic categories and doctrine of levels of natural order, supplies the right tools for such a project. For in effect this environmental cosmology is an exercise in appreciating the value of nature. But before turning to such an ethical vision, it is necessary to look at some of the more recent efforts to reconstruct the three traditions by providing more appropriate models for environmental ethics.

Kohak's Phenomenological Moral Sense

In *The Embers and The Stars,* Erazim Kohak records his reactions while living in the New Hampshire woods and building a cabin. His methodology is phenomenological in the sense that he attempts to describe his experiences as they actually occurred, without the interference of philosophical presuppositions. In this way, he threw an epoche around his existence in the hopes that it would reveal to him the moral sense of nature. The result of this effort is a book that is at once evocative, important, and influential. Nevertheless, it is necessary to express severe reservations about the validity of such a philosophical enterprise. His book raises all the problems attendant upon the phenomenological tradition. How much of this supposedly "pure description" is really autobiographical, being largely the reaction of one kind of temperament to coming to grips with nature and the demands it places on human beings? Can one strip away culture to such an extent that a pure apodictic state of consciousness becomes available? And does one have the sheer verbal power to describe this experience exactly as it occurred? Furthermore, is Kohak's recourse to personalism as an ultimate ground for environmental thinking sufficient for the construction of an appropriate ethical vision?

Among the major themes of this "philosophical inquiry into the moral sense of nature"[12] are *Theoria, Physis, Humanitas,* and *Credo.* Each deals with questions essential to environmental ethics. *Theoria* is the methodology employed by Kohak to ground his ethical vision. It seeks to evoke a sense of the inherent worth of nature rather than to derive it systematically from a set of principles. By employing the phenomenological tool of epoche, Kohak seeks to reestablish a sense of the ethical dimension of nature, a sense that has been covered over by the interruptive presence of technological devices. His phenomenology is meant to compel assent to the proposition that there is a "continuity of the vital and the moral order... ."[13]

And "to recover the moral sense of our humanity, we would need to recover first the moral sense of nature."[14] This brings us to a discussion of *Phusis* where it is imperative to reexperience the sense of the innate value of the natural world.[15] Now, there is much in this to agree with. Over and over again this cosmology has been at pains to endorse a vision of nature as filled with value. But there is also much missing. Phenomenology in the end must have recourse to metaphor and poetry and that is what gives the lie to its pretensions. By this sharp judgment I mean the fact that phenomenology has always presented itself as some form of apodictic science. But here, where its warrants and its evidence are most wanted, it resorts to metaphor to evoke a mode of consciousness felt in particular natural moments. I do not doubt that such moments exist. Neither do I dismiss their value; however, one cannot build a systematic axiology of nature on such partial insights.

The weakness of this method of securing value for nature becomes apparent when the question of the ethical ground of nature is raised. In a section termed *"Humanitas,"* Kohak affirms the basis of the moral ground of nature to be the dwelling of human beings within it. We witness, cherish, protect, and enlarge the goodness of nature. It is the person that guards natural value. Furthermore, it is only on the basis of extending the personal into nature that we can grasp its inherent worth.

Now this sounds on target and even rhetorically satisfying, but how can it serve as the ground of an environmental ethics? Does it not commit the fallacy of the misplaced category? In the end, the human being remains the sole source of the identification and preservation of natural value. For all Kohak's imposing language and homespun experience, we are no better off. The stolid, overwhelming cultural presence of scientific materialism remains in place.

In the end, as Kohak himself asserts, it is a matter of trust and belief in the efficacy of personalism as a philosophic creed.[16]

This cosmology has been at pains to articulate and systematically defend an alternate way of viewing nature as valuable. The model I have selected is that of the aesthetic event that, through its environmental interactions, forges a distinct perspective on the universe and thereby compels us to envision it as an expression of value, unique in its importance and to be understood through the cosmological categories of inscape, contrast, pattern, and transmission. Also, despite his frequent invocation of Whitehead's name, Kohak does not understand that Whitehead regarded the category of the person as much too narrow to do justice to the creative power residing at the base of all natural processes. Finally, there remains the fundamental difference between phenomenology and cosmological speculation. Phenomenology rests content with an attempt at the sheer disclosure of the things themselves in their essential being. Speculative philosophy, on the other hand, seeks to articulate the ways in which events compose themselves so as to express their various modalities of value. This insistence on composition as a key to environmental reality marks the difference between these methodologies. It also is the reason why aesthetics is so central to the environmental vision this cosmology defends. Given his presuppositions, Kohak must find his ethical sources in the philosophical system of personalism. Just how productive such a starting point for environmental ethics can be, remains a continuing question.

Deep Ecology

Arne Naess is the founder of that school of environmental ethics that has come to be termed "deep ecology." Though there remains much dispute about its fundamental meaning, its basic principles and program revolve about the norms of life and value.[17]

These are themes I have deployed in the construction of this environmental cosmology. What, therefore, distinguishes deep ecology from this environmental vision? The differences are many and profound. There is, first of all, the question of definitions. I have offered specific definitions of life and value. In this cosmology, life means the clutch at vivid immediacy that marks a bid for freedom that breaks the shackles of the past. Similarly, value is defined in terms of degrees and kinds of intensity whereby process attains unique modes of environmental syntheses. Furthermore, on the level of systematic form and adequate application, I have provided a set of categories and hypotheses that, taken together, apply vaguely to environmental events. Naess's deep ecology does not exhibit such concern for formal system and application. Given Naess's contributions to semantics as well as his early commitment to the programs of the Vienna Circle, such an absence of empirical application and theoretical structure is more than a little surprising. In fact, I would maintain that deep ecology commits the fallacy of confusing general hypotheses with vague ones.

What results from such a failure to distinguish the objectively vague from the generally applicable is an ersatz "system" of thought that hovers uncertainly between scientific and religious modes of thinking. The scientific side is made manifest in the suggestion that this mode of thinking applies equally to all states of affairs. It thereby mimics the claims of the natural sciences to lay down in law-like fashion the universal dimensions of reality. The religious side is expressed in the adjective, "deep." Like Tillich's definition of religion as that which deals with matters of ultimate concern, the term "deep" has no limiting dimension. One can always ask a deeper question when it comes to matters of ecological concern: It is this attempt to reach what is simultaneously a universal and an ultimate level of discourse that gives deep ecology such appeal. On the one hand, it appears to be in keeping with the spirit of the age; that is, it is aligned with the disciplines of scientific materialism. Such is the power of the term ecology. On the other hand, there is the obvious religious appeal built into the term "deep." (By contrast, I have defined "depth" as an environmental ideal that stands in coherence with the other ideals of intensity, integrity, and wholeness.) Insofar as Naess foresees no end to the inquiry necessary to fathom the depth of the relational connections that make up environmental realms, he is really substituting a form of religious thinking for a philosophical methodology. If one can, by definition, always "go deeper" into these fundamentals, then also by definition, we have left the realm of rational discourse and have entered domains better understood through faith claims and religious practices. Naess is not unaware of this move. In fact he has gone on to call his thinking an "ecosophy." This term, an amalgam of the Greek word for home, *oikos,* and the Greek word for wisdom, *sophia,* indicates that we are in the presence of a way of thinking, acting, and believing that has moved beyond what is normally meant by philosophy, science, or religion. Now, there is nothing inherently wrong in such an attempt to forge a new way of living, but it does mean that the dialectics of dealing with it in an intellectually responsible manner become exceedingly difficult. For one is dealing with a movement that at one and the same time presents itself as a philosophy, a science, an ethics, and a political movement.[18]

Therefore, as regards the ethical importance of the deep ecology movement, it is appropriate to see in it an initial cultural gesture to shake off the bonds of scientific materialism. But to grant it more than that would be, I believe, to overlook its many shortcomings. Intellectual movements can significantly shift the emphases of a culture. Indeed, they can bend the curve of culture. But it is the hard work of forging and articulating new categoreal schemes that in the end does the heavy lifting required to reconstruct in depth a civilization's form of the good. The difference between deep ecology and this cosmology built on the principles of Platonic naturalism is the difference between an intellectual movement and a philosophy.

The Ecocentric Model

One of the major difficulties confronting those forms of ethical theories that owe too much to the analytic tradition is finding moral standing for such holistic entities as species and natural systems. This is what makes the ecocentric model so interesting. In seeking to provide a new model for environmental ethics, J. Baird Callicott draws heavily on the pioneering work of the great American conservationist Aldo Leopold. It is Leopold's redefinition of the good in terms of environmental matters that is at the heart of this ecocentrism. Leopold held that: "A thing is right when it tends to preserve the integrity, stability, and beauty of the biotic community. It is wrong when it tends otherwise."[19] By shifting the focus away from individuals and onto the systems within which they reside, Leopold and, by extension, Callicott redefine the locus of ethical concern. This doctrine turns the usual form of ethical debate on its head. It is no longer ethically sound to look at individuals and compare their values and interests; rather, what is necessary is an estimate of how well or how poorly they contribute to environmental regions. Now, this immediately moves the discussion away from any privileging of persons or humans in terms of the value of entities. The ecocentric model deals a death blow to all forms of anthropocentric ethics. The relevant and final determinant of any natural being's worth is: Does it contribute in a fair and fitting fashion to the environment in which it dwells?

The major discipline needed to assign such worth is of course ecology. And it is precisely here at this ethical juncture that ecology would appear to earn its title as the "subversive science." But does it really? For if we are to take the ecocentric model literally, what is at stake in such ethical deliberations are not values but facts. It is facts that will decide if and how and when an entity contributes positively or negatively to its environment. Or so it would seem from Callicott's interpretation of Leopold's land ethic.[20] How far are we to take the preeminence of facts? It does seem as though a very frightening form of fascism lurks in the future. How about eugenics? Where does one draw the line when it comes to "contributing" to environmental well-being? And where does one ecological niche end and another one begin? Who decides where the boundaries are to be drawn? If it is the scientists, then are we not right back into the dogmas of scientific materialism? Only this time the scientists are using the language of values to disguise their strictly factual orientation.

This is why I have been so insistent on the importance of drawing categoreal distinctions. It is also why I have worked to create an aesthetically oriented language for this cosmology. For all its good intentions in moving environmental thinking away from an exclusive preoccupation with human interests, an unqualified ecocentric model does not have the kind of intellectual flexibility to make the important distinctions that will be required of such an avowedly "functionalist" ethics. Lawrence Johnson has made an important attempt to fill in the gaps in this type of thinking, but it remains rooted in a contractual utilitarian model of thinking.[21] Most especially, there needs to be some nuance brought to the idea of individual life and what constitutes both its value and its right to be at the center of an ethical system. Still, the ecocentric model brings to the discussion an important truth: The environmental system within which an entity exists can change the very essence and meaning of an individual entity. Thus, a molecule subsisting in a living system can be entirely different from a molecule subsisting in a nonliving one. There are, in other words, times when contexts can radically change the very meaning and importance of individuals. The biocentric model of environmental ethics brings this truth into focus.

The Biocentric Model

A variation on the ecocentric model is a form of environmental ethics that concentrates on the primacy of life in all ethical matters. John Cobb and Charles Birch, the authors of *Liberation of Life,* are good representatives of this point of view, and so also is Paul Taylor in his *Respect for Life.* I begin with the Birch and Cobb work which in many ways expresses a position similar to this cosmology. Inspired by Whitehead's metaphysics, it lays out an impressive argument for reconstructing the field of environmental ethics. Its most important point is what may be termed the Ecological Thesis:

> The ecological model holds that living things behave as they do only in interaction with the other things which constitute their environments. ...[T]he ecological model proposes that...the constituent elements of the structure at each level operate in patterns of interconnectedness which are not mechanical. Each element behaves as it does because of the relations it has to other elements in the whole, and these relations are not well understood in terms of the laws of mechanics. The true character of these relations is..."internal relations."[22]

What this means is that nothing can be understood in isolation from other things. As this cosmology argued in Part One, it is the relation between events in an environment that make up reality. The shorthand way of saying this is: *"The Process is the Reality."* The ecological model of life maintains that life is the outcome of the systems within which it finds itself. This restates my earlier position that life is therefore never self-sustaining.

Another similarity is the fact that the authors of *The Liberation of Life* refuse to offer a formal definition of life. Instead they provide a series of characteristics that are true of the forms of life now known and quote with approval both Aristotle's dictum that "life is the power of selfnourishment and of independent growth and decay"[23] and Sir Peter Medawar's observation that "life is an abstract noun never used in laboratories."[24]

Birch and Cobb maintain that life is best understood as a spreading center of individualized creative order that exists within a less well-ordered universe.[25] Again there is considerable similarity between my analysis of life and that of the authors of this work. Life is seen to be individualized, that is to say, it is a protest against the conformity of its surroundings. Furthermore, life is not bound to a single responsive chord but rather can modulate its responses according to the environmental situation within which it exists. Therefore, life is a form of order that is essentially anarchic in the sense that its responses are not conformally programmed. Life disrupts the orders within which it finds itself in order to sustain its own unique form of order. Within the exchange of all these orders are to be found the forms of feeling that make up what I earlier called "the world of feeling."

Life is therefore the rare, mysterious emergence of creative individualized order set within the wider order of continuing entropic decay. Life stands, if only for a moment, against the general tendency of the universe to run downward toward waste and triviality. The authors eloquently state the consequences of this point of view; but in the authors' development of this theme "life" quickly becomes a synonym for God. In their chapter entitled "Faith in Life," they provide a nuanced and compelling account of the God of process thought and the God of the New and Old Testaments. God is Life just as Spirit is God and Life is the Spirit of Love. A detailed analysis of this aspect of their argument lies beyond the scope of this essay. Suffice it to say that their use of the God/Life sign is a reasoned one that neither wallows in sentimentality nor conjures up suprarational sources of evidence.

Birch and Cobb push the dialogue further by stressing the importance of trusting life and reconstructing our sense of justice. The meaning of placing trust in life involves essentially a religious commitment grounded in the human need for wholeness, hope, and integrity. Of equal importance is the reconstructed sense of justice provided by Birch and Cobb. For them, once the fostering of life itself is seen to be the goal of our dwelling on earth, there is a compelling need to reconfigure our personal, cultural, and economic priorities. In a series of concluding chapters, they argue for the importance of sustainability rather than growth. Socialist and market economics are also to be revised in the light of the commitment to life. Third World and feminist concerns are to be viewed as manifestations of the call of life. Similarly, the concepts and practice of agriculture, energy use, and transportation require a thorough recasting.

In sum, *The Liberation of Life* is an important contribution to the development of an appropriate environmental ethics. Its advantages over other schools of thought are numerous. It is grounded in a metaphysics of events in process. It takes seriously the question of internal relations as definitive for understanding the value of nature. It is both realistic and eloquent about the forms, processes, and meaning of life. It brings together into a practical whole a religious, social, and political vision that is both reasonable and radical. Indeed, I judge it the century's best theoretical and practical environmental ethics.

And yet it, too, has difficulties and problems. Most especially, it remains too wedded to the intellectual framework and discourse of scientific materialism. In some ways this is of course inevitable. We are citizens of this century and stand in awe of the discoveries of the biological and physical sciences. (Also, Charles Birch holds the Challis Chair of Biology at the University of Sydney.) Still: I would assert that Birch and Cobb do not take sufficient advantage of Whitehead's radical recasting of scientifc materialism. More particularly, they do not employ his central aesthetic vision and his understanding of beauty as the ground of all ethical discourse about nature and its processes.

Earlier, in Chapter Eight, I insisted on what I called "The Primacy of the Aesthetic." My reasons were historically embedded in the history of American philosophy as well as the way in which the goodness of nature was summed up in the concept of "The Good, the Fair, and the Fitting." As regards The Liberation of Life, I suggest that its authors miss an important opportunity to employ what Whitehead in *Adventures of Ideas* calls the "Major Form of Beauty." In succeeding chapters this concept will grow in importance and application. Here, I use it to suggest how aesthetics can function as the ground of a reconstructed environmental ethics. As previously noted, Birch and Cobb are fully aware of the terrors that attend life. Their solution is to appeal to faith. Now, this is an acceptable response, but I believe that the authors are under an additional intellectual obligation to show how this faith can work out in practice. It is precisely here that the relation between truth and beauty —what Whitehead calls "the truth of discovery"—comes directly into play. For rather than relying on the faith that life has the capacity to solve its own problems, I argue that the human race can further weaken the bonds of scientific materialism by seeing all such "life conflicts" as invitations to transpose conflict into contrast. On one level this may appear merely a scholar's quibble. For obviously, the authors intend to encourage the use of critical intelligence to resolve life's quandaries. But I maintain that the truly radical act would be to insist that all such efforts be viewed as aesthetic acts seeking to find in nature a space for the good, the fair, and the fitting. In this way, the ethical, the scientific, and the aesthetic receive appropriate emphasis. I shall revisit this question when the issue of the relation between technology and nature is discussed in Chapter Eleven.

There is another version of the biocentric ethic that deserves attention. In *Respect for Nature,* Paul Taylor has constructed a coherent, articulate system of biocentrism that demands an absolute respect for living beings. Professor Taylor's work is distinguished by careful intellectual analysis, coherent and systematic development, and a genuine sense of reverence for the natural world. The difference between Taylor's account and my own resides in Taylor's allegiance to the Kantian tradition. An earlier section of this chapter detailed the basic postulates of that approach to ethical questions. It rests upon a sharp distinction between the natural and the human worlds. Taylor, therefore, must find a means to bridge this gap so that the insights of the deontological tradition can become applicable to the world of nature. He carries this out through a number of useful distinctions drawn from the tradition of analytic philosophy. These distinctions deal with the differences between inherent worth, intrinsic value, and inherent value. Briefly put, inherent worth refers to the actual value achieved by something. Inherent value and intrinsic value refer to the way in which such worth is to be measured. In keeping with the Kantian tradition of the distinction between *noumena* and *phenomena* (things in themselves and things as they show themselves to knowers), there is a radical distinction between the two activities. The intrinsic and inherent value of an entity is the outcome of how we assess its merits. As a result, the move from a split world of reality and appearance to a unified world of inherent worth can be carried out by expanding the categorical imperative to include all those entities that have inherent worth. Upon examination these entities turn out to include all living entities, since they have their own good as an essential part of their own being.[26] They are therefore in possession of a power similar to that of the rational moral agent.[27]

Taylor's work is a brilliant expansion of the Kantian position, but it also shares its defects. The key to its difficulties resides in the term "belief-system," which undergirds the ethical system. I am more than willing to testify to the elegance, compassion, and affective power of Taylor's system, but none of those qualities make it more than what it claims to be: *A belief system.* This renders the system vulnerable to the objections that can be brought to bear on any faith system. Kant himself detailed these problems in *Religion within the Limits of Reason Alone* and *The Groundwork for a Metaphysics of Morals.* Suffice it to say here that the appeal to faith, no matter how grounded in reason, remains a fideistic gesture.

The difficulties are compounded when Taylor offers us no set of normative measures with which to judge the excellence of living things. Like all good Kantians, Taylor retains his allegiance to the intellectual framework and discourse of scientific materialism. Throughout this essay, I have tried to indicate the folly of pursuing this line of thought concerning what Taylor calls "the inherent worth of living things."

Here, once again, we encounter the intellectual hegemony exercised by the massive cultural force of quantitative scientific analysis. If a philosopher as skilled, astute, and talented as Taylor is compelled to fall silent when faced with the abstractions of scientific materialism, then surely it is time to offer an alternative categoreal scheme. That was the rationale behind my efforts in Part One to present a theory of normative measures leading to an axiological cosmology. In sum, Taylor's *Respect For Life* is an ingenious attempt to construct a biocentric environmental ethics based on the Kantian deontological tradition. But in the end, it must resort to an "outlook" to ground its ethical principles and moral code. In my judgment, an outlook is not a cosmology and offers neither the intellectual strengths nor the powers of application to be found in such a philosophical method. Once again it is a matter of building up, acquiring, and practicing an aesthetic attitude toward what Taylor calls the "inherent worth" of living beings. An ethics not grounded in an aesthetics must inevitably turn into an act of faith in something other than the values experientially felt in the environment.

The Natural Humanism of Holmes Rolston

A much tougher form of environmental realism informs Holmes Rolston's *Environmental Ethics.* For him there is no justice in nature, only the law of claw and fang. To contrive to portray nature as some type of moral system is to completely misunderstand the actual natural situation. There is neither right nor wrong in nature. Nor is there justice or injustice.[28] Now, this is a decidedly cold dash of water in the face of those who would romanticize nature out of all proportion to its actual *modus operandi.* It is part of Rolston's commitment to a realistic naturalism that drives him to such a statement. But his realism does not prevent him from acknowledging the actual values achieved in nature. In fact it appears, on the surface at least, that Rolston's natural good is quite similar to the one advanced by this cosmology. This is especially so when he speaks of painful goods, the morally satisfactory fit, and the biologically satisfactory fit. Here we arrive at a fundamental problem besetting Rolston's environmental ethics. It is what Frederick Ferré has called an "ethical incoherence," by which he means the radical disconnection between two types of ethics—there is one ethic for natural environments, a tough form of biological naturalism rooted in a realistic sense of the struggle that characterizes all natural processes.[29] As Rolston says, this is "found" in nature and ought to be respected as nature's way of working with the facts of life so as to establish satisfactory fitting values. Side by side with this sense of a painful good we humans strive to create an interhuman ethics that works against the predator/prey dyad of the natural environment. This is an ethic that urges cooperation in place of conquest and kindness in place of compulsion. But all this arrangement does is repeat on a humane natural scale the deontological split between the natural and the moral. In fact, it makes the split worse, for it asserts that nature's goal of seeking a satisfactory fit is itself a value. At least the Kantian sphere was consistent in its refusal to allow value to be spoken of on the natural side of things.

Rolston is aware of the fact that he is trying to have it both ways; that is to say, establish an environmental ethics beside a social ethics. In fact, he tries to make a virtue of this incoherence by asserting that humans must straddle both ethics and act so as to endorse the major dimensions of both.[30] In making this distinction between capstone and foundational values, Rolston's humane naturalism sounds very much like a contemporary version of the Aristotelian tradition. We need a type of civic, public phronesis to guide our interaction with the environment. But the problem is that there are no intellectual resources given that could span the gap between the natural and the social domains. On the practical side of things, no coherence means no continuity established between these realms of value. What Rolston needs is an environmental cosmology that can cross between these realms and adjudicate between what is fair and fitting on one side and what is good and beautiful on the other. It is not so much that he does not see the problem. The defect lies in the absence of any flexible resources with which to begin the task of envisioning a continuing realm of value that starts at the foundational end with natural processes and culminates in the capstone values of the human culture. Such flexibility is one gift of cosmological thinking.

Postmodern Naturalism

By far one of the strangest efforts to deal with the problem of creating an appropriate environmental ethics has been suggested by those committed to postmodern philosophy. That school of thought appears prepared to abandon all forms of Enlightenment reason—both scientific and moral—on the grounds that it is precisely this form of thinking that has brought about our current environmental predicament. Three good examples of this type of thinking are Robert Pogue Harrison's *The Forests,* Neil Evernden's *The Social Construction of Nature,* and Max Oelschlaeger's *The Idea of Wilderness.* The central postmodern premise made popular by Derrida by way of Heidegger's condemnation of all forms of "metaphysical thinking"(and one to which all three thinkers give allegiance) is that contemporary reason is an ontotheological monster that eats up the differences in the world by reducing all things to a single flat, homogenized plane on which our technologically driven culture can work its will to power. The themes are familiar enough. The sacred has been lost. The self is a mere social construct. History is at an end. Philosophy must be replaced by a more radical form of thinking that no longer seeks to capture everything in its logical nets. More specifically, in terms of environmental ethics this postmodern naturalism receives its most radical expression in the proposals of Oelschlaeger, Harrison, and Evernden to abandon completely the concept of "nature." Given the present dominance of scientific materialism, the argument goes, the idea of nature as presently understood signifies, in Richard Rorty's previously cited phrase, only "A World Well Lost." It is better to abandon it than seek to reconstruct its meaning.

The strategy behind this postmodern effort to avoid the use of the term "nature" is the assumption that suspension of a particular conceptual tool is the equivalent of destroying its presence in consciousness. By outlawing the term "nature," this type of postmodern naturalism hopes to encourage a fresher appreciation of nature and its processes. But legislating language has never been terribly effective. And in conceding to modernism the use of the term "nature," little is really gained while much is lost. Such postmodern gestures do appear a bit like grandstanding. Pouting has never solved the world's difficulties.

Let us begin with Harrison. His book is an extraordinary tour de force, for he traverses much of Western culture in search of the semiotics of forests. From Dante to Shakespeare to Wordsworth to Beckett to Benjamin to Zanzorro with many stops in between, the meaning of forests for human culture is expertly and evocatively plumbed. In tracing this shifting panorama, he finds in Vico's theory of historical *ricorsi* a map for these intriguing twists and turns. As Vico memorably puts it: "This was the order of human institutions: first, the forests, after that the huts, then the villages, next the cities, and finally the academies."[31]

Harrison's conclusions are quintessentially postmodern. The forests and their deforestations and the rise of the cities and their loss of restraint reveal that human culture is frozen in an historical era mired in the overwhelming expression of the will to power. There is no place to rest. There is no place to be still. There is no place to be at home. In the most literal sense imaginable, we are aliens on our own planet. This unnatural "logos" bred out of the steel womb of the technological has distorted the authentic meaning of creativity.

While there is no immediate way out of this morass, we can at least accept our plight. We can attempt to dwell in our very estrangement from the natural. In accepting this condition we once again experience the true dimensions of our freedom. For humankind is condemned to be the poet of the natural. In learning once again to name the natural, we take up the human burden of undertaking the creation of meaning. For life is an experiment of meaning even when that meaning entails the radical endorsement of our failure, loss, finitude, and dislocation. In accepting this postmodern condition humans take a first step toward a return to the forests. Lost in the forest, we may yet find our way. Lost because we have no forest left, we are bereft of our natural heritage. It is our relation to nature that must be reclaimed if authentic existence, language, history, and experience are to reemerge. What must occur is a breakthrough whereby a more original experience of the natural comes into play in our world. Only in that sense will a more authentic form of the world of culture begin to assert itself in the words and affairs of the human realm.

What must first be cleared away so that the true origins of the interplay between the human and the natural can emerge is the relation between history and nature.[32] And so once again, silence is the aesthetic counsel of the wise.

Neil Evernden's *The Social Construction of Nature* is more direct in its assault on our culture's understanding of nature. For we have been blinded to nature's value by our technological culture.[33] Now, the remedy for this absence of an ethical vision appears quite similar to the one I have suggested. We must lose control of our world and let its strangeness begin once again to dazzle our being. Once this occurs, a new and more radical aesthetics of nature might emerge.[34] Loss of control is frightening but so also is loss of the very environment that we need in order to survive. The remedy offered by Evernden is the radical one of a violent overcoming of the present age's semiotics of nature so that new forms of wild otherness can emerge to capture our attention: "What catastrophe might set the sparrow free of the 'ossified signifier' that seals it in Nature!"[35]

Once again the influences of Heidegger/Derrida, *logos,* and the "Text" show themselves. But I do not think that strange, forced, or exotic language will alter our relation to nature. Neither will verbal plumage camouflage the real fact that we have lost sight of the value of nature. Restoring that sense of worth requires more than a novel vocabulary. It is, rather, a cosmological undertaking.

I am not opposed to professors of literature plying their trade, but I do believe they have things more than a little backward when they claim to change the world by changing a vocabulary. For all its prominence in contemporary postmodern philosophy, the "Text" remains a derivative, secondhand, and effete form of experience. One can hardly expect it to pull off the cultural miracles claimed for its powers.[36]

As I have argued, such an approach leaves the one who would be a lover of wisdom only on the first rung of Plato's ladder of knowing.

Indeed, we need to be engaged by fresh images, for that is the very first step toward knowing the Good. But if we leave it there, we turn ourselves into children ever delighted and ever distracted by whatever comes along next. We neither deserve nor can afford a child's innocence. The climb out of the cave and the descent back into it require cosmological speculation, articulated categoreal schemes, and their appropriate application. That, to my mind, remains philosophy's responsibility. Anything less turns philosophers into literature professors and literature professors into philosophers. I recommend a rereading of Plato's *Sophist.* Furthermore, this postmodern poetics of nature is neither kind to Aristotle's understanding of the relation between science and poetics nor a valid interpretation of the complete role of the citizen in the *Polis.*

Max Oelschlaeger *The Idea of Wilderness* is a monumental study of the intellectual history of the environmental movement in America. As such, it serves as a fitting conclusion to this dialectical survey of the value of a postmodern philosophy of nature. One finds in his work a similar retreat to natural domains as a necessary precondition for renewing our sense of the creative. In fact, it is the paleolithic mind that is offered as a standard for an authentic engagement with nature. Mystery, the sacred, and appropriate terror before the power of the natural were then still in full bloom. Something akin to such an awe must be rekindled in human beings if the natural world is to be saved from ecological doom. At present, there is too much arrogance and too much confidence in the power of our technological culture. Until nature once again becomes an abode of mystery, what is really at stake in changing our attitude toward the natural will elude us. Hence the saving power of the wild places. With the wholesale triumph of modernism, human consciousness has become profoundly inured to the feeling of reverence before nature and its processes. While not exactly returning us to the Stone Age, a postmodern view of nature would alter, widen, and deepen the interpretative vision that now strangles our view of the wilderness.[37]

What are the elements of this new vision and what are its intellectual tools? The vision is "cosmic synergism," but with what tools shall this vision be shaped, articulated, and shared with others. There is no ultimate ground between facts and values, ends and means. This is what I mean by intellectual irresponsibility. I have nothing but respect for Oeschaelger's scholarly research. But how can any thoughtful person end such an intensive intellectual labor with such foolishness? No ultimate distinction between facts and values, or between ends and means? Surely, Western intelligence is not that enfeebled by its ontotheological adventures!

Furthermore, in all this there can be detected the perfume of romanticism. Also, though it is nowhere admitted, such a vision is heavily dependent upon the continuing success of the contemporary economic model. In fact, there is about all this a decidedly bourgeois contentment with the world as presently arranged. It is as though all we need is just a little more nature and a little more backpacking. But that has always been the way of postmodern thinking. It has a decided preference for the economic comforts of industrialized capitalism and a romantic nostalgia for the piney woods. Indeed there does remain an unknown future awaiting new forms of thinking even as the achievements of the past continue to weave a spell. The postmodern view makes much of irony as the appropriate mode of addressing the modern condition. Is it not therefore doubly ironic that postmodern naturalism would cast out nature for the sake of saving it?

But it is not enough to merely object to the conclusions of others. Given the reality of our environmental crisis, a far more vigorous response is called for. The next chapter provides a vision for a reconstruction of the discipline of environmental ethics.

Chapter Ten

A Normative Environmental Ethics

What is most required for the development of the discipline of environmental ethics is a shared sense of moral discernment. It was precisely to encourage such a movement that the environmental cosmology of Part One was constructed. Couched in the form and language of aesthetics, the environmental cosmology seeks to encourage a kind of appreciative intelligence that is attuned to the workings of value in the natural world.

It has been argued that this cosmology provides a level of engagement that is suited for framing and presenting an ethical vision. Therefore, the ground has been prepared for this chapter's effort to present an ethical vision based on normative measures appropriate for identifying what is of worth in nature and what, therefore, possesses a claim on our moral attention.

This chapter begins with a discussion of the relation between cosmology and ethical vision. It then defends the unique power of human consciousness to choose appropriate norms for judging the value of nature and its processes. Specific norms for estimating both intrinsic and instrumental values in nature are then offered for consideration. The chapter concludes by putting these ethical categories to work in an actual natural environment. Hopefully, by the end of this discussion a willingness to consider both the appropriateness and the effectiveness of such an ethical vision will have been gained.

Cosmology and Moral Vision

This study offers an ethical vision for the environment that runs counter to prevailing ethical systems. I believe that such an alteration in moral discernment is indispensable for beginning the renewal of our attitude and conduct toward the natural sphere. Ethics is in the business of identifying, safeguarding, and developing what is valuable. A major premise of my argument is that contemporary versions of environmental ethics lack the intellectual power and discipline for this task. I further claim that the value of nature and its processes can best be understood through the systematic categories speculatively laid out in this cosmology. Important connections and distinctions can be derived from the cosmology's application to nature and its processes. In offering this ethical vision I hope to answer this fundamental question: What is important about nature and why?

The first thing required for an effective vision is establishment of a perspective that simultaneously grants both optical width and personal engagement. This is precisely what the Greeks meant by *Theoria*. Thus, the second thing needed for an effective vision is an act of imagination. I tried to supply this by deploying the main lines of Whiteheadian process metaphysics. What was provided was a vision of the environment as interwoven sets of ever-novel events that yielded up harmonic integrities of value. It is a theoretical vision that asks the reader to imagine vast interlocking patterns of value falling and rising interminably with the advance of time. Some of these patterns interlock so as to form the familar features of nature as we know it on this planet. Thus, oceans and mountains, deserts and plains, lakes and rivers, clouds and storms are complex, interdependent moments of value that spin through the world of nature. And so, too, are the living creatures, from the tiniest amoeba to the giant Sequoia. Other patterns of events, perhaps in far distant galaxies, form webs of value less well known to us. But whether it be here on earth or in intergalactic space, each has its unique value in itself. Each transmits that value to others within its environment. Each event, therefore, has a level of instrinsic value and each has the capacity to be of instrumental value to another. Sometimes their uniqueness is submerged within the vast systems in which they dwell. They are merely a blip on the moving horizon of time. But their value still registers and still counts. Sometimes they reach such a peak of individuality that entire systems are transformed and begin to serve their particular ends. But the point not to be missed is that the vision demands that each and every event be taken for what it is *in itself, for others, and for the whole:* An occasion of value precious in its uniqueness.

An ethical vision also needs the qualities of width and specificity. In this it also resembles cosmology which was seen to need both vagueness and applicability. Width derives from narrowness woven onto vagueness. Now, this cosmology has sufficient vagueness (again in the algebraic sense of the variable "any," not in the sense of fuzziness or ambiguity). Likewise, by employing the term "event" the ethical vision gains considerable width. Any environmental entity qualifies for consideration under the term, event. Narrowness comes in when the events take on through *adequate application* more and more specificity. This particularity is gained through the use of simplicity and complexity as naming the important components of events. Also, a high degree of specificity is achieved through detailing the essential and the conditional features of events. In addition, what was earlier termed the diachronic and the synchronic axes of events can be brought into play to highlight those temporal dimensions most important in a specific environmental region. Finally, the vertical and horizontal dimensions of environmental processes point toward specific types of events at work in particular regions. All of these distinctions—the simple and the complex, the essential and the conditional, the diachronic and the synchronic, and the vertical and the horizontal—make possible a high degree of narrowness in selecting out certain types of events even as an element of vagueness is also effectively preserved within the environmental analysis. That said, it should be obvious why this ethical vision has built into it an indispensable width.

Engagement is a difficult quality to measure. What engages one person bores someone else. In this ethical vision the act of engagement is encouraged by asking moral agents to see themselves as immersed in a vast sea of values. Everything they encounter in the present moment is a value. Everything that lies in the past is already an achieved value and everything that will come to be is a future value. Surrounded by value, I would assume that the sincere moralist would have little trouble with engagement. This ethical vision's problems do not reside in finding the presence of value. Importance and worth is everywhere. The central difficulty for a moral agent in this ethical vision is how to distinguish among types of value and how to rank them so as to preserve their uniqueness and at the same time make room for adequate comparisons. In a word, this axiological cosmology, and the ethical vision that accompanies it, is in dire need of effective tools for moral discernment. It is the level of cultural participation that is of primary ethical concern. And that is why norms and consciousness form the subject matter of the next section.

Norms and Consciousness

I have termed this cosmology an exercise in Platonic naturalism. It is time to reap some benefits from this somewhat awkward, if not indeed shocking, phrase. Plato's supposed "other worldliness"—his "Platonic" side, if you will—has become so much a part of the received interpretation that it is difficult to step back and see his deep concern for the actual world and its workings. But a glance at the *Republic, Statesman,* and *Philebus* serves as a reminder that most of his speculative genius was meant to be used to understand this world and its temporal becoming.

In searching for the forms at this level of the temporal world Plato was trying to identify those normative measures that made things the way they were. In seeking for justice, he sought the measure by which we know that justice has been achieved. And so on, with both the measuring of pleasure and with the distribution of power at which the statesman is supposed to excel. If all things are mixtures of the ideal and the actual, then one practical question that always needs asking is: How are they mixed? Plato's answer is they are mixed according to certain standards or measures which make up the distribution of elements characterizing each temporal thing.[1]

Now what I propose to do is to take this insight and transpose it to the domain of environmental ethics. In so doing, we gain an ethical vision as well as a remarkably flexible set of tools for moral discernment. And that is why I continue to call this cosmology an exercise in Platonic naturalism. It is Platonic in the sense that it seeks for the norms that measure out the axiological weight of events. It is a naturalism in the sense that it confines the discussion to this natural environment.

How do we know these norms? Recall that in this cosmology consciousness was defined as **the experience of the affirmation of a negation.** When we are conscious we are aware of what is there and what is not there. We do this by reason of the effective presence of ideal normative measures. What saves this cosmology from being just another version of an already old-fashioned and discredited idealism is the clear acknowledgment that the ideal—whatever it is—is never quite in fact realized. This avoids the intolerable modes of interpretive idealization that gave idealism a bad name in the first place. There is no need to turn this cosmology into another refuge for neurotic thinkers who are always seeking the security of what can never be.

Furthermore, there is no need to view this ethical vision as a form of stipulative assertions that border on intellectual fascism. The norms put forth are done so publicly and hypothetically in hopes of engaging spirited public debate on what is most important to us—our environment and how we are to care for it. I gladly volunteer to be the first to withdraw a normative measure if it is shown to be off the mark, irrelevant, or simply wrong.

Nor is it the case that all norms are either relative or subjective. Normative measures are always in use in all forms of discourse, from the most practical to the most theoretical. Rather, the real question is whether the norms proposed are sufficiently normative. The question to be asked concerning norms is: Do they hit the mark or not? It is only through open and honest public debate on this question that progress can be made on the construction of a systematic environmental ethics.

More is to be said about this "affirmation of a negation" that is at the heart of human consciousness. When I see two unequal lines, how do I know they are unequal? Do I actually see the inequality? That cannot be, because there is no inequality to be seen. There are only two lines to be seen. Empirical observation does not yield the optical vision of inequality. I "see" inequality because of something that is not there, *viz.,* equality. This is what Plato means when he tells us in the *Republic* that we know the visible by means of the invisible.[2] We judge something to be what it is by reference to a standard that is not fully there in a physical sense. It is not there in the quantifiable exactness of observable material extension precisely because the standard is an ideal. As a possible, this normative measure is experienced by the mind as a conceptual feeling. With sufficient reflection, this conceptual feeling can become a standard by reference to which what is there can be judged. It can be evaluated as either moving toward fulfilling that normative measure or falling away from it. This is what is meant by normative thinking and this is what is at the heart of Platonic naturalism's attempt to create an ethical vision for the environment.

I have already alluded to the sense of the alternative that haunts our conscious judgments. Here it is a question of recognizing that the very same process is at work when we go about the task of ethically envisioning what is a good way for an environment to be. Consciousness is naturally embedded in normative thinking. It is not a question of arbitrarily inventing such norms and applying them in some haphazard fashion. In fact, our public discourse is already saturated with normative measures of all sorts. And most of them, unfortunately, are quite off the mark. The real question is: What are the correct norms?

Norms for Intrinsic Natural Value

In putting forth this sketch of an ethical vision, I am aware of the need to provide a unified vision that also supports a maximum of diverse values. Also, there is a need to identify two types of environmental values, intrinsic value and instrumental value. In dealing first with instrinsic value I am not overlooking the need to account for how these values are transferred around environmental systems. Still, there is a need in the first place to identify what types of values are being moved about the environment. The categoreal scheme lists four ways to identify the major processes at work in environmental regions: inscape, contrast, pattern, and transmission. The first three are concerned with the intrinsic value achieved by environmental events and the last concerns their instrumental value. Within each category there are processes at work that can be judged as living up to or falling away from normative standards that mark off a good way for inscape, contrast, and pattern to be.

Thus, every inscape, contrast, and pattern can be judged to uphold the following standards in varying degrees.

I suggest that the normative measures for intrinsic environmental value are: Intensity, functional simplicity, patterned complexity, and novelty. To the degree that environmental inscapes, contrasts, and patterns express these standards, to that same degree the importance of their value is to be understood. Looking at each norm for intrinsic value we find the following.

Intensity is the outcome of the special way in which an event compresses its environmental world so as to express a unique harmony of essential and conditional features. The more it can combine simplicity with complexity, so much the more intense is its value. The most effective way of doing this is through the act of contrast, whereby differences are put into unique unities. There has already been ample discussion of intensity of experience as a major environmental measure.

Functional simplicity results from an event's unique determinateness as a singular environmental expression. As the outcome of the economy with which it harmonizes its environment, functional simplicity establishes the relevant limits of its environmental world. The range of this value extends from low-level ordering that excludes most environmental influences to high-level inclusion of startling width. The more structured the harmony, the more elegant is its inclusionary process. As the ordering principle of environmental harmony, functional simplicity can so structure events as to let a unique center of experience emerge as a controlling presence. This dominant functional simplicity can eventually reach the stage whereby a center of experience emerges. At this point, we are talking about the emergence of effective subjectivity, real individuality, and, ultimately, personhood.

Patterned Complexity is the usual way in which a harmony extends its reach so as to include more and more environmental richness in its essential features. Such patterns usually function through the use of vague representatives that stand in for a multiplicity of environmental factors. Neurological systems are successful instances of this type of harmony. And when united to a high degree of functional simplicity, possibilities of real personhood emerge. As far as we know, the human brain functioning as human thought is the richest expression of this normative measure.

Novelty is the normative standard by which nature's creativity in this instance can be measured. The measure of novelty stretches from that which is new simply because it is a new repetition of an old pattern right on up to the most outrageous concept that has yet to be thought. Obviously, novelty for its own sake is not a sufficient warrant of environmental excellence. If that were the case, the HIV virus for all its novelty of inscape, contrast and pattern should be the most valuable environmental event to appear in this century.

Taken together, these four normative measures provide an extremely reliable way of appreciating the intrinsic value of environmental events. The measures take into account the harmony that is at the heart of every environmental happening, but they also provide significant flexibility for discerning the very real qualitative differences that can exist between events. By providing a range of measures covering events as far apart as a subatomic reaction and an act of human agency, this ethical vision can account for exactly that diversity of intrinsic value that is so much a part of nature's goodness. At the same time, it provides a unified vision of intrinsic environmental value by locating value within the embrace of a single cosmological scheme.

Types of Instrumental Value

It is the category of transmission that provides the working tools for understanding instrumental value in nature. Instrumental value is another name for how values become transferred around environmental systems. Given the enormous increase in our technological power, there is no doubt that it is this part of environmental ethics that needs the most attention. Recall that the category of transmission was devised to deal with the way in which feelings are moved around environmental systems.

It is my hypothesis that an environment is really best understood as worlds upon worlds of feelings. These feelings come in four different types: physical feelings, conceptual feelings, propositional feelings, and feelings of stillness. Physical feelings are the outcome of the constant repetition of past events so that little or no feelings of novelty pervade an environment. The material world with its preponderance of physical forces and objects was offered as the prototype of this world of physical feelings. A certain "rock hard" and substantial statistical regularity was expressed throughout its domains. This is where the laws of nature reign supreme.

On the other hand, it was seen that there are also environments characterized by a dominant sense of the real presence of possibility. Quick change and sudden alterations in scope and size and mood were among its noted features. These environments were dominated by the influx of conceptual feelings. They are places where the rigid laws of nature have not closed off all possibilities of novelty. Still, these regions are more unsettled than they are alluring, for no directions or concretely possible outcomes are to be discovered in the conceptual feelings that dominate environmental transmissions.

A sense of real possibility rather than just pure possibility, however, hangs over those environments in which propositional feelings of high intensity could be felt. These are the regions that set forth halfway houses between the actual and the possible. They lure change by reason of hints and suggestions. Plants in their heliotropic spirals are lured by propositions. Animals that hunt know when they are in the midst of an environment transmitting high-profile propositions. And, of course, humans are superbly adapted to detect such propositional lures. The felt presence of likely radical novelty is an indication that an environment saturated with propositional feelings is at hand. Finally, there are feelings of stillness that express a sense of fullness and completeness spreading through natural environments. They are rare and exceptional and require separate analysis.

How then do these feelings get transmitted throughout an environment? Or what is their instrumental value? I maintain, first, that physical, conceptual, and propositional feelings transmit change in decidedly different ways throughout an environment and, second, that these instrumental values can be identified through the levels of order, stability, and variety they transmit across an environmental region.

First, as regards the transmission of different kinds of value throughout environmental regions. An environment in which there is a dominance of physical feelings operates through force. It compels order by reason of the sheer compulsion inflicted on its members. Physical feelings are the equivalent of conformal patterns of force that repeat themselves without letup. Repetition, temporal sameness, and a vast massive regularity are the ways in which physical feelings show their environmental presence. When physical feelings are in control, there is little likelihood of the emergence of radical novelty. Unless, of course, other physical forces displace the webs of order already in place. Regions characterized by the massive presence of physical transmission are extremely resistant to change. But when change does arrive, it does so suddenly and with a fury that only natural physical transmission can produce.

On the other hand, the transmission of conceptual feelings throughout an environment has little instrumental value. It amounts to a randomness that borders on the chaotic. As such, unorganized feelings of possibility are largely ineffective when it comes to being instrumental in environmental happenings. It is only when they become organized as propositions that environments begin to feel their instrumental value.

Propositional feelings spread through environments when enduring patterns of environmental order take shape. I am talking about the emergence of real individuals within the vast process of environmental happenings that is called nature. When a set of events can be strung together so as to achieve a certain degree of effective consecutiveness, then real individuality begins to emerge as an important environmental trait. When in addition this string of events is alive, then entire sets of propositional feelings become felt throughout an environment. Finally, when this living individual can express a degree of personal order, we have arrived at that level of environmental complexity that harbors the possibility of important, creative environmental change. Propositional feelings are for the most part confined to structured living systems that come to dominate various environmental settings. It is through them that nature expresses the kind of environmental instrumentality that concerns this ethical vision. Here, of course, we are on the verge of technology as an important environmental presence. The next chapter deals directly with this issue.

In sum, values are transmitted around environmental systems through the way of force, the way of chance, or the way of persuasive lures. This brings my analysis to the second part of the hypothesis concerning instrumental value, which maintains that the transmittal of feelings throughout an environment results in the establishment of three different types of change by which natural instrumental values can be appreciatively understood: Order, stability, and variety.

Order is the single most powerful way in which nature enforces environmental behavior. Some orders, like the transmittal of physical feelings, severely restrict the actions of their members. Others serve to promote freedom. Either way, order is the most direct instrumental value in any environment. Order is present when a degree of regularity is found in the activities of its members. Such regularity is derived from the way in which members of the order conform to the conditions laid down for their coming to be. Order, therefore, carries with it a necessary reference to givenness. It is order that gives to things the conditions which their essential features harmonize. By sheltering individual entities from certain perspectives, order restricts opportunities for change and thereby enhances the strength of its constituents by emphasizing those dimensions of harmony that have proven environmental worth. It is for this reason that order always brings in its wake a certain massiveness and rhythmic regularity. Lastly, order is naturally associated with goodness, since it guarantees a set of conditions that are apt for specific harmonic satisfactions. Therefore, the enjoyment of order is a precondition for successful environments.

Stability provides a sense of the regular and consistent transmission of feelings pushing through an environment. It is important not to confuse stability with sameness. The doctrine of harmony underlying this vision of environmental ethics suggest that the way to stability is through variety, not sameness. A harmony requires identity and difference for its achievement. Too much identity blunts harmony by denying the relevance of the complex. Furthermore, a narrow form of identity prevents access to patterned complexity. Likewise, the functional simplicity of particular events does not necessarily exclude variety. It is the very width of the environment that tests the breadth of functional simplicity. Finally, intensity and novelty demand that a strong individuality register its influence throughout a richly stable environment.

Variety arises from the active presence of novelty. Its presence is a sign of great tensile strength resident in a harmony. Without the novelty provided by variety a very weak form of order would prevail throughout an environment. Sameness has no defense against real instances of novelty. It is a commonplace of ecology that variety produces stability. Thus, it is the freedom enjoyed by the members of an order that fosters the flexibility required to respond to novel situations. There is no metaphysical necessity to the customary opposition of order and freedom. In fact, variety's important instrumental value depends upon the appropriate conjunction of these two notions.

Instrumental value is one side of the environmental situation and intrinsic value is the other. Through order, stability, and variety good changes are transmitted throughout environments. Such instrumental change can take place either by force, by chance, or by persuasion. That depends on the kind of feelings being transmitted throughout an environment. But no matter what the instrument of change might be, the environmental outcome is always the same—a new occasion with specific intrinsic value emerges within the environment.

A Case Study

Appraising instrumental value involves the assessment of change, which has many forms, each of which disturbs environmental stability in a different way. The minimal form of such change would be the rhythm of time marking out the passage of events in the forward movement of process. The maximal form would be the complete rearrangement of all the forms of order in an environment. Nuclear holocaust would be an extreme example. In between lies a complex range best understood by focusing on the levels of environmental order involved. The most direct way to change anything is to alter the order in which it sits. A trivial change marks out slight alterations in the nexus of connections binding environmental entities. An insignificant spatial shift is an example. Vague changes occur when the major representative entities in an environment no longer hold their place. As a result, the systematic uniformity of an environment undergoes alteration. A stony field moves ever so slowly toward the softness of a meadow. When narrowness impresses itself upon an environment, clearly identifiable changes are sighted. For example, the intense activity of a beaver radically alters environmental dimensions. Changes in width come about through the melding of narrowness and vagueness. Thus, the narrow quest of the mining company bores into environmental vagueness producing a radical shift in the width of the land's values.

In assessing change the normative categories of this cosmology serve as measures whereby the worth of change can be defined. What matters are the relevant shifts in harmonic emphases. An important consequence of this analysis is that no change can be automatically condemned as violating the normative structure of an environment. Each change is to be specifically evaluated by reason of its contribution to the family of harmonies within which it lies. By discerning the value of each environmental transmission, this ethical vision takes on the kind of specification needed if it is to be an effective guide to action.

This environmental cosmology should combine with its ethical vision to provide useful measures for moral discernment in specific environmental situations. One such case study would be the hunting of mountain lions in the western United States. The parties involved would include the mountain lion, any affected cattle and sheep ranchers, and the hunters and naturalists. Let us step back from traditional partisan positions and look at this situation through the vision provided by this environmental cosmology. Obviously, a mountain lion is a harmony; indeed, it is a complex set of entwined harmonies nesting within each other. Its simplicity of functioning is demonstrated by its superb hunting ability. Its complexity is equally manifest in the many ways in which it engages with the environment. Seeing, smelling, spoor marking, mating, cub rearing, and so forth are signs of its complex environmental interaction. That its life is intense is sensed in its roar, its stealth, and its predatory power. Its novelty is not so obvious, for ethology tells us that its behavior is fairly predictable. The transmission of value that it contributes to an environment is found in the way it culls weak, infirm, and aged members from the animal population.

What stands out in all this is its lack of novelty. But from the standpoint of a vanishing species, the mountain lion is intensely unique. It therefore exhibits novelty by reason of its rare presence in the environment. Here we change the perspective of the ethical vision and see the mountain lion as a unique order within the unique order of its habitat. The reciprocity between both orders is such that they secure for each other relevant stability and endurance through the changes resulting from their interactions.

But the act of moral discernment does not stop there. By employing the four levels of environmental order, an ethical vision of the mountain lion begins to emerge. It is a harmony of narrowness woven onto a backdrop of vagueness such that a singular intensity of experience is achieved. It is precisely this depth of experience manifested by the predator that attracts the hunter or naturalist. Similarly, the rancher is acutely aware of the narrow aim of the lion as it stalks its range. In deciding on a good way of acting, we must take into consideration the norms governing the mountain lion, the environment, and interested human parties. They, too, have norms that measure their actions. Begin with the naturalist. There is little need for decision here, since observation is the goal. The rancher's normative measure is only slightly more complex: Removal of the predator is the goal. The means employed to carry out this task should respect the value of the lion, the sheep. and the environment.

It is, of course, the case of the hunter that is most difficult. But the normative measures developed in this cosmology point toward a clear answer. What normative measures could the hunter find to justify the killing of the lion? Two suggest themselves: The thrill of the hunt and recreation. the thrill of the hunt involves the intense experience of tracking the animal and the skill and daring required to vanquish so powerful a prey. The value of the hunted lion lies in its representational function as an animal extraordinarily dangerous and elusive. In other words, what the hunter really hunts is the depth of experience embodied by the lion. The hunter seeks the power of the hunted. Our civilization has granted us means to do this without the danger faced by earlier hunters who also sought the spirit of the lion (and had need of its meat for life purposes). Modern hunting techniques render such totemic rituals futile. Regarding recreational value, there are so many other forms available that the selection of hunting amounts to an arbitrary act of the will. Performed from the safety of the guided expedition, such an act has no redeeming value when compared with the value of the lion.

Let us assess the hunter in the same way that we measured the lion. The modern hunter is a case of narrowness woven onto further narrowness. The environment becomes a thin slice of space and time, harboring one entity whose fate it is to supply atavistic energy to the hunter. Whatever energy is expended by the hunter is given over entirely to this end. The vagueness so necessary for width of experience is eliminated by reason of the intention of the hunter. While it remains true that a successful hunt leaves the participants with a significantly intense experience, that moment is utterly finished when the prey is slain. True enough, tales of bravery and effort will be told, but the fact remains that it was the lion that supplied all such value. The human contribution to the environment in this case is nil. The reason is startlingly simple: The human was not in the environment as a human but as another animal. What was left behind in the pursuit of the prey were features of human being that we are under an obligation to fulfill: fairness, compassion, and judicious interaction that contribute to an environment. It is the failure to measure up to these norms that condemns the activity.

What has occurred in this case study is that the stature of the human has been reduced. There is indeed a simplicity of functioning as the hunter narrows down his interest to the taking of the prey. But in this case, I would call such an activity "simple minded." The many dimensions of the environment are reduced to a single one: There is somewhere here something to kill. The hunter is all gun. Indeed, intensity prevails, but what is transmitted throughout the environment is destruction.

On the basis of its categories, this cosmology through its ethical vision sees the contemporary version of this type of hunting as having no good place in the mountain lion's terrain. It is neither fair nor fitting. The value obtained by the hunting party is minimal compared to what is destroyed. Here, it is not, as Utilitarianism would have it, a question of the greatest good for the greatest number. Nor is it, from a deontological perspective, a matter of the "rights" of the mountain lion. In this ethical vision what is to be discerned are the actual values at play in the situation. It is the axiological basis of the cosmology that allows for this assessment of the relative values that are in conflict.

Since the empirical side of cosmology demands a specific application of its vague principles, an ethical vision of the kind here offered mirrors in the closest way possible the actual workings of the environment itself. It establishes a symmetrical relationship between abstract normative structures and concrete activity. The axiological principles specified in the act of ethical judgment are the direct outcome of the vague categories employed in the cosmology. When applied to questions of action, they become regulative principles governing the actions of all environmental participants. The rules of the game are part of the game itself. In this way, my Platonic naturalism avoids the idealistic fallacy that forces deontological systems to conjure up extreme versions of personhood. Furthermore, being based on a cosmological system, this ethical vision does not need to fall back upon a version of nineteeenth-century liberalism with its insistence upon the primacy of human freedom. As Plato pointed out, the best kind of human thinking is that which takes its rise from the good, the true, and the beautiful. Thus, the thinking of the sort practiced here derives its power from the validity of its coordinated categories. This does not mean that such a normative environmental ethics will be followed. The reality of human freedom prevents such a guarantee.

It would be unfair to accuse this ethical vision of generalizing from experience. Rather, the movement of thought is from the vague to the specific. In their tendency to generalize, "generals," as Peirce pointed out, move thought away from the concreteness of experience. Vague principles, on the other hand, require application if their truth is to be known. Reference to the actual world in its dynamic formation narrows vagueness into a set of related categories anchored in wide environmental activities. Used properly, this vision suggests a broad wisdom characteristic of ethics as a practical science. This practice involves nothing less than the doctrine of harmony applied to the discipline of ethics itself. Systematic philosophy seeks to grasp the world in one self-reflective comprehensive view. One test of the adequacy of a philosophic system is the universal applicability of its fundamental principles. What is true of the activities of things in the environment is also true of the ethical vision that directs good action in that same environment. What is true of the mountain lion is what guarantees its proper place in the environmental system. The judgment of this ethical vision simply reflects that accomplishment.

Hopefully, this case study demonstrates the possibility of bringing together into a unifying vision the realms of actuality, value, choice, and action. Its unity is its simplicity. Its interpretive and explanatory power is its complexity. It needs specific interdisciplinary application of its principles for growth of understanding. It recognizes the unfathomable complexity of the order of nature as well as the inherent creativity of its creatures. It allows for the rather precise identification of the value of particular things even as it affirms the continuity of all things. It stands open to correction on all fronts because its presuppositions are publicly acknowledged. It can bring together all these opposites because it establishes the ground of their actuality.

Throughout its many modes, harmony achieves this union of opposites by establishing a realm within which complexity and simplicity can play their chosen roles. Whatever the results of these complex decisions, the environment continually manifests the simple presence of harmony which results in fair and fitting displays of value. Commitment to such a vision will allow environmental ethics to take an important step beyond its present efforts. When ethical principles must be tortuously rearranged in order to deal with environmental issues, it is a sign of their inadequacy. The cosmological perspective of this study generates an ethical vision of values expressing themselves throughout the environment. By framing an understanding of such relations within the explanatory power of a categoreal scheme, a genuinely effective environmental ethics becomes normatively possible.

Respecting Value

A preeminent virtue to be cultivated in this ethical vision is respect. But respect must be earned. One of the reasons for this laborious effort to construct an environmental cosmology was to earn back for nature the respect it lost when it was savaged by scientific materialism. When value was thrown out of nature by a fact-obsessed ideology, respecting nature on its own terms was made deeply problematic.

The history of Western philosophy has once before witnessed a similar attempt to restore respect for nature's value. I am referring to Spinoza's heroic attempt in *The Ethics* to overcome the disastrous results of Cartesian dualism. Then, as perhaps even now, that effort was widely misunderstood. Whatever be the ultimate judgment on this classic of metaphysics, cosmology, and ethics, Spinoza does put forth a norm-driven account of nature that demands respect for nature as the fundamental good. He also encourages us to develop a central emotional response to life that he calls "Fortitudo" which I translate as "Strength of Mind."[3]

In my judgment, something very much similar to Spinoza's "Strength of Mind" is required to meet today's environmental crisis. What is needed is the "Strength of Mind" that can hold together in a single unitary vision the processes of nature and the values they create and transmit. Only a strong mind can keep together what the culture has so expertly trained us to tear apart. Our culture educates us in the arts of analysis. We are not taught to hold the world together in a unity. When Spinoza calls for another kind of knowing to stand beside imagination and scientifc reasoning, I believe he intends something very close to the ethical vision that I have been describing. His *scientia intuitiva* is an act of a strong mind that can see the whole as expressing itself concretely throughout the parts. Because of his conviction that all things are together in a fundamental unity, a wide and deep involvement in concrete life is essential. Anything less cheats our experience.[4]

Now, obviously there are great differences between the process cosmology I have articulated and Spinoza's system. But what is shared is as important as what is different. Both Spinoza and this cosmology agree in reversing the traditional relation between wholes and parts. Scientific materialism maintains that parts are simple and wholes complex. One begins always by analyzing down to the simplest part. Spinoza and process thought regard parts as complex and wholes as simples.[5] A strong mind is required to see the whole in which the part sits. Only this vision will grant true comprehensive knowing. Further, there is general agreement that each part of nature is connected to every other part and what is required is the development of the intellectual strength to grasp this implicate order.[6] In short, only an appropriate idea of the whole will suffice to give us a concrete sense of the particular parts of nature. Finally, Spinoza shares this cosmology's conviction that the natural environment is saturated with value. In his case he calls *Natura* both *naturans*—the unending expression of divine power—and *naturata*—the face of God inscribed on and manifested in nature's achievements. I call it, more prosaically, "value" (perhaps that is merely the caution brought about by some 300 years of scientific materialism). What matters most is that Spinoza provides a template for environmental thinking that makes it impossible to think about nature without at the same time thinking about value.

Therefore: Respect is to be accorded to that which is valuable in itself, for others, and for the whole. To provide this respect on the scale of environmental goodness calls for an uncommon strength of mind. In attempting to understand environmental goodness as an expression of the fair and the fitting, I ally my thought with the

Platonic and American naturalist traditions. The final reason why respect should be accorded nature is the simple fact that in natural environments beauty is the name of the good.

I am under no illusions that gaining this respect and developing the strength of mind needed to communicate it to others will be easy. But I take heart from the words with which Spinoza closed his *Ethics:* "All things excellent are as difficult as they are rare."[7]

Chapter Eleven

Nature, History, and Technology

Technology has carved its initials all over our century. From media to space travel to nuclear war to computers to internets and on and on, it is technology that defines this age. It is the very signature of the times. Now, in the face of this awesome fact, philosophy in the last few decades has turned inward and away from a genuine confrontation with technology as a cultural force.

It is the school of postmodernism that is at the bottom of this failure of nerve. This chapter will trace the origins of this philosophic movement back to Heidegger and his conception of the history of being in the West. In addition, it will look at the suggestions for reforming technological culture put forward by the American Heideggerean, Albert Borgmann. It will raise the question of everyday technological goodness and its presence and absence in contemporary civilization.

Furthermore, it will confront postmodernism's position with the thought of Whitehead on the place and meaning of technology in our age. In doing so, I will have an opportunity to apply the cosmological categories constructed in the first part of this study. Technology will take on the ontological status of a propositional contrast, and its place in our age is to be judged by how well it comports itself with certain other normative measures used by Whitehead to understand the rise and fall of great civilizations.

In effect, this chapter allows us to take up the question of the destiny of nature at this moment in history. Heidegger and Whitehead are the two great systematic metaphysical philosophers of our century. Their confrontation over the question of nature, history, and technology will be a memorable one, not unlike the already mentioned *Gigantomachia* of the *Sophist.*

Heidegger's History of Being

Heidegger's analysis of technology is composed of a number of parts. There is first the assessment of technology as the culmination of Western metaphysics and its passion for control. Then there is a shift to a phenomenological portrayal of technology's basic structure through the presentation of its being as *Gestell* (the Enframing). Finally, technology is seen as the destined outcome of the flawed beginning of Western metaphysics—the fateful beginning from Plato onward to Nietzsche that necessitates the return to authentic origins as experienced in the Presocratics and poets such as Holderlin. The conclusion Heidegger reaches is that expressed by Holderlin in his poem, "Patmos": "But where danger is, grows the saving power also."[1] I shall argue that Heidegger is eminently correct but not for the reasons he thinks.

From his earliest explorations in *Being and Time* to his last works, Heidegger sought to answer a single question: "What is the meaning of being?" Despite the many pathways taken, he never settled on a satisfactory answer. Rather, he came to view the entire history of Western philosophy as some sort of case study in amnesia. For it is the forgetfulness of being rather than its recollection that marks our path. Being's truth is hidden even as it is partially revealed in the many names granted it in the course of the devolution of Western metaphysics. Be it Plato's forms, Aristotle's *ousia*, Spinoza's substance, or Leibniz's monads, each time being is named its essence slips away. That, indeed is the very meaning of the Greek term for truth: *Aletheia*, the disclosed, the unveiled that always retains its alpha privative.

The waters of *Lethe* rise until in modern times every being is engulfed in a sea of nihilism that masks itself as the assertion of an enormous appetite for and will to power. It is modern technology that comes to express this metaphysical fall from ontological grace. An unbridled lust for domination searches into the most secret places, even into the human heart where it turns all beings into *objects for use*. Nature, once understood as abundant *Phusis*, is now simply there, exposed and ready for use, spread out before us like so much supply. As *Gegenstand*, it is object for our self-determining subjectivity. Technology satisfies our need to control being by turning everything into a utilitarian *Gestalt*.

How technology brought this about is the question Heidegger seeks to answer through his famous characterization of *Technik als Gestell*. Understood as the "Enframing" that marks all dimensions of modern thought and culture, technology throws a frame of reference around experience, forcing us to see the world as sets of objective opportunities for exploitation. Everything, including the human race itself, is now seen as "a standing-reserve."

For Heidegger, this did not come about by accident. The end of philosophy was already present in its beginning. It is the destiny of the West to come to completion as precisely this self-assertive technological will-to-power. Though the intermediate reasons leading to this fall are many, one cause outstrips all others in importance. We —philosophers in the West—have forgotten what it means to be. Our lack of thoughtfulness culminates in Nietzsche's metaphysics of the will. What is left for us are "The Tasks of Thinking."[3] Our destiny is to seek alternative paths back to the authentic First Beginning, when philosophy was in touch with the meaning of being. The thoughtful way back to that past event of appropriation *(das Ereignis)* is essentially a poetic one, for it is the struggle of the *Poietes* to carpenter a world through authentic language that joins the kindred paths of thinkers and poets.[4] Heidegger's struggle to retrieve the history of Western philosophy authentically is also, at the same time, a *Dekonstruktion* revealing the forgetfulness of being rotting its core. The recourse to poets like Holderlin, Trakl, and Rilke are attempts also to seize the ontological difference (harbinger of Derrida's *differance)* obliterated by philosophy's ontotheological hegemony. The otherness of being that was displaced by logocentric thinking seeks a space where it can be both experienced and authentically expressed. The search for this Originary Place occupies all of Heidegger's remaining thoughts. His final naming of it has already been heard: It is the patient quest for *das Ereignis*—

that event of appropriation that authentically brings the human being—*Dasein*—into the nearness of what has been forgotten. While technology is the dominant event of our culture, it is not by any means the saving power itself. As Heidegger would have us learn: It harbors the possibility of restoring an authentic *Da*, a "there" where *Sein*, being, can show itself. What is required is a Turning whose arrival is no more at our disposal than being itself.[5]

Now, the seeds of the major themes of postmodern philosophy are to be found in this sketch of Heidegger's position on technology. There is the condemnation of a metaphysics of presence that seeks to control reality. There is an invitation to new voices and new styles of philosophizing. And finally, there is the judgment that the hopelessness of the present situation calls for the radical revision of all forms of philosophizing. It is precisely the categories and systems of Western philosophy that have brought culture to this impasse. The development of postmodern forms of philosophizing follows inevitably from this apocalyptic vision.

A worthy representative of the Heideggeran interpretation of technology is Albert Borgmann's *Technology and the Character of Contemporary Life*.[6] Borgmann excoriates everyday technological experience for splitting the world: A "diremption" that makes holistic experience impossible in everyday life. His argument develops Heidegger's position by extending the discussion of technology to include its impact on the character of our life and the ways in which that deleterious result is a necessary outcome of technology's essential structure. He also suggests types of therapy for our age so that the dysfunction attendant on technological addiction can be alleviated. All in all, Borgmannn's work represents this decade's most extensive critique of technology from the perspective of American hermeneutic phenomenology. According to Borgmann, technology is this age's single most serious challenge to authentic human existence. Its pervasive cultural presence is such that it represents everything and nothing at the same time. Its invisible cultural presence brings about an inevitable mood of disengagement. A tone of happy, effortless living dissolves the stresses of existence into a continuing series of charmed present moments. Rather than seeking involvement in being, we are satisfied to let human beings wallow in the shallow forms of commodious living. The result is that our being and being itself become covered up, forgotten, and distanced from their true belonging together as authentic modes of disclosure.

Meanwhile, the river of being running through history eludes us as we settle into modes of being that conceal our true relationship to being and its many modes of disclosure.[7] The essential means for effecting this massive cultural forgetfulness is through the "device paradigm" which dissolves the engaging seamlessness of the world.[8] It is this absolute "diremption" of means from end and the simulataneous identification of experience with a commodity that establishes disengaged displacement as the character of contemporary life.

What seals off this cultural phenomenon and makes it invisibly triumphant are the modes of discourse operating in contemporary society. They are three in number and represent the major ways in which technological culture is justified, covered up, or revealed in its true nature. *Apodeictic, paradeictic,* and *deictic* modes of discourse name the ways in which what Heidegger called *Logos* gets covered up and/or authentically revealed in our time. If language is indeed the house of being, then each of these ways of laying out the dimensions and meaning of the real strongly determine the destiny of our age. Understanding their essential differences is crucial for reversing the tide of forgetfulness that besets the present age.

Apodeictic discourse represents that mode of explanation characteristic of the natural sciences as they seek the unvarying universal characteristics of things in general.[9] Thus, scientific discourse provides us with a world rendered homogeneous through explanation. By laying out the conditions and laws through which explanation can be necessarily derived, forms of apodeictic speech level down the world into controllable forces whose ultimate meaning escapes us. The emphasis is always on power through a uniform explanation. What is left out is the *meaning* of what is controlled. This inevitably occurs within the domain of apodeictic discourse, for the significance of what is explained is forgotten in the rush to get down exactly as possible the laws and conditions of all phenomena whatsoever. Apodeictic discourse produces for technological culture a generalized theory of natural laws.

Paradeictic discourse apes apodeictic discourse but is epistemologically deficient when it comes to producing universal laws and conditions of predictability. Most readily seen when the social sciences seek the certitude of of the physical sciences, paradeictic discourse picks out a set of features which it then declares through use and professional agreement to be the very heart and soul of the matter in question. A ready example might be the use of social

Darwinism in the work of the sociobiologist E. O. Wilson. In isolating these patterns, paradeictic discourse approximates the device paradigm of technology, since "they exhibit in a more diffuse way the circularity and lack of demonstrability that we have found in metaphysical paradigms."[10] Metaphysics here means "apodeictic" because from the hermeneutic point of view all metaphysical thinkings are failed versions of the West's ontotheological crusade. And this indictment also includes such modern pretenders to the crown as the natural sciences.

Just as the device paradigm distances us from the experience to be had, so also paradeictic discourse moves us away from the very object we are trying to understand. Based as it is on the detection of the presence of vaguely similar characteristics, paradeictic discourse prevents a deeper analysis of things. No authentic disclosure of being can come forward and show itself.[11]

When social sciences like economics, history, or psychology fasten on to paradigmatic explanations that rub out crucial distinctions for the sake of uniform application of explanatory laws, then they have committed the fallacy of the device paradigm. What is covered over is the richness of the phenomena and what is handed over for consumption is an explanation that this is one more instance of "the law of..." The meaning of the activity is lost. Its rich significance is displaced through some easily replicable paradigm now knowable by reason of some professional jargon. Leithic amnesia lurks inside paradeictic discourse. Obviously, both these types of discourse dominate our cultural speech. They are enshrined in the Academy as well as the vast funding agencies of our government. Nevertheless, they remain a variant of a more foundational form of speech.[12] Deictic discourse concerns itself with origins, points of orientations, beginnings, and makings—in short, this type of discourse founds worlds and is akin to the creation accounts of great civilizations. It seeks to express the source which grounds beings, events, and things. It is poetical in the strict Heideggerean sense of world-founding. To name is to bring into being an entire realm of meaning that summons up significant meaning. If the reader detects a certain liturgical whiff to all this, he or she would not be far wrong. For when it comes to putting deictic discourse into practice, it converts into types of rites which Borgmann calls "focal things and practices."

The last part of Borgmann's work is dedicated to finding a way out of our technological malaise. The first move, he suggests, is that we opt for a reform of the device paradigm itself. This would be in opposition to all functionalist critiques that would argue for reforms within the technological paradigm itself. Because cultural amnesia arises from the device paradigm, the needed presence of engagement can be felt only when that grip of oblivion is loosened.

There are some three ways to release ourselves from the clutch of technology and reengage the world: *deictic discourse itself, the challenge of nature, and focal things and practices.* Deictic discourse questions technology's gift of commodious availability. For "it discloses something to us and elicits active assent; it moves us to act ."[13] It lays a normative claim on our being through its ultimate strength in demanding engaged attention in a concrete way. One direct way in which deictic power announces itself is in the experience of wilderness. Nature challenges us because it is "the experience of something in its own right, of nature in its primeval character, that seeks appropriate testimony in our deictic thinking."[14] What nature challenges us to do is recognize that the smooth continuity between means and ends so characteristic of contemporary life is in the end only partially real. It is an appearance that is dependent upon a profoundly reworked order of things for its continuing existence. The shock of meeting being in its own right can call forth appropriate engagement.[15]

Such originary learning takes on concreteness in focal things and practices. Focal practices, things, and events center and illuminate our lives by integrating means and ends in one rewarding experience—an event of meaning that does not rely on the technological paradigm of concealed means and availability of product as commodity. Borgmann stresses two such practices: running and "the culture of the table." Both provide engagement that is direct, strong, concrete, and purposeful. These are actions that disclose deictically the belonging together of being and being human.[16]

In the everyday world, the web woven by the device paradigm is too thick and impenetrable to find much goodness in it. We must find ways to step outside its keep in order to encounter again the freshness of being and the shock of its arrival.[17] What Borgmann asks us to do is to awaken from our deep technological sleep so as to experience once again, and in a new way, the terror and joy, the fright and delight of human dwelling on earth.

Now all this can be traced back to the fundamental dualism that infects all thinking inspired by Heidegger. For the master himself, that dualism showed itself in the distinction between "ontological and ontic" and "existential and existentielle" in the opening sections of *Being and Time*.[18] In fact, being lost in everydayness is the very sign of inauthentic *Dasein*. Here Borgmann extends the sway of inauthenticity to the use of technological devices. We must locate extraordinary places and take up pure practices unsullied by technology's presence if we are to secure a lasting goodness for ourselves and the communal culture we share with others.[19] So technology can be used if we are careful not to let it stain our essential being. This, of course, is exactly the stance taken by Heidegger in his address to the townsfolk of Messkirch. As he put it: "we can say yes and we can say no."[20] Borgmann tells how to go about preparing for this task of yes and no. But we are left without the normative measures required to carry out such a project.

Whitehead's Understanding of Technology

No such apocalyptic tone infects Whitehead's reflections on technology. There is caution, as when he inveighs against the desecration of the Thames in *Science and the Modern World*.[21] But there is also appreciation for its ability to break the iron shackles of past physical boundaries and assist the human soul in its journey toward freedom and dignity.[22] These presystematic and postsystematic observations are grounded in the systematic speculative metaphysics formulated in *Process and Reality*. In examining the place reserved for technology in that work, we find the roots of his generosity toward technology's place in everyday life. Where Heidegger senses doom along with the glimpse of salvation, there Whitehead secures a specific ontological place where lures for culture's advance or decay invite our engagement. What is more, he provides select normative measures whereby the values awaiting our actions can be judged.

Process and Reality sees the actual world as an ever-novel mixture of actuality and possibility. As the Categories of Existence indicate, there are two extremes on this continuum of process: fully actual beings termed "actual occasions," and potentials for specific determinations termed "eternal objects." Between these limits there exist a number of beings whose specific mode of being is determined by the relative mixture of actuality and possibility that they express.

Now, I argue that technology as a cultural phenomenon and artifact exists as a specification of Category Six: "Propositions or Matters of Fact in Potential Determination or Impure potentials for the Specific Determination of Matters of Fact or Theories."[23] I have already elaborated the place of propositions within the category of transmission in this environmental cosmology. But it is well now to develop this category somewhat further.

I argue further that human beings authentically experience technology in the present moment when it takes on the character of a proposition. As lived, concrete experience, technology provides a halfway house between the possible and the actual. As culturally funded and embedded, technology has the being of a contrast. It brings together diverse modes of being so that new depths of reality are exposed, experienced, and expressed. In between technology felt as a propositional lure for feeling and technology as a culturally funded and institutionalized contrast, lie the problems so often associated with modern life.

To begin, let us once more note that a contrast is not a comparison but rather a mode of expressing the specific being of an entity. And that specification is always of the same form: *It puts difference into a unity that respects the identity of that difference.* A contrast is a way of being that brings together what is usually understood as separate and apart.

It is the special existential structure of a proposition that gives it the tensile strength to hold together that which normally slides apart.[24] A proposition has three components: a predicative pattern, a set of logical subjects for that pattern, and an existential subject that entertains the fruitfulness of the propositional feeling arising from the contrast holding between the pattern and the logical subjects. As was seen earlier in the discussion of cultural participation, it is largely through the felt experience of propositions that novelty gains effective cultural entrance to the mesocosm inhabited by human beings.

The first element of a propositional event is a predicative pattern suggestive of a certain form or mode of being that could be realized in the actual world. This pattern is that part of the unity of the proposition that can be felt as germane to a specific existential situation. In nonsystematic language, the predicative pattern uproots a bounded situation by intimating an alternative meaning. It carries the sense of "maybe," "could," or "might be." It intimates the presence of a difference lurking at the edge of a seemingly settled existential domain.

The second element of a propositional structure is the set of "logical subjects" potentially destined for unification with the predicative pattern. These logical subjects have lost much of their own objective presence and by being so loosened, become a type of indicative system pointing toward a potential realization in the actually determinate world they inhabit. Under the pressure of propositional feeling, their mode of being shifts from the facticity of the world to the status of "bare its," deeply suggestive of new modes of realization in the actual world. Icarus and Daedalus felt the propositional lure of flight and so did the Wright brothers; each with different results.

The reference to the actual world brings the discussion to the final component of the structure of propositions. Propositions are meant to be *entertained by an existentially active subject.* In the case of technology, this usually means the members of a particular culture whose boundaries are being challenged by the proposition in question. Galileo was prepared to entertain a new theory of the heavens; his worldly judges were not. The importance of entertainment as the mode in which propositions properly function cannot be overestimated. It is not the truth or falsehood of the proposition that is crucial but rather the dynamic drive toward alternatives that it asserts. Propositions call forth responses from the actual world and these responses existentially determine the world's fate.

In concluding this discussion of Whitehead's theory of propositions, it is important to recognize just how firmly Whitehead grounds his thought in the Western metaphysical tradition. Rather than jettison this body of knowledge, he goes to the heart of that tradition by making the ontological status of propositions a response to the ancient problem of the One and the Many. A proposition is a felt reaction to an existential situation wherein no place for an authentic response is permitted. The place of resolution is closed off in two possible ways. Either the One is too rigid to tolerate difference, or the Many have overrun the situation such that no satisfactory response appears possible. For the One, we can substitute the reigning cultural orthodoxies; for the Many, substitute all those who would challenge such unities. A new contrast between physical actuality and conceptual possibility is offered. What is foremost is that this new alternative be *culturally entertained.* Judgments concerning usefulness and goodness are a later matter.

As Heidegger might express it, propositions announce the hermeneutic command that the cultural world must be interpreted. But unlike Heidegger, Whitehead offers significant normative standards whereby the importance of civilizations can be measured. These standards comprise the elements of his philosophy of civilization. In *Adventures of Ideas,* Whitehead marks out five normative measures whereby the significance of great civilizations can be measured. This study has used them extensively in previous discussions. They are *Truth, Beauty, Adventure, Art, and Peace.*[25] Truth is the carryover of value from the past and the future into present experience.[26] Beauty is the special way in which harmonies of increasing intensity are achieved in the actual world. We have already seen the service which the truth of discovery renders beauty. Adventure is the drive toward novel modes of experience. Art is the primary way in which the creative advance of the One and the Many are granted the push of contrastive unity that elevates them to the level of civilized modes of cultural participation. Peace is the sense of accomplished involvement in the whole that humans experience when they accept the reality of their finitude.

Each of these normative measures is to be used to assess both the being of technology as a propositional lure for feeling and as institutionalized cultural form. The measure of the truth of technology is how much value it brings into our lived experience. The measure of beauty is the degree to which technology harmonizes previously fragmented experiences. Adventure is had when technology opens up new domains of experience that drive toward increased beauty and truth. Art is technology in its instrumentalized guise as inexhaustible lure for feeling and actualized modes of syntheses.[27] Peace is experienced when we refuse the Faustian bargain and accept our place in the scheme of things. Thus understood, technology is neither boon nor bane. It is an opportunity to engage process on a new level.

Whitehead's construction of an open space for the possibilities of technology stands in stark contrast to the demonization of technology by Heidegger and Borgmann. Whitehead can clear such a place because he reaffirms the tradition of Platonic naturalism that asserts that the authentic name of being is the Good.

On the opposite side, it is precisely Heidegger's failure and refusal to name being that leads to the elimination of technology as the birthplace for the good. From the opening pages of *Being and Time* to his last utterances, Heidegger (and *a fortiori,* his followers) condemned Western philosophy's attempts to name being as an exercise in forgetfulness. In fact he keeps his harshest criticism for those philosophers who would form their thought around the terms, *Value and Goodness.* It is in the Sixth Appendix to the essay "The Age of the World as Picture" that he explicitly yokes together system building, the modern age, and its urge to flatten everything into objectivity. Axiological thinking prepares the ground for the contemporary appearance of technology as the self-assertive will to power that is the ultimate nihilisitic destiny of the West.[28]

In terms of their attitudes toward technology, Whitehead and Heidegger face in opposite directions. For Heidegger, it is the past that keeps the secret, and it is through an "originary thinking" capable of clearing a new and forgotten ground for being that technology will bring forth its saving grace. This hoped-for salvation has nothing to do with technology, for "technology's essence is nothing technological."[29] Whitehead faces the future convinced of the possible danger and goodness of technology. It is neither good nor bad in itself but is to be entertained as a lure for feeling. When judgment comes later, the success or failure of technology must be measured not simply in terms of truth but also by reason of beauty, art, adventure, and peace.

When a philosophy like hermeneutic phenomenology confines its understanding of truth and interpretation to the act of sheer disclosure, it exposes itself to all the dangers of a romanticized "Event History" culminating in the *Geschick* of peoples, nations, and races. In such supercharged atmospheres, it is the everyday goodness of the lived world that suffers neglect. Because of this tendency toward the grandiose, the question of the everyday ethical import of technology tends also to be forgotten. It is a worthy postmodern irony that the central questions of our culture get pushed aside, even as we are urged to remember some distant originary event whose very existence is questionable in the extreme.[30]

The root of the difference between speculative philosophy and hermeneutic phenomenology resides in their respective understandings of the role of philosophy. For Whitehead, categories are not *prima facie* evidence of a disguised will to power that would cheat us of full experience. They are, among other things, the central way in which we engage experience. They are abstract but their destiny is to lead us into the concrete. Indeed, they can disfigure experience, but it is the business of philosophy to judge them harshly when they do so. It is not categories per se that are the enemy. It is, rather, inadequate categories that do not apply adequately to experience that are the problem. In this sense, Borgmann may be correct in assessing the baleful impact of the device paradigm. But the solution does not lie in jogging, communal meals, or wilderness trips. The "Saving Power" comes from hard thinking that renews the categoreal scheme underlying a culture's activities and concerns.

It is, of course, the reconstruction of our culture's categoreal scheme that Whitehead took as the central task of modern thinking. By making technology a way of mixing the actual and the potential, Whitehead gives us a civilized way to suspend judgment long enough to engage technology's potential contribution in a normatively axiological way. It is also Whitehead's achievement to have systematically elaborated such a scheme of normative measures. We are not left in doubt as to the relations between truth and beauty, art and adventure, and the peace characteristic of great civilizations. In terms of everyday goodness, technology for Whitehead is already here. There is no advantage to be gained by regarding it as some form of Mephistophelean virus. Nor does salvation lie in viewing technology as a powerful narcotic whose addictive force has seized our essential being.

I would argue that technology is an interpretation of the world. But its semiotic power resides in the special way it suspends the mixed world of the actual and the potential. It does not prevent engagement, but rather, in its propositional form, it lures us forward into an incredibly rich interpretive matrix of relations, a matrix that is as much concerned with the future as it is with the past—one that can bring forth the novelty sadly lacking in our impoverished consciousness.

To the extent that Borgmann and Heidegger envision our everyday being as disengaged through the device paradigm, they are correct in indicting the bad use of technology in everyday life. But focal practices, deictic discourse, and the challenge of nature do not alter the ontological place they reserve for technology: Nihilism's last historical gesture is technology. By not abandoning metaphysical speculation, Whitehead secures an ontological place for technology that exactly accords with its place in everyday life. In a process world, technology has a double status. As a proposition, it functions in the present moment as a lure for alternative modes of realizing value in the temporal world. As an institutional cultural phenomenon, it functions as a mode of contrastive being luring us into the stream of inexhaustible novelty that is the very meaning of being itself. It is our ethical duty to assess the goodness of these ways of being both in terms of their connections with the past and their importance for the future.[31]

In this Whiteheadian sense, everyday life is already suffused with implicit references to truth, beauty, art, adventure, and peace. It is the task of philosophy to make explicit these connections through a systematic interpretive scheme that unites the multiform dimensions of experience without sacrificing their essential differences. To the extent that technology provides us with the opportunity to do this in everyday life, it is one more semiotic process available for the enrichment of human existence.

It is speculative philosophy, not originary thinking, that provides an interpretive network wide enough to do justice to the continuum of human experience. The tools offered by hermeneutic phenomenology are too wedded to an intuitive grasp of the truth of being as sheer disclosure to do much good when it comes to appreciating and correcting everyday technological being. In addition, there lurks the temptation to romanticize a secret hidden past and thereby promote a false vision of authentic existence as somehow sharply different from our everyday lives.

Whitehead agrees with Plato's understanding of philosophy as the aim to rule well. Among other things, ruling well in our time has come to mean interpreting well. It is in the sense of respecting the past and guarding the future well that Whitehead's normative philosophy excels. He has fashioned better tools with which to experience the truth, beauty, unity, and goodness of the present moment. Everyday life and technology form a bond that invites the deepest engagement for the sake of being and being human.

Phusis, Techne, and the New

In "The Letter on Humanism," Heidegger declares that "language is the house of being." This dictum has formed the basis of a major shift in certain modes of contemporary philosophy. More precisely, as we have seen, it is the ground of the postmodern substitution of "the Text" for experience. For Heidegger, the understanding of being is layered into the language that humans use to describe their experiences. Thus, language understood as *Logos* is the royal road to the authentic understanding of being. This is the ground of Derrida's "grammatological" methodology as well as Rorty's insistence upon the importance of "final vocabularies" for the interpretation of contemporary culture. Indeed, Heidegger's saying has brought about a whole new style of cultural reflection. It is no longer experience in all its richness that is at the center of philosophical effort. Now it is the text—be it a poem, a novel, or even a word—that is the new *a priori.* Everything worthy of philosophical examination passes through the lens of language. It is the text (and even sometimes the subtext) that is the philosopher's stone. For better or worse, postmodern philosophy now restricts its efforts to textual analysis and criticism. The loss in potential richness of experience is obvious. We are reduced to secondhand versions of reality and depending on the quality of the text selected, often to second-rate experience as well.

Whatever the final judgment on the appropriateness of this new style of philosophy, it can be done well or poorly. One of Heidegger's more compelling textual examinations is his treatment of the Greek term for nature, *phusis.* Heidegger's understanding of *phusis* is contained in his *Introduction to Metaphysics* where he identifies the Greek experience of nature as connecting with "a self-blossoming, emerging power."[32] He thus aligns himself with the tradition that sees creativity as the basic category for understanding nature.

It is therefore even more remarkable to find no comparable concern for the Greek term *techne* in Heidegger's thought. True enough, *"technik"* and technology receive full treatment. There is, however, no similar attempt to retrieve an understanding of the Greek experience of *techne.* This is all the more regrettable for, as will be seen, there is an authentically direct connection between nature and technology, *phusis and techne.*

Techne is derived from the Greek word, *tikto,* which means give birth by being a mother.[33] For example, in the Greek Orthodox Church, the Virgin Mary is often called *Theotikos*, the mother of God. Now, given the frequent condemnation of technology's supposedly "male" aggression toward "mother" nature, this is a surprising finding. What is now regarded as the very symbol of patriarchy,

Western technology, had an original matriarchal association.

The sense of this maternal *techne* must be carefully respected; otherwise, it will turn into one more "ossified signifier" that prevents thought rather than encouraging it. Recall that Chapter Five argued that the ultimate character of space was seen to be that of a *Chora* or Receptacle. This "foster mother of all becoming" gave room for that which was other than itself to come to be. It allowed this difference to assert itself to the full limits of its power. As the nurse that nourished, the receptacle was precisely that which let be that which it was not. In carrying out this duty, *techne* in its original sense had for the Greeks the primary meaning of letting the different emerge from *phusis*.

I therefore argue that in the beginning of Western metaphysics *phusis* was understood to be *techne*.[34] As an original experience, the technological harbored in itself the power to let the different be, to let the other grow and declare its otherness. As bearer of otherness, *techne* fulfills very precisely the qualities usually attached to the maternal signifier. Like space, it lets that which is different come to be within its precincts. It neither crushes originality nor betrays a false love of the *outré*. It simply (dare I say it?) "naturally" lets difference be different.

Now, the cultural significance of this retrieve of the original Greek experience of technology can scarcely be exaggerated. For it brings Western metaphysics (*pace* Heidegger *et. al.*) face to face with the central modern problem of being. I term this "the problem of the new." It must be recalled that even according to Heidegger, being historically appears in "mittences" or epochs. Now, it is my argument that the problem of being in the contemporary age is not *á la* Heidegger a problem of forgetting the meaning of being. I argue that in our time the problem of being is the problem of the new.

By this I mean the simple cultural fact that our century has experienced a more direct revelation of fundamental novelty than any other time in history. Further, I argue that this emergence of novelty affects our understanding of the most common, the most ordinary, and the most fundamental dimensions of our experience. I am referring to the fact that our understanding of space and time has been totally reconstructed during this century. Further, I argue that our understanding of matter and its relation to energy has been equally revolutionized. Finally, I argue that this radical reconstruction of these most fundamental concepts in our world experience is what makes this "the metaphysical century" *par excellence.*

When the fundamentals of our world are torn loose, then it is time to do metaphysics once again. I have also argued that now is precisely not the time for a failure of nerve. This is the challenge that Whitehead accepted at the beginning of the century. It remains the challenge at its end. Cosmology is not some arcane "new age" discipline. Rather, it is the way in which civilization reconstructs and rearranges its metaphysical categories so as to continue to fulfill its responsibility to measure appropriately the value of nature and our place in it.

Consider the following sources of the new that have become commonplaces in our time:

- In the Macrocosmos: Relativity Theory
- In the Microcosmos: Quantum Physics
- In the Biocosmos: DNA and the Genetic Code

For each of these revolutions in our understanding Whitehead has attempted to provide a response that enables us to recover a measure whereby we can appreciate the values of the natural world. Unlike Heidegger and his postmodern followers, Whitehead does not counsel silence in the face of the new. Rather, as the foregoing chapters on natural space and natural time demonstrate, he offered new categories with which to understand both the facts and the values inherent in the new spacetime schemes made possible through the revolution carried out by the new relativity theories. Similarly, at the microcosmic level, Whitehead's theory of actual occasions and their epochal coming-to-be and perishing is a cosmological response to the new quantum physics and the implications of the quantum jump for our understanding of the relation between matter, spacetime, and energy. Finally, Whitehead's definition of life as the impulse toward originality moving the creative process forward in incremental stages is the equivalent, cosmologically speaking, of the information processing powers now found to reside in the genetic code.

What unifies Whitehead's response to what James Bradley has called the "paradoxes of the new" is his insistence on the absolute importance of the "event" as the fundamental category of the process that is the reality of nature. Furthermore, as I have consistently argued, Whitehead's model of the event as a process structured through normative aesthetic measures is a deliberate effort to return to nature a proper sense of its own value. Just how powerful this idea of the aesthetic event is for an appropriate understanding of the relation between history, nature and technology is the concern of the last section of this chapter.

From Conflict to Contrast

In Chapter Two, I proposed that there were three levels of participation—the physical, the living, and the cultural—and that each level was determined by the structural normative measure selected to house the determinate forms of value specific to each environmental region. In terms of the category of contrast, different levels of participation are achieved through different modes of engagement with reality. Thus, contrast is limited at the physical level since it is repetition, conformity, and spatiotemporal thickness that is most prominent in such environments.

Contrast widens at the level of the living environment, since the physical undergoes a kind of reversal whereby the actual is strongly wed to the possible. Dynamic patterns of the actual and the possible emerge as life in its "quickness" moves toward the immediate, the novel, and the vivid. Thus, the contrast that life presents is a unity coexisting between what is and what could be. As Chapter Two argued, this results in a quality of instability affecting all forms of life. The watchfulness qualifying living beings is a direct sign of this natural sense of precariousness. Change is afoot and alertness is a survival tool.

But humans can do much more than live on the edge of surprise. They also can build cultures. The type of contrast characteristic of the civilized environment lays special emphasis on the future. Through forms of active cultural imagination issuing into semiotic richness, the future loses its emptiness and becomes crowded with lures for feeling. The possible and the actual stand forth in sustained patterns of expression. The resultant propositions become the warp and woof of a culture's sense of the important. Through its aesthetic, religious, scientific, and technological interests, a particular culture shores up life's instability. Furthermore, through a variety of physical, living, and cultural embodiments, forms of civilized process rise up and dominate the environment. Finally, a culture, in our time in the form of the modern city, emerges as the very expression of the new.

What has happened in this process is ***an enlargement of opportunity achieved through the power of limits provided by appropriate forms of contrast.*** I stress this definition because of its importance for the argument of this essay in cosmological speculation. Enlargement, opportunity, power, limits, and contrast are its essential elements. In a process universe every determinate event is a process of selection. The infinitude of possibility is compressed within the confines of a finite event. Something is admitted; something is left out. Within the parameters of selection lie the range of values selected. It is precisely the limits imposed by the measures chosen that either widen or lessen the values that eventually express themselves throughout the environment.

This is the ground of the doctrine of harmony that underlies my environmental cosmology. Physical experience is primarily a matter of settling for the least conflicted harmony. This is what is meant by the phrase "massive averageness." The physical world screens out difference for the sake of conformity. Aesthetic experience, on the other hand, is grounded on increasing levels of contrast that do not eliminate difference but enhance it through increasingly rich harmonic unities. In *Religion in the Making*, Whitehead states: "All aesthetic experience is feeling arising out of the realization of contrast under identity."[35] Therefore, to the degree that an event can incorporate difference into its process of becoming, to that same degree it expresses an aesthetic value throughout an environment. Also, the intensity of value achieved is a function of the degree of contrast achieved. Finally, contrast always carries out the same task: It converts conflict into contrast.

The process whereby opposition is transformed into harmony is the outcome of assigning appropriate limits to different dimensions of experience. This is the great secret of beauty in its major form. Through the truth of discovery it makes room for the genuinely new. It does so because it sets novel limits that wrestle new value from the womb of nature. This means that ***limit is power***. No self-respecting postmodernist could agree to such a proposition. It goes against the spirit of the age. Some sort of Nietzschean aesthetic spontaneity or Derridean excess would be more in tune with the present mood. But consider the following three examples of the power of limits. First, in terms of nature it is precisely the limits established by its patterns and proportions that is the ground of its successful functionings.[36] Similarly, appropriate human building depends absolutely on the limit provided by selective architectural forms.[37] Finally, it is precisely the limits established by its forms that gives the Zen garden such a sense of freedom.[38]

Limit is power because it makes real in space and time what once existed only in possibility. Here, "realization" has the sense of "authoring" and "making real" developed by Hall and Ames in *Thinking Through Confucius*.[39] A limit is a boundary separating what is from what is not. It is therefore on the edge between conflict and contrast. A weak limit shuts down process and invites conflict. A strong limit opens up alternatives and yields a further sense of the possible. It is this unfathomable sense of depth that signals the presence of great art. Aesthetics becomes the vehicle whereby limits can be expanded and conflicts transmuted into contrasts.

Thus, the relation between history and nature is continuous, for there is no radical break between the technological, the natural, and the human. What history discloses is a series of conflicts and contrasts. To the extent that such conflicts prevent the enlargement of experience, then history and nature are in a mutual decline. When contrast transmutes conflict, then nature and history disclose the greater depths that lurk beneath the surface of the continuum spanning the natural and the human.

As previously argued, this is the reason why C. S. Peirce insisted on the ontological relation between the logical, the ethical, and the aesthetic. Here we have a suggestion as to the next step to be taken by the tradition of Platonic naturalism that threads its aesthetic ways through the history of American philosophy. To deal with "real novelty" requires the active presence of both metaphysics and aesthetics. Metaphysics supplies the limits needed to keep civilization appropriately in tune with creativity and aesthetics offers the feeling of enlargement needed to make room for the new. The next step in advancing the tradition of Platonic naturalism in American philosophy involves the creation and development of the discipline of foundational ecology as the praxis of the new in the contemporary age.

Chapter Twelve

Foundational Ecology

A double danger lurks in the aesthetic emphases of this study. We can mistake beauty for truth. We can also fail to see the real relation between beauty, truth, and effective action. What I term foundational ecology is an attempt to avoid both dangers and at the same time put to work the insights gained through the application of this systematic cosmology. This chapter deals with the following themes: aesthetic sensibility, strength of mind, a respectful will, and ecological practice. Each theme builds upon its predecessor so that this study culminates in an emerging picture of what needs to be done to reconcile the natural and the human.

Aesthetic Sensibility

Throughout this study an important distinction has been drawn between the rational and the aesthetic orders. It is a distinction first made by Whitehead and then carefully developed and elaborated as a major tool of comparative philosophy in the work of David Hall and Roger Ames. Specifically, the aesthetic order is one that privileges the particular over the general, the unique over the universal.

It reverses the usual order of Western logic by assigning priority to that which must be felt in its own right rather than being subsumed under some larger category. Thus, the categories of this speculative philosophy—inscape, contrast, pattern, and transmission—are designed to highlight the ways in which natural environments compose themselves in order to express the drive toward creative particularity that is at the heart of nature. Now, in dealing with the presence of this aesthetic order in Chinese thinking, Hall and Ames use the term "correlative thinking." I mean something very similar by the term "aesthetic sensibility," by which I designate a kind of environmental thinking that stresses recognizing the presence of insistent particularity in ecological activities. Other terms have also been employed throughout the course of this study. For example, I have referred to the doctrine of *haeccitas* to be found in the philosophy of Duns Scotus and the fresh creativity of the spontaneous *Tao*. In each of these instances I am reaching out for the means to express the absolute uniqueness of every environmental event.

In the discussion of symbolic reference as the primary way in which environmental ideals are naturalized, the argument was made that ideals are felt by the body. This is the most important reason why I use the term aesthetic. Aesthetic here means the actual feelings felt by the human body as it enacts its modes of environmental perception. Aesthetic sensibility therefore names the best way to participate in the world of feelings described in Part One as the structural ground of a process universe. To be sensible in an aesthetic way is to be attuned to the ideal environmental values actualized in specific environmental regions.

Therefore, the first and indispensable step in initiating the discipline of foundational ecology is the need to deepen human sensitivity to the aesthetic value residing at the base of nature. This can be done in several ways. One important way is to insist on the concreteness of the signifiers to be employed in the cosmological system. This is what lies behind Whitehead's insistence on the need to employ imaginative language in constructing a cosmological scheme. This is the reason why the frequent reference to poetry in this study is no mere ornament. Rather, I am seeking to evoke the "feel" of the themes about to be philosophically examined. Another potential contribution to developing aesthetic sensibility lies in training the human person to appreciate the compositional excellence of nature. As I have argued, it is precisely the way in which events "fit together" that constitutes their goodness. Value, essential and conditional features, and simplicity and complexity are joint partners in the axiological structures that make up all natural processes. It is the aesthetic consequences of these modes of interaction that constitute both their internal and their instrumental values.

Any valid recommendations to improve aesthetic sensibility must in the first place respect the relation between aesthetic feeling and intelligence. One's feelings are not simply given through naive reaction to the environment. Locke's *tabula rasa* is a fiction. One can be more or less skilled in noticing the aesthetic fit characterizing natural environments. Furthermore, our modes of awareness are filtered through the lens of cultural participation. It is a scientific commonplace that our cultural experience shapes our modes of perception. In a culture overly attuned to rational generalizations, it is precisely the differences and particularities in nature that are most likely to be missed or ignored.

Given the stress laid on creative uniqueness by this process cosmology, it is imperative to find new ways and means to identify the different. And when it is recalled that an increasing gradient of individuality is the mark of the emergence of the most important natural values, the need to refine our aesthetic sensibility grows even more critical. In addition, the capacity to achieve a certain level of tensile strength is what admits events into the stream of the actual. Finally, as Chapter Eight argued, life itself arrives only in forms that express temporal acts of genuine individuality. It is within all these manifestations of individual particularity that the values of nature show themselves. Without the ability to identify such uniqueness, we are blind to the very values we should be most ready to identify and defend.

In addition, the type of beauty experienced at the level of cultural participation involves the functional presence of high consciousness. While this may mean more intense forms of beauty, it also necessarily means the real possibility of more intense forms of ugliness. Risk, success, and failure are entwined within and about all cultural events. Immense pleasure entails immense pain.[1]

Aesthetic sensibility, therefore, does not merely mean the ability to appreciate significant form or harmonious proportions. It also means the power to identify the beautiful and the ugly and to be responsible for such judgments. This new responsibility is made even more difficult by reason of the fact that it is the unique, the different, and the particular that is the heart and soul of the major form of beauty.[2] As Kant argued in *The Critique of Judgment,* the beautiful and the sublime are connected by the power to claim our undivided attention.[3] This compelling character of the aesthetic is the result of the looming presence of that which exists in its own right and therefore in its own otherness. It is otherness in its purity that beckons aesthetic sensibility.

Now it is no small feat to be able to stand in the presence of otherness. By definition there is nothing in our own being that naturally prepares us for it. This is why the next step in creating the discipline of foundational ecology involves what I term developing strength of mind.

Strength of Mind

I borrow this phrase from Spinoza's *Ethics,*[4] where it translates the Latin word *fortitudo.* For Spinoza, strength of mind is the primary virtue needed to conduct one's life in intimate connection with a good that ever nourishes itself. Without strength of mind a happy life is inconceivable. What is this *fortitudo* upon which so much depends? Here is Spinoza's description of the *"Liber,"* the person who has realized true freedom in a concrete way in the conduct of his or her daily life: "The free person hates no one, is angry with, envious of, indignant with no one, despises no one, and is minimally proud."[5]

Spinoza tells us that the strength of mind required to live in this way results from the appropriate combination of two other emotions: "high spiritedness" and "generosity." Now, I maintain that high spiritedness names what I have been calling in this study "normative thinking." I also maintain that generosity names what in this study has been called "respect."

High spiritedness connects with normative thinking through the fact of the absolute importance of ideals in determining the true nature of reality. Thus, the nobility of life's aims is directly related to the search for appropriate normative measures with which to gauge such modes of nobility. The doctrine of normative measure is central to the construction of the cosmological scheme in the first part of this study. Briefly, I argued that every event that comes to be, does so in accordance with a normative measure that marks the degree of reality attained by the event in question. This doctrine brings excellence and reality together in an existential synthesis such that "how a thing comes to be constitutes what that being is."[6] The good and the actual are in tandem. Degrees of excellence measure degrees of reality: The high spiritedness that marks nobility of character is only possible when humans are willing to assume responsibility for the norms they use to measure the presence of the good in the world. And, of course, they are also responsible for marking out the presence and degrees of evil as well.

The need for strength of mind becomes even more apparent through a review of the category of contrast. Recall that contrast is both a central category in the cosmological scheme as well as the critical agency in the creation of the major form of beauty. In both instances what is required is the power to hold together in a unity that which has a tendency to fly apart. High spiritedness is required to encourage such a search for wider and more expansive ideals that can transmute conflict into contrast. The sheer energy needed to refuse the less taxing act of exclusion is a sign of the presence of an enthusiasm for life and its goodness.

In a similar way, generosity is indispensable for attaining an appropriate level of strength of mind. First, there is the need to be willing to go the extra mile in order to attain the excellence signified by the effective presence of instantiated ideals. Then there is the fact that only a form of intellectual generosity can win through the ordeal of sifting and sorting measures so as to bring about what is best for each situation. Finally, generosity is precisely the feeling required to find room for the strange otherness that the major form of beauty always summons up through the truth of discovery. The unique, the particular, the fresh inscape of every natural event is precisely what calls for generosity. How else can its own special *haeccitas* be acknowledged, respected, and protected? In this cosmology generosity means enlargement of experience.

To be generous also means to have something good to give. What is the goodness found in generosity? I believe that generosity encourages the establishment of relations rather than solitary existence. To be generous is to acknowledge the existence of others and their needs. The primary need of any event is its right to exist. When generosity is an effective environmental presence, then the forging of relations in and through others becomes an essential mode of being. Relationships replace the effort to be independent of all others. A substance universe with its definition of primary being as "that which needs nothing but itself in order to exist" makes generosity a second-rate emotion. The radical independence inherent in each substance works against the habit of generosity characteristic of the free person in a norm-driven culture.

By making relationships primary, generosity lays open a field of being closed to the narcissistic preoccupation with self so characteristic of postmodern thought. Generosity refuses to see the world as a mirror of one's self-interest. It reverses such narrow cultural habits and insists on the real presence of the other in environmental affairs. Generosity makes impossible what Santayana called "the solipsism of the solitary ego." The fact that such a state of affairs remains a real cultural possibility is evident in the all too numerous philosophical essays that deal with "the problem of the other." In a culture marked by a rich process of cultural participation, the other is not "a problem." Rather, the other is a necessity for one's own growth and well-being.

Generosity is the royal road to intense internal relations. Its tendency to be open to the reality of others also harbors a potential danger, for it can be overwhelmed by the needs of others and thereby neglect its own proper concerns. This is why generosity requires balance through high spriritedness or normative thinking. Normative thinking is an exercise in proportionality, for it always seeks just the right balance beween conflicting demands and needs. A correct normative measure hits the mark between extremes. It supplies exactly the right limit that grants power to a situation. Therefore: The appropriate combination of high spiritedness and generosity demands knowledge of conflict and contrast, limit and power, measure and goodness. Good and evil are dimensions of the aesthetic realm normatively understood.

All this brings us back to strength of mind. A mind has to have an extraordinary strength to seek balance in place of excess. In a culture driven by consumption and materialistic desires, excess is a manifestion of success. Moderation—*Sophrosune,* what the Greeks insisted was the key to the form of the good—is often considered a form of weakness. This is what gives the term "harmony" such a hollow ring. We tend to see it as a weakness, as though the willingness to compromise indicates a lack of backbone. Harmony is often taken to mean some "warm and fuzzy" mode of shallow coexistence. Nothing could be further from the truth. It is a sign of towering strength to find room for the other in one's own corner of the universe. The only way to achieve such forms of harmony is to be well schooled in various normative measures that transmute conflict into contrast. A measure is a limit. It includes and excludes depending on where the line is drawn. When a limit is set, a value appears. Harmony is the sign of strength of mind at work.

The effective presence of harmony is also a sign of wisdom for wisdom means knowing where to draw the line. The compositional art (of which natural processes are a prime example) is all about drawing the appropriate lines. Wise lines create balance. Proportion and balance are the gifts of wisdom. Above all else the emerging discipline of foundational ecology requires the acquisition of wisdom. As I argued in the preface to this work, civilizations are measured by their understanding of what is important. This sense of importance arises from the perspectives they adopt, which in turn issue into specific modes of expression. The values that emerge are a witness to the level of wisdom achieved by a civilization's understanding of the form of the good.

I argued in previous chapters for the important relation between the major form of beauty and spiritual strength. I also discussed the relation between forms of spiritual strength and what I called the sacred depths of life. Here, strength of mind unites with spiritual strength to point the way toward the indispensable contribution the mind makes to spiritual growth and development. Strength of mind is the sign of spiritual strength. In an earlier discussion of life it was pointed out that only a conscious being can experience what was called the "sacred depths of life." Because the body provides an extraordinary volume of novelty, the human person has the power to reach through contrastive levels of experience and thereby come into the real presence of affirmed negation. This state of consciousness drives the person toward the axes of the environmental ideals of depth, wholeness, intensity, and integrity. It is this moment of exceptional feeling that is often understood as "holiness."[7] I have also called it spiritual strength. The exact term is not important but its relation to Spinoza's *fortitudo* can be plainly stated. Holiness and beauty, and consciousness and truth are dimensions of experience that show human beings just how deep is their connection with nature. Without the strength of mind that results from normative thinking and respect, these levels of experience can be neither reached in a living way nor sustained in a culture. Foundational ecology is as much a matter of spiritual growth as it is of wise use of natural resources.

In conclusion, the major form of beauty was seen to be the ultimate act whereby "the many become one" through the experience of enlargement. This expansion of the natural to include the different is the sign of generosity. When it comes to dealing with the world of natural processes, it is the finest human gesture. When real difference emerges because of the room provided by conscious human action, then the good, the fair, and the fitting are brought to clear expression. This act of supreme goodness depends upon the cultivation of a respectful will.

A Respectful Will

The last element of Plato's classic conception of the tripartite soul is the will. Aesthetic sensibility concerned the proper training of feelings. Strength of mind dealt with the acquisition of normative thinking as a habit of mind. A proper training of the will concludes this reconstruction on a natural level of Plato's concept of the tripartite soul. More than anything else, our culture needs to ground its will in respect. Now, respect only comes about when values are recognized.[8] Fear can bring about restraint, but that is no closer to respect than ice cream is to turkey. A culture whose ecological foundations are bound up with fear is destined to turn destructive. Repression only leads to the return of the repressed in more virulent and violent forms.

This study has challenged the reigning assumptions of contemporary scientific materialism. It has not done so out of an ignorance of science's extraordinary achievements. Neither is this study an appeal for a return to Luddite sensibilities. An open and welcome place for technology is part of this cosmology's systematic reinterpretation of culture. My major objection to scientific materialism has always been its refusal to grant a place for values in nature. It should now be obvious just why my challenge to scientific materialism has been mounted with such vigor. Respect comes from recognizing value. A system of thought that forbids even the mention of value is bound to foster disrespect. There is no possibility of restoring respect for nature without at the same time reconstructing the theoretical underpinnings of scientific materialism.

In taking up the challenge of providing an axiological cosmology for environmental philosophy, I have offered three major reformulations of the paradigms that make up the intellectual framework of contemporary scientific materialism. From the beginning, I have insisted on the fallacy of representing nature as a mechanical device that is devoid of "life and motion." My effort to redescribe nature as "a world of feelings" was meant to respond to Plato's demand in the *Sophist* that we become more childlike. Second, in describing the various orders of nature I have deliberately adopted an aesthetic vocabulary. In systematically employing Whitehead's brilliant suggestion that order is more a matter of aesthetics than of rational configuration, I have attempted to recognize value as the very heart of natural processes. I developed a systematic redescription of natural space and time in order to demonstrate how one could speak concretely about the values achieved by these seeming abstractions. The third revision in the system of scientific materialism concerned the recognition of normative measures as a vital part of the working of natural processes. This restoration of normative thinking is a response to Plato's second demand in the *Sophist:* That we find room for the ideal in our understanding of the world of becoming.

Now, it may seem disingenuous to call so complicated a program of theoretical reconstruction an effort to become more "childlike." But I believe that it is precisely the wisdom of the child that is needed to restore balance to our environmental behavior. What do feelings, aesthetic grounds of order, and normative thinking have to do with being childlike? The answer lies in the childlike word, "Both." It refuses the gambit of either/or and demands the real presence of an "And." Therefore, the speculative categories developed in this cosmology demand a childlike desire to seek contrast instead of conflict. It is wisdom to seek harmony rather than exclusion, unity instead of separation, and beauty instead of the ugliness of exclusion. The wisdom of the child consists precisely in its sense of wonder and astonishment at the plenitude of the world of being. To condemn the child for wanting to have it all completely misses the point. The child is aware of the limits of power. In its own way it knows that a limit is a form of power. What it seeks to do is enlarge the limits of its world and thereby increase its power. In this way the child is already an artist seeking that form of contrast that will allow it to have both. This is its wisdom: That limits can be expanded by the right use of intelligence.

Now, what empowers the child to ask for both is precisely its respect for value. I do not believe that the child's desire for both is simply a matter of greed. It is the intensity of the values that lures forth the special wisdom which asks for both. Therefore, seeking to have it both ways is not always a sign of ignorance and greed. It is much rather the human desire to live in a beautiful world.

My point is easily caricatured. It is not an invitation to childish behavior. Exactly the opposite conclusion should be drawn. The child desires "both" because it intensely feels each value. Furthermore, it is precisely the ability to feel each value that causes the will to pause in its choosing. This restraint on the will can only be derived from the intensely felt value itself. The first move towards childlike wisdom is therefore growth in the ability to feel the values of the natural world. I have already called this growth "aesthetic sensibility." The second step in growing into childlike wisdom involves recognition of the aesthetic order of the natural world. Such recognition entails a recognition of the natural world's inherent relational essence. The final step in growing up into wisdom is the recognition of the connectedness of the processes of nature. This awareness leads to the equally important conclusion that knowledge of normative measure is the very ground of the strength of mind needed to create the contrasts that allow humans to have "both."

I believe Spinoza meant something very much like this when he wrote at the end of his *Ethics* of the need to relate to things, others, and nature as an adult and not as a baby.[9] Now these three things —things, others, and nature—represent a precise summary of the themes of this study.

For they are the events that make up both the human and natural environments in which we seek to achieve our measure of dignity and happiness. But neither aesthetic sensibility nor strength of mind nor a respectful will amount to much without some form of practice. Foundational ecology is as much a matter of doing as it is a matter of feeling, thinking, and willing. In conclusion, I offer some modes of praxis that can inform a foundational ecology.

Ecological Praxis

The cosmology developed in this study makes action dependent upon modes of participation. In turn, the appropriateness of these modes of participation rests upon the selection of the right normative measures. The three levels of participation singled out in this cosmology are the physical, the living, and the cultural. Each has distinctive normative measures that determine what is fair and fitting at each level of action. Good ecological praxis depends upon measuring up to these ideals.

Physical participation is marked by the presence of repetitive conformity that results in the storage of massive quantities of energy. A sense of enduring averageness comes to dominate the physical landscape. This builds up layers of stability upon which all living and cultural events will come to depend. This rhythm of regularity is the distinguishing feature of the physical realm. It is the conformal character of physical participation that grounds the scientific laws found to be immanent within the natural environment. In turn, humans in the conduct of their daily lives come to depend on the steady availablity of such things as fresh air, clean water, appropriate seasonal cycles, and so forth.

The appropriate normative measure to use in judging good action at the level of physical participation is intensity. It is the transmission of energy in its many usable forms that permits all other levels of natural process to function. The physical realm transmits the base level of support all forms of life need to prosper. When its intensity fades, everything else is endangered.

The key to preserving the intensity of the physical realm lies in respecting the conformal character of its structural processes. It is these cycles of repetition and regularity that force enormously intense levels of power to build up and become available for living creatures. It would be an act of outrageous disrespect to empty out this vast reservoir of energy. The truth of nature conservation movements lies in their clear recognition of the importance of these resources. In fact, the essentially conservative character of these movements is precisely what is needed to protect the physical environment. For it is the past that dominates environments at the level of physical participation. Conformation of the present to the past is the very sign of the physical. The dominant temporal shape of physical environments is repetition of the past. And it is this dominant temporal order that guarantees the smooth transmission of energy throughout physical nature. What the physical level excels at is this recycling of the past in the present.

Foundational ecological praxis at the level of physical participation involves in the first place altering the images we use to structure our understanding of physical nature. For too long, human beings have regarded natural physical resources as inexhaustible. The great contribution made by nature conservation movements has been to help alter this sense of an independently existing source of available physical resources. These resources are only inexhaustible to the degree that we do not interfere with the regular repetition of the past into the present. Each time human beings enter the physical realm, that rhythm is threatened.

But pure conservation spells death to nature, for it thwarts the very processes of novelty that give rise to life itself. Ecological praxis must involve more than a mere attitude of preservation. An environmental philosophy encouraging only the repetition of the past would leave nature bereft of the very freshness it needs to renew itself. It is for this reason that foundational ecology must also deal with participation at the level of living nature.

The normative measure best suited to judge the goodness of participation at the level of life is integrity. To live is to bring together into a forceful and active unity greatly diverse patterns of process. To live is to exhibit a maximum level of coordination of difference. Life lives in the present through an appropriate contrast of otherness and identity. The very fact that life needs food—that which is other—is a sign of its significant power to integrate what is different in its own processes. To transform the other into one's self takes many forms, ranging from the annihilation of the other to the transformation of the other to a parasitic relation on the other to a symbiotic relation with the other.

In terms of this cosmology, the norm of integrity should encourage life to seek a balance in its acts of transformation. When life fosters more life, it is on the way toward its own liberation as an important environmental presence. But the word integrity itself also means balance and harmony. As we have seen, it is not always in the nature of life to seek balance. A sense of proportion does not come readily to life and its exuberances. Left to itself life tends to lose balance. It is therefore all the more imperative to arrive at a sense of proportion at the level of living participation.

I have already praised the practical recommendation set forth in Birch and Cobb's *Liberation of Life.* They stand as important contributions to the emerging discipline of foundational ecology. There is, however, another culture well skilled in the practice of achieving balance in life. I am referring to the Chinese understanding of living a balanced life as the greatest of human achievements.[10] Integrity, balance, and proportion are the key to the good use of physical forces, resources for living, and modes of conduct. *Tao, Yin, Yang,* and *Te* are the Chinese concepts central to the practice of good living. "Living fully balanced in the present moment" names the goal of Chinese thought and culture. *Tao* is the way by which life achieves its own self-expression. As original, as spontaneous, and as expressing itself in the present moment, *Tao* is the essential form of creativity that this cosmology envisions as the pivot of nature. *Tao* can only be explained in terms of itself. It does not owe its being to the past and therefore does not yield to explanation through modes of analytic reduction based on efficient causality. As the form of life itself, *Tao* dwells entirely in the present. Its being is its expression and its self-justification. *Tao* is the way of life itself.

If *Tao* is the way of life, then *yin* and *yang* are the ways through which *Tao* achieves the balance necessary for living fully in the present. *Yin* names the passive, female side of nature that through its receptivity tirelessly receives the creative action of the cosmos. *Yang* is the active, male side of the cosmos that endlessly expresses itself in new forms of creativity. The receptive is balanced by the creative. The female integrates the male. The active is proportionate to the passive. *Yin* and *yang* assert the ways in which that which is other joins what it is not in order to nourish and foster life. Every difference can issue into an identity if it be rightly respected. The *Tao* is the gift of a childlike trust in the power of contrast to create beauty instead of ugliness.

Finally, *te* marks the presence of the power that springs from the appropriate balance of *yin* and *yang*. In closing the circle of the Chinese concept of life, *te* is the manifestation of the effective presence of energy on the physical level and virtue on the living level. What happens through the norm of intensity can also come about through the norm of integrity. In being able to use the same word for excellent performance on the physical and the living levels of nature, the Chinese seeker after wisdom is at a distinct advantage. It is precisely the ability to mark out a continuous curve which spans different levels of environmental activity that our culture lacks. We have lost the power to unite the realms of fact and value. The Chinese have never stopped seeing the value of the natural and its relation to the human goodness.[11]

The images of life that presently dominate Western culture tend to equate the good life with the satisfaction of material desires. Obviously, if a foundational ecology is to take hold, a new image of the good life needs to be created. Once again, I have recourse to Spinoza's *Ethics*. In trying to grasp the possibilities of human life, Spinoza presents two stark options. We are either on a path toward preserving and expressing our life through self-affirmation or we are moving away from such an affective condition. The emotion that accompanies affirmation he calls joy; its opposite he calls sadness. Life is therefore its own self-enjoyment and the ground of its own self-affirmation. Put more directly, Spinoza maintains the following theses:

- Joy will always conquer sadness.
- Virtue is the result of our happiness.
- Happiness does not result from virtue.
- Life is therefore its own reward.[12]

The image suggested for appropriate physical participation was based on a sense of the massive achievements of the past. To engage life in a good way requires an image that focuses on the present. Due to its relentless pursuit of future desires, such images are largely absent from our culture. It is for this reason that images from the East seem to be far more suitable for expressing the sense of contentment with the present life. The self-contained Bodhisattva, the poised Taoist sage, and the supreme bliss of the Buddha are directly eloquent expressions of self-enjoyment and self-affirmation.

There is a fine irony in this recourse to Eastern images in order to convey a right sense of living. The West has struggled to gain all the means necessary for living and now does not know what it means to be alive. The simple act whereby the self-enjoyment of life is experienced has eluded our culture. In its place there are a hundred thousand substitutes but none of them provide a clue as to how to live in the present moment. In a cultural denouement worthy of the worst excessses of existentialism, Western instrumentalism has devoured itself. We no longer enjoy the act of life itself. Loss of the sense of the value of life brings its own vengeance. No more is life its own reward.

Living participation stresses the importance of the present moment. What Eastern modes of spirituality bring to the fore is the real possibility of transmitting modes of stillness through succeeding present moments. When carried through on a regular basis this act of temporal enlargement provides the room necessary to regain a sense of life's own enjoyments. The category of transmission includes more than the transference of physical, conceptual, and propositional feelings. Feelings of stillness can also be transmitted throughout environmental regions. And this, of course, includes that environmental region we call the human person. Meditational practices, types of spiritual yoga, some forms of the martial arts, and other ways to enlarge the present moment of living human consciousness have become more and more available to Western persons. While I in no way intend to promote the excesses of New Age pseudophilosophy and religions, I believe these practices do suggest an alternative way of experiencing life that is consonant with the ethical and aesthetic dimensions of this cosmology.

Thomas Merton, Western monk and lover of Asian spirituality, offers an extraordinary expression of the joy with which the Zapotecs of Mesoamerica experienced life itself:

> The "reality" and "identity" of archaic man was, then, centered in sensuous self-awareness and identification with a close, ever-present, and keenly sensed world of nature; for us, our "self" tends to be "realized" in a much more shadowy, abstract, mental world, or indeed in a very abstract and spiritualized world of "soul." We are disembodied minds seeking to bridge the gap between mind and body and return to ourselves through the mediation of things, commodities, products, and implements. We reinforce our sense of reality by acting on the external world to get ever-new results.[13]

Unstated in Merton's description of the joy with which one can experience life is the type of cultural participation that promotes such a different understanding of the meaning of life. The norms for measuring cultural participation are the two remaining ideal environmental values: Wholeness and Depth. The possibility of constructing a foundational ecology worthy of nature resides most especially in renewing cultural participation. Without the kind of transformation of consciousness that cultural participation can bring about, the tenets, dogmas, and doctrines of scientific materialism will continue to reign supreme and unquestioned.

The final praxis in moving toward a foundational ecology deals with reconstructing the cultural level of participation in a world beset by a form of life that denies the very values it seeks to promote. Cultural participation completes the temporal triad by stressing the role of the future in human experience. It does so by bringing to the fore the way its cultural perspectives ensure a future shaped by what it regards as the importances of the past and the present. It attempts to promote those modes of unity and potential through the normative measures of wholeness and depth. Therefore, this concluding analysis of cultural participation sums up the role of environmental ideals in altering humankind's attitude toward the processes of nature.

Wholeness is the outcome of the power of real unity to bring together in a form of completeness the diverse essential and conditional features of environmental processes. As such, it depends on the category of contrast as well as enlarged interpretations of simplicity and complexity. On a cultural level wholeness is the triumph of the major form of beauty. Its basic character has been detailed in Chapter Three and involves the ways in which wholeness registers the real unity of simplicity and complexity within a cultural event. What is essential establishes a simple unity within complex conditions that can be wholly felt as expressing the value in question. Similarly, the synchronic level unites with the diachronic to establish patterns of wholeness that spread throughout the culture. Such a sense of completeness is rarely achieved in cultures but when it does occur, it is marked by an extraordinary convergence of the horizontal and vertical levels of experience. The private joins the public; the historical merges with the personal and what is internal to natural processes receives complete external expression.

This sense of an overwhelming cultural wholeness is what spurs efforts to preserve and continue such values. The future becomes a means whereby the cultural consensus is sustained and strengthened. Of course, such efforts are doomed to failure. One cannot stop the process of change. Process is ever on the move. Cultural wholeness may be achieved for a time but always fades in the face of the creative impulses at work throughout the natural environment. Complete and absolute perfection is a false notion. There are only modes of wholeness that shine forth for a time and then recede before the onrush of process in its physical, living, and cultural forms. Such is the consequence of the harmony of the One and the

Many. The many which become one are always increased by another one. Imbalance follows on the heels of balance. Disjunction succeeds conjunction. No matter how pleasing, wholeness is always but for a moment. Ironically, the future which is the temporal mode of greatest interest at the cultural level is also that which eventually subverts all expressions of wholeness.

Images of wholeness tend to be false ones. Often wholeness is confused with an image of eternal perfection that just does not exist at the cultural level. Monumental architecture, religious statuary, and pompous temples to art share in the pretensions that affect this sense of a false eternity. Rather than using such bogus modes of expression to pay a compliment to wholeness, I prefer to demonstrate its importance by showing how closely aligned it is to the felt experience of depth.

Depth is experienced when layers of value are so coordinated that real potentiality beomes a felt presence to the culture at hand. The components of cultural experience take on intense contrast such that great beauty and great novelty become equally available as felt cultural experiences. Furthermore, as Chapter Three also pointed out, the depth values are signalled by the concentrated presence of propositional feelings. This is what drives cultural participation toward the future. Depth implies lures and lures imply novelty. The gift of depth is the direct feeling of real potentiality as the central expression of a cultural process.

Depth and wholeness belong together at the cultural level of participation because at the ideal level all norms tend toward continuity. As we have already seen, convergence is the very nature of the ideal environmental values. It is inevitable that when speaking of one, the other looms into view. What happens in a culture marked by depth and wholeness is the opportunity to pursue great values with great intensity. A mood of expectation appears to attach itself to cultural events. In addition, there is in the air, so to speak, a seriousness that has been stripped of its heaviness. There is a joyous lightness to be felt among the people. A culture in the grip of wholeness and depth has managed somehow or other to unite present, past, and future without compromising any of these temporal modalities. What is small has been sidelined and what is great approaches. It is not possible to say how it all will turn out. Such are the limits of a process cosmology.

In some ways I have already concluded this study for we are now solidly within the domain of the cultural. And while the point of the discussion is to reconstruct our understanding of ecological praxis, I have begun to trench on the subject matter of another study yet to be carried out, the city and its urban values. I therefore end this study with a summary of the steps needed to ground a new discipline I choose to call foundational ecology. On the level of renewing the human interaction with nature there is a need to increase aesthetic sensibility, develop strength of mind, and encourage a respectful will. Given the ability to carry out such a project, it becomes possible also to envision undertaking a reconstruction of the types of participation through which ecological praxis takes place. The will might treat the physical level with the respect it deserves. The mind might have the strength to understand the real beauty residing at the heart of nature's process. And human beings might be able to feel the exceptional wholeness and depth that their culture can bring to encounters with the natural world.

None of this is guaranteed. Cosmological speculation does not deal with assurances. Here we are dealing with the reality of human freedom. At the end, this cosmology guarantees freedom only in this sense: Human freedom resides in the capacity to manage our experience. Our freedom acts in tandem with our sense of responsiblity. At the very least, this cosmology has articulated the measures by which we can most appropriately exercise our freedom. Less than that shows we have not yet learned to value nature.

NOTES

Preface

1. These concepts are articulated in the first four chapters of Alfred North Whitehead, *Modes of Thought* (New York: Free Press, 1968). Hereafter *MT*.

Chapter One

1. Plato, *The Sophist,* 249 c-d, as translated by F. M. Cornford in *Plato's Theory of Knowledge* (London: Routledge and Kegan Paul, 1937), p. 242.

2. A thorough defense of the method of speculative cosmology is to be found in Robert Neville, *Reconstruction of Thinking* (Albany: State University of New York Press, 1981).

3. Alfred North Whitehead, *Process and Reality,* corrected edition by David Ray Griffin and Donald W. Sherburne (New York: The Macmillan Company, 1978), Part I, Chapters I–III. Hereafter *PR.*

4. *PR,* p.5.

5. *Ibid.*

6. Charles Sanders Peirce, *The Collected Papers of Charles Sanders Peirce,* ed. by Charles Hartshorne and Paul Weiss (Cambridge, Mass.: Harvard University Press, 1931–1958), Vol. 5:448. Hereafter *CP.*

7. See Albert Borgmann, *Technology and The Character of Contemporary Life* (Chicago: The University of Chicago Press, 1984), pp. 1–34, for an extended discussion of these methodological points.

8. *PR,* p. 5.

9. *Ibid.*

10. *Ibid,* p. 24.

11. *Ibid,* pp. 25–26.

12. See also Whitehead's important distinction between the two types of "process", Transition and Concrescence. See *PR* II, Chapter X. These distinction are parallel to the diachronic and the synchronic orders.

13. For an overview of this vexed issue see Barry Smith, ed., "The Intrinsic Value of Nature," *The Monist* 75, No. 2 (April 1992): pp. 119–278.

14. For Whitehead's detailed argument concerning these matters see *Science and The Modern World* (New York: Free Press, 1967) Chapters III–V. Hereafter *SMW.*

15. *Ibid.*, p. 54.

16. *PR,* p. 21.

17. See Michael LaFargue, *The Tao of the Tao Te Ching* (Albany New York: State University of New York Press, 1992). 43 [1], LaFargue devises a new numbering system for the Sayings. The first number is Lafargue's revision; the number in brackets is the old version.

18. See *Gerard Manley Hopkins,* ed. W. H. Gardner (Baltimore: Penguin Books, 1963), pp. 122–128.

19. For a systematic discussion of these distinctions between the logical and the aesthetic orders see David Hall and Roger Ames, *Thinking Through Confucius, op. cit.,* pp. 131–137. These distinctions will grow in importance as this study proceeds. The original distinction is to be found in MT, p. 97 ff.

20. The phrase comes from Richard Rorty's Consequences of Pragmatism (Minneapolis: University of Minnesota Press, 1982) pp. 3–18.

Chapter Two

1. Aristotle, *Metaphysics,* Book IV, Chapter 7, 1011 b 26, in *The Complete Works of Aristotle,* ed. Jonathan Barnes. Vol. 2 (Princeton: Princeton University Press, 1984), p. 1597.

2. See Jane Jacobs, *The Death and Life of Great American Cities,* Part Three, "The Forces of Decline and Regeneration" (New York: Random House, 1961).

3. The development of normative thinking has been the lifelong task of Robert Neville. See his *Cosmology of Freedom, op. cit.,* Chapter Three, "A General Theory of Value," pp. 52–86, for the basic arguments underlying this axiology of thinking.

4. *PR,* p. 105.

5. *Ibid.*

6. David Hall, in *Uncertain Phoenix* (New York: Fordham University Press, 1982), has explored this primal sense of emptiness. See "The Uncarved Block," p. 251 ff.

7. See *PR,* p. 339.

8. This is the dominant motif in Susanne Langer's masterful *Mind: An Essay on Human Feeling,* 3 vols. (Baltimore: The Johns Hopkins University Press, 1967), See especially Vol. I, pp. 73–106.

9. See Mary T. Reynolds, "The City in Vico, Dante and Joyce," in *Vico and Joyce,* ed. Donald Verene (Albany: State University of New York Press, 1987) pp. 110–122.

10. *Philebus,* 23b–27c.

Chapter Three

1 See *PR*, pp. 110–115.

2. *Ibid.*, p. 111.

3. *Ibid.,* p. 111.

4. *Ibid.,* p. 112.

5. *Ibid.*

6. See Jean Gabbert Harrell, *Profundity* (University Park, Pa.: The Pennsylvania State University Press, 1992), for a compelling account of the experience of depth as primordial and universal throughout human experience.

7. See Laura Westra, *The Principle of Integrity* (Lanham, Md.: Rowman and Littlefield, 1994), for a useful employment of integrity as a foundation for environmental ethics. Though insightful, her work, like others in the field, suffers from a lack of systematic organization and development.

Chapter Four

1. *PR,* p. 122; *AI,* p. 181 ff.

2. *PR*, pp. 62–64; 311–312.

3. *MT,* pp. 71–72.

Chapter 5

1. Native Americans have an exceptional sense of this quality of space. See *Black Elk Speaks,* recorded by John G. Neihardt (New York: Pocket Books, 1972), *passim.*

2. See Jorge Luis Nobo, *Whitehead's Metaphysics of Extension and Solidarity* (Albany: State University of New York Press, 1986), p. 131 ff.

3. *Timaeus*, p. 59 ff.

4. See *PR,* pp. 61 ff.

5. See Nobo, *op. cit*. pp. 222.

6. See T. S. Eliot, *Selected Essays* (New York: Harcourt, Brace and World, 1932), *passim.* Also, Marjorie Hope Nicolson has provided a comprehensive analysis of the same experience in *The Breaking of The Circle* (New York: Columbia University Press, 1960). She has also exquisitely analyzed the human experience of mountains in *Mountain Gloom and Mountain Glory* (New York; Norton, 1960).

7. The classical text on this phenomenon is Mircea Eliade, *The Sacred and The Profane* (New York: Harper, 1959).

8. It is important to note here the connection between this mode of spatial originality and the Chinese concept of *Tao* previously discussed.

9. The metaphysical implications of this cultural narcissism are brilliantly expressed in William Desmond, *Desire, Dialectic and Otherness* (New Haven: Yale University Press, 1987).

10. See Brian Martine, *Individuals and Individuality* (Albany New York: State University of New York Press, 1984) for a thorough discussion of this critical metaphysical issue.

11. See Paul A. Bogaard, "Whitehead and the Survival of 'Subordinate Societies,'" *Process Studies* Vol. 21, No. 4 (Winter 1992): pp. 219–226, for an interesting discussion of how such normative measures effect important decisions in chemistry and related fields.

12. See Barry Lopez's compelling description of spatial intensity in *Arctic Dreams* (New York: Bantam Books,1987), pp. 243 ff.

13. Kathleen Norris has written of the exceptional ways in which space can generate the integration of experience. See her *Dakota: A Spiritual Geography* (New York: Ticknor and Fields, 1993).

14. *AI,* p. 256.

15. See Norman MacLean's wonderful description of an experience of spatial wholeness suffused with stillness, *A River Runs Through It* (Chicago: The University of Chicago Press, 1976), p. 105.

16. The phenomenological tradition has produced a number of brilliant analyses of the experience of lived depth. See Susan Cataldi, *Emotion, Depth and Flesh* (Albany: State University of New York Press, 1993). The *locus classicus* for this tradition is, of course, Maurice Merleau-Ponty, *The Phenomenology of Perception,* translated by Colin Smith (New York: Humanities Press,1962). The problem all such studies face is their lack of systematically developed categories.

17. This, of course, is the great value of John McPhee's examination of geological explorations. See "Basin and Range," in *Words from the Land,* ed. Stephen Trimble (Salt Lake City: Peregrine Smith, 1989).

Chapter 6

1. F. Bradford Wallack, *The Epochal Nature of Process in Whitehead's Metaphysics* (Albany: State University of New York Press, 1980), p. 285.

2. See David Bohm, *Wholeness and The Implicate Order* (London: Ark, 1983); Ilya Prigogine, *From Being to Becoming* (San Francisco: W. H. Freeman, 1980) for discussions of how the epochal theory of time comports with the findings of relativity theory and quantum physics. Also, see David Ray Griffin, ed. *Physics and the Ultimate Significance of Time* (Albany: State University of New York Press, 1986) for an excellent collection of important essays on these topics.

3. David Hall has consistently argued for the importance of acknowledging alternate possible worlds. See his "Logos, Mythos, and Chaos," in *New Essays in Metaphysics, op. cit.,* pp. 1–24.

4. This is the significance of Susanne Langer's insistence on the importance of "the act." See Mind: *An Essay On Feeling, op. cit.* Vol. 1, Chapter 8.

5. See Robert Neville, *Recovery of the Measure* (Albany: State University of New York Press, 1989) for a systematic development of the metaphysics of time (and space).

6. See the work of George Allan for a compelling analysis of the roles of the past and the future in our lives: *The Importances of The Past* (Albany: State University of New York Press, 1986) and *The Realizations of The Future* (Albany: State University of New York Press, 1990).

7. Richard Rorty, "Matter and Event," in *Explorations in Whitehead's Philosophy,* eds. Ford and Kline (Bronx, New York: Fordham University Press, 1984), pp. 68–103, argues differently. But his position, I believe, is undercut by his own uncritical allegiance to scientific materialism's dogmas.

8. As was the case with liminal space, Mircea Eliade also offers the classical statement on full time in *The Sacred and The Profane, op.cit.,* Chapter II.

Chapter 7

1. See Charles Birch and John Cobb, *The Liberation of Life* (Denton, Texas: Envionmental Ethics Books, 1990) and Erwin Schrodinger, *What is Life?* (New York: Cambridge University Press, 1967) for discussions of the problematics of formal definitions of life.

2. I have already cited Susan Cataldi and Merleau-Ponty for their work on the perception of lived space. Their work is also helpful in recovering

a sense of the human body as an active participant in the world. The sense of what Whitehead called the "withness of the body" is expressed quite well by Edward Casey's "Voluminous Depth" in *Merleau-Ponty Vivant,* ed. M. C. Dillon Albany: State University of New York Press, 1991), pp. 1–30.

3. *PR*, p. 243.

4. Michael LaFargue, *op. cit.,* 64 [34].

5. See Robert Neville, *The Puritan Smile* (Albany: State University of New York Press, 1987) and David Hall and Roger Ames, *Thinking Through Confucius, op. cit.*

Chapter 8

1. *The Collected Works of C. S. Peirce,* ed. Hartshorne and Weiss (Cambridge, Mass: Harvard University Press, 1931), 2:198 and see 2:196–200 for a complete presentation of the doctrine.

2. Again, see the discussion of the logical and aesthetic orders to be found in Hall and Ames, *Thinking Through Confucius, op. cit.*

3. See Arthur O. Lovejoy, *The Great Chain of Being* (New York: Harper & Row, 1960).

4. See Michael LaFargue, op. cit., 3 [67].

5. Aristotle, *The Nicomachean Ethics,* in *The Complete Works of Aristotle,* ed. Jonathan Barnes, Vol. II (Princeton: Princeton University Press, 1984), pp. 1729 ff.

6. William Desmond draws important and telling distinctions between agape and eros in *Desire, Dialectic and Otherness, op. cit.*

7. See Stephen David Ross, *Art as Inexhaustibility* (Albany: State University of New York Press, 1982) for a sustained application of the principle of plenitude to the idea of contrast and the depths of art.

8. See *AI,* Part IV.

9. *Ibid.*

10. See *AI,* cc.XVI, XVII, XVIII.

11. *Ibid.,* p. 266.

12. See *PR*, "The Category of the Ultimate," pp. 21–22.

13. See *The Philosophical Writings of Duns Scotus,* trans. Alan

Wolter, O.F.M. (Indianapolis: Hackett Publishing Co., 1987), p. 166 And the rich poem "Duns Scotus's Oxford," by Gerard Manley Hopkins.

14. See *Republic,* p. 504 ff; the *Symposium,* and the *Phaedrus.*

15. See *AI*, p. 260 ff. for Whitehead's understanding of the ways in which truth, appearance, beauty, and consciousness interact.

16. See Arnold Berleant, *The Aesthetics of Environment* (Philadelphia: Temple University Press, 1992) for a powerful indictment of this cultural tendency and equally important suggestions on how to reverse this trend.

Chapter 9

1. See Eric Katz, "Searching for Inrinsic Value," *Environmental Ethics* 9, No. 3 (Fall 1987): pp. 231–41.

2. The classical text is *The Critique of Practical Reason,* trans. Lewis White Beck (Indianapolis: Bobbs Merrill, 1956).

3. See Barry Smith, ed., *The Intrinsic Value of Nature, The Monist* 75, No.2 April 1992.

4. See Tom Regan, *The Case for Animal Rights* (Berkeley, University of California, 1983).

5. Christopher D. Stone, "Should Trees Have Standing?" *Southern California Law Review* 45 (1972): pp. 450–501.

6. This is Richard Rorty's position. See David Hall's nuanced and sensitive critique: *Richard Rorty, Poet and Prophet of the New Pragmatism* (Albany: State University of New York Press, 1994).

7. Peter Singer, *Animal Liberation* (New York: Avon, 1977).

8. See my essays: "Being, Feeling and Environment," *Environmental Ethics* (Winter 1985): pp. 351–364, and "The Nature of Things," *The Journal of Speculative Philosophy* VIII, No. 2 (1994): pp. 97–112.

9. See William M. Sullivan, *Reconstructing Public Philosophy* (Berkeley: University of California, 1986) and Bellah *et.al., The Good Society* (New York: Knopf, 1992).

10. Alaisdar MacIntyre's work is the best contemporary representative of this Aristotelian tradition. See *After Virtue,* 2nd edition (Notre Dame: University of Notre Dame, 1984).

11. See Whitehead's insightful comments on the relation between Plato and Aristotle, *AI,* pp. 146–150.

12. Erazim Kohak, *The Embers and The Stars* (Chicago: The University of Chicago Press, 1984).

13. *Ibid.,* p. 12.

14. *Ibid.*

15. *Ibid,.* p. 56.

16.. See *Ibid.,* p. 209.

17. See Warwick Fox, *Towards A Transpersonal Ecology* (Boston: Shambhala, 1992), pp. 114–115.

18. For a balanced assessment, see Max Oeschlaeger, *The Idea of Wilderness* (New Haven: Yale University Press, 1991), pp. 305–307.

19. Aldo Leopold, *A Sand County Almanac* (New York: Ballantine, 1966), p. 266.

20. J. Baird Callicott, *In Defense of the Land Ethic* (Albany: State University of New York Press, 1989).

21. L. Johnson, *A Morally Deep World* (Cambridge: Cambridge University Press, 1991) tries to expand the dimensions of the good from an analytic orientation but its lack of systematic articulation and cosmological thinking tells against it.

22. Charles Birch and John Cobb, *The Liberation of Life, op. cit.,* p.82.

23. *Ibid.,* p. 16.

24. *Ibid.,* p. 11.

25. *Ibid.,* p. 43.

26. See Paul Taylor, *Respect for Nature* (Princeton: Princeton University Press, 1986), pp. 59–192.

27. *Ibid.,* pp. 79–80.

28. Holmes Rolston, *Environmental Ethics* (Philadelphia: Temple University Press, 1988), p. 39.

29. Frederick Ferre,"Persons in Nature: Toward An Applicable and Unified Environmental Ethics," *Zygon* 28, No. 4 (December 1993): p. 446.

30. Rolston, *op. cit.*, pp. 229–230.

31. Quoted in Robert Pogue Harrison, *Forests* (Chicago: University of Chicago Press, 1992), p. xv.

32. *Ibid.*, p. 242.

33. Neil Evernden, *The Social Construction of Nature* (Baltimore: The Johns Hopkins University Press, 1992), p. 126.

34. *Ibid.*, pp. 129–130.

35. *Ibid.*, p. 132.

36. *Ibid.*, pp. 132–133.

37. Max Oelschlaeger, *op. cit.*, pp. 320–321.

Chapter 10

1. The best contemporary presentation of the normative dimension of Platonic naturalism is Robert Neville, *The Cosmology of Freedom, op. cit.*

2. *Republic*, 509 ff.

3. *Ethics,* III, Props. 58–58. The best interpretation of Spinoza remains Paul Wienpahl's masterful *The Radical Spinoza* (Albany: State University of New York Press, 1979). The final chapter of this work leans heavily on Spinoza's sense of the importance of strength of mind.

4. I have sketched the broad outlines of Spinoza's importance for the contemporary world in "Spinoza's *Scientia Intuitiva," Philosophy and Theology* II, No. 3 (Spring 1988): pp. 241–257.

5. See W. Sachsteder, "Simple Wholes and Complex Parts: Limiting Principles in Spinoza," in *Philosophy and Phenomological Research* XLV, No. 3 (March 1985) for a clear discussion of this very important methodological distinction.

6. This is also David Bohm's point in *Wholeness and The Implicate Order, op. cit.*

7. Baruch Spinoza, *The Ethics,* trans. Samuel Shirley (Indianapolis: Hackett Publishing Co., 1982), Part V, Prop. 42, scholium.

Chapter 11

1. See Martin Heidegger, *The Question Concerning Technology,* trans. William Lovitt (New York: Harper, 1977), p. 42. See Frederick Ferre, *The Philosophy of Technology* (Englewood Cliffs: Prentice Hall, 1988) for a beautifully clear examination of the major cultural and philosophical themes implied in contemporary technology.

2. Martin Heidegger, *The Question Concerning Technology, op. cit.,* pp. 3–35.

3. See Martin Heidegger, *The End of Philosophy and The Tasks of Thinking,* trans. Joan Stambaugh (New York: Harper, 1973).

4. See Martin Heidegger, "Building Dwelling Thinking" in *Poetry, Language, Thought* (New York: Harper & Row, 1971), pp. 143–162.

5. Martin Heideger, *Question of Technology, op. cit.,* p. 110.

6. Albert Borgmann, *Technology and The Character of Contemporary Life* (Chicago: The University of Chicago Press, 1984).

7. Borgmann, *op. cit.,* p. 180.

8. *Ibid.,* p. 47.

9. *Ibid.,* p. 72 ff.

10. *Ibid.,* p. 75.

11. *Ibid.,* p. 75.

12. *Ibid.,* p. 77.

13. *Ibid.,* p. 72.

14. *Ibid.,* p. 181.

15. *Ibid.,* p. 186.

16. *Ibid.,* p. 190.

17. *Ibid.,* p. 204.

18. See Martin Heidegger, *Being and Time,* trans. Macquarrie and Robinson (New York: Harper & Row, 1967), Sections 3 & 4.

19. Borgmann, *op. cit.,* p. 204.

20. See Martin Heidegger, *Discourse on Thinking,* trans. Anderson and Freund (N.Y.: Harper, 1966), pp. 43–57.

21. *SMW,* p. 196.

22. *AI,* pp. 3–100.

23. *PR,* pp. 32–33.

24. See Anthony Steinbock, "Whitehead's 'Theory' of Propositions," *Process Studies* 18, No. 1 (Spring 1989): pp.19–29.

25. *AI,* p. 366.

26. See Robert Neville, *Reconstruction of Thinking, op.cit.,* and

Recovery of the Measure, op. cit., for a systematic interpretation of the place of beauty and truth in our contemporary culture. Also David Hall's *The Civilization of Experience* (Bronx, New York: Fordham University Press, 1973), for a sustained analysis of Whitehead's philosophy of culture.

27. See David Ross, *A Theory of Art, op. cit.*, for the connection between ontological inexhaustibility, contrast, art, and technology.

28. Martin Heidegger, "The Age of the World as Picture," *The Question Concerning Technology, op. cit.*, pp. 141–143.

29. *Ibid.*, p. 4.

30. See James Bradley, "Whitehead, Heidegger and the Paradoxes of the New," *Process Studies* 29, No. 3 (1991): pp. 127–150, as well as my own "Deconstruction and The Philosophy of Culture," *Process Studies* 17, No. 3 (Fall 1988) pp. 141-151.

31. See George Allan's works on temporality, *The Importances of the Past* and *The Realizations of the Future, op. cit.*

32. Martin Heidegger, *Introduction to Metaphysics*, trans. Ralph Mannheim (New Haven: Yale University Press, 1959), pp. 180–194.

33. Liddell and Scott, *Greek Lexicon* (Oxford: Oxford University Press, 1972).

34. See David Hall, *Uncertain Phoenix*, *op. cit., passim.*

35. *RM,* p. 111.

36. See Gyorgy Doczi, *The Power of Limits* (Boston: Shambhala, 1985), for a stunning introduction to the power of limit and proportion in nature and human culture.

37. See the seminal work of David Seamon, *The Geography of the Lifeworld* (New York: St. Martin's Press, 1979). More than any one else working in the field of phenomenology, environmental design, and architecture, he has grasped the essential connection between normative measure and excellence in building.

38. See the Zen concept of "Basho" in Yuasa Yasuo, *The Body* (Albany: State University of New York Press, 1987), *passim.* Also, see Mara Miller, *The Garden as an Art Form* (Albany: State University of New York Press, 1993).

39. Hall and Ames, *op. cit.*

Chapter 12

1. Whitehead's chapter on "Beauty" in *Adventures of Ideas* is required reading for any course in foundational ecology. It goes to great lengths to articulate the good as well as the evil introduced into the domain of human culture once states of aesthetic consciousness become a dominant factor in the world of natural processes. See *AI,* Chapter XVII.

2. *Ibid.,* pp. 259 ff.

3. See Immanuel Kant, *The Critique of Judgment*, trans. J. H. Bernard (New York: Hafner, 1951), Second Book: The Analytic of the Sublime.

4. See *The Ethics of Spinoza,* trans. S. Shirley, *op. cit.* III, Prop. 59; IV, Prop. 73. Hereafted cited as *Ethics.* I also repeat my recommendation of Paul Wienpahl's great work, *The Radical Spinoza, op. cit.*

5. The translation is from Wienpahl, *op. cit.,* p. 135. See *Ethics,* Part IV, Prop. 73 Scholium.

6. This is Whitehead's category of explanation IX. See *PR,* p. 27.

7. See Robert Inchausti, *The Ignorant Perfection of Ordinary People* (Albany: State University of New York Press, 1991), for a sensitive and compelling portrait of how this works out in real-life situations.

8. See my previous discussion of "Respecting Value" in Chapter Ten, Cosmology and Moral Vision.

9. *Ethics* Part V, Proposition 39.

10. See Tu Wei Ming, *Confucian Thought: Selfhood as Creative Transformation* (Albany: State University of New York Press, 1985), for a convincing presentation of both the possibility and the importance of culturally adopting such a point of view.

11. See Roger Ames, "Putting the Te back into Nature," in Callicott and Ames, ed., *Nature in Asian Traditions of Thought* (Albany: State University of New York Press, 1989), pp. 113–144.

12. See Wienpahl, *op. cit., passim* for this sense of the real message of the *Ethics.*

13. Thomas Merton, *Preview of the Asian Journey.* ed. Walter Capps (New York: Crossroad, 1989), p. 87–88.

BIBLIOGRAPHY

Allan, George. *The Realizations of the Future.* Albany: State University of New York Press, 1990.

______. *The Importances of the Past.* Albany: State University of New York Press, 1990.

______. "The Primacy of the Mescosm," in *New Essays in Metaphysics.* Edited by Robert Neville. Albany: State University of New York Press, 1987.

Ames, Roger. "Putting the Te Back into Nature," in *Nature in Asian Traditions of Thought.* Edited by Callicott and Ames. Albany: State University of New York Press, 1989.

Aristotle, *Metaphysics and Nicomachean Ethics,* in *The Complete Works of Aristotle.* Edited by Jonathan Barnes. Princeton: Princeton University Press, 1984. 2 vols.

Bellah, Robert, et. al. *The Good Society.* New York: Knopf, 1992.

Berleant, Arnold. *The Aesthetics of Environment.* Philadelphia: Temple University Press, 1992.

Berry, Thomas. *The Dream of Earth.* San Francisco: Sierra Club Books, 1988.

Birch, Charles, and Cobb, John. *The Liberation of Life.* Denton, Texas: Environmental Ethics Books, 1990.

Bogaard, Paul. "Whitehead and the Survival of Subordinate Societies," *Process Studies* Vol. 21. No. 4, 1992.

Bohm, David. *Wholeness and The Implicate Order.* London: Ark, 1983.

Borgmann, Albert. *Technology and The Character of Contemporary Life.* Chicago: University of Chicago Press, 1984.

Bradley, James. "Whitehead, Heidegger and the Paradoxes of the New," *Process Studies* Vol. 29 No.3, 1991.

Callicott, J. Baird. *In Defense of the Land Ethic.* Albany: State University of New York Press, 1989.

Casey, Edward. "Voluminous Depth," in *Merleau-Ponty Vivant.* Edited by M.C. Dillon. Albany: State University of New York Press, 1991.

Cataldi, Susan. *Emotion, Depth and Flesh.* Albany: State University of New York Press, 1993.

Confucius. *The Analects*, as translated in Hall and Ames. *Thinking Through Confucius.* Albany: State University of New York Press, 1987.

Desmond, William. *Desire, Dialectic and Otherness.* New Haven: Yale University Press, 1987.

Dillon. M.C., editor. *Merleau-Ponty Vivant.* Albany: State University of New York press, 1991.

Doczi, Gyorgi. *The Power of Limits.* Boston: Shambhala, 1985.

Duns Scotus. *The Philosophical Writings.* Translated by A. Wolter. Indianapolis: Hackett, 1987.

Eliade, Mircea. *The Sacred and The Profane.* New York: Harper, 1959.

Eliot, T.S. *Selected Essays.* New York: Harcourt, Brace and World, 1932.

Evernden, Neal. *The Social Construction of Nature.* Baltimore: The Johns Hopkins University Press, 1992.

Ferre, Frederick. *The Philosophy of Technology.* Englewood Cliffs, N.J.: Prentice Hall, 1988

_____. "Persons in Nature: Toward An Applicable and Unified Environmental Ethics," *Zygon* Vol. 28 No. 4, December 1993.

Ford, L., and Kline, G. *Explorations in Whitehead's Philosophy.* Bronx, N.Y.: Fordham University Press, 1983.

Fox, Warwick, *Towards a Transpersonal Ecology.* Boston: Shambhala, 1990.

Grange, Joseph. "Being, Feeling and Environment," *Environmental Ethics.* Winter 1986.

_____. "The Nature of Things," *The Journal of Speculative Philosophy* Vol. VIII No. 2, 1994.

_____. "Spinoza's *Scientia Intuitiva," Philosophy and Theology* Vol. II, No. 3, Spring 1988.

_____. "Deconstruction and the Philosophy of Culture," *Process Studies* Vol. 17, No. 3, 1988.

Griffin, David Ray, editor. *Physics and the Ultimate Significance of Time.* Albany: State University of New York Press, 1986.

Hall, David. *Richard Rorty, Poet and Prophet of the New Pragmatism.* Albany: State University of New York Press, 1994.

_____. *Eros and Irony.* Albany: State University of New York Press, 1982.

_____. *Uncertain Phoenix.* Bronx, New York: Fordham University Press, 1982.

_____. *The Civilization of Experience.* Bronx, New York: Fordham University Press, 1973.

_____. "Logos, Mythos, Chaos," in *New Essays in Metaphysics.* Edited by Robert Neville. Albany: State University of New York Press, 1987.

_____, and Ames, Roger. *Thinking Through Confucius.* Albany: State University of New York Press, 1987.

_____. "Rationality, Correlativity and the Language of Process," *The Journal of Speculative Philosophy* Vol. V No. 2 .

Harrell, J.G. *Profoundity.* University Park, Pa.; The Pennsylvania State University Press, 1992.

Harrison, Robert Pogue. *Forests.* Chicago: University of Chicago Press, 1992.

Heidegger, Martin. *The Question Concerning Technology.* Translated by William Lovett. New York: Harper, 1977.

_____. *The End of Philosophy and The Tasks of Thinking.* Translated by Joan Stambaugh. New York: Harper, 1973.

_____. *Poetry, Language, Thought.* Translated by Albert Hofstadter. New York: Harper, 1971.

_____. *Being and Time.* Translated by Macquarrie and Robinson. New York: Harper, 1967.

_____. *Introduction to Metaphysics.* Translated by Ralph Mannheim. New Haven: Yale University Press, 1959.

_____. *Discourse on Thinking.* Translated by Anderson and Freund. New York: Harper, 1966.

Hopkins, Gerard. *Gerard Manley Hopkins.* Edited by Catherine Phillips. New York: Oxford Univeristy Press, 1986.

_____. *The Poems and Prose of Gerard Manley Hopkins.* Edited by W.H. Gardner. Baltimore: Penguin Books, 1953.

Inchausti, Robert. *The Ignorant Perfection of Ordinary People.* Albany: State University of New York Press, 1991.

Jacobs, Jane. *The Death and Life of Great American Cities.* New York: Random House, 1961.

Johnson, L. *A Morally Deep World.* Cambridge: Cambridge University Press, 1991.

Joyce, James. *Finnegans Wake.* New York: Viking, 1986.

Kant, Immanuel. *The Critique of Judgment.* Translated by J.H. Bernard. New York: Hafner, 1951.

_____. *The Critique of Practical Reason.* Translated by Lewis White Beck. Indianapolis: Bobbs Merrill, 1956.

Katz, Eric. "Searching for Intrinsic Value," *Environmental Ethics* Vol. 9. No. 3, Fall 1987.

Kohak, Erazim. *The Embers and The Stars.* Chicago: University of Chicago Press, 1984.

Langer, Susanne. *Mind: An Essay on Feeling.* Baltimore: The Johns Hopkins University press, 1967. 3 vols.

Leopold, Aldo. *A Sand County Almanac.* New York: Ballantine, 1966.

Lopez, Barry. *Arctic Dreams.* New York: Bantam Books, 1987.

Lovejoy, A. O. *The Great Chain of Being.* New York: Harper, 1960.

Maclean, Norman. *A River Runs Through It.* Chicago: University of Chicago Press, 1976.

Martine, Brian. *Individuals and Individuality.* Albany: State University of New York Press, 1984.

MacIntyre, Alasdair. *After Virtue.* 2nd Edition. South Bend, Ind.: Notre Dame University Press, 1984.

McKibben, Bill. *The End of Nature.* New York: Random House, 1989.

McPhee, John. *Basin and Range.* New York: Farrar, Strauss, Giroux 1981.

Merleau-Ponty, Maurice. *The Phenomenology of Perception.* Translated by Colin Smith. New York: Humanities Press, 1962.

Merton, Thomas. *Preview of the Asian Journey.* Edited by Walter Capps. New York: Crossroads, 1989.

Miller, Mara. *The Garden as an Art Form.* Albany: State University of New York Press, 1993.

Neihardt, John, ed. *Black Elk Speaks,* New York: Pocket Books, 1972.

Neville, Robert. *The Cosmology of Freedom.* New Haven: Yale University Press, 1974.

______. *Reconstruction of Thinking.* Albany: State University of New York Press, 1981.

______. *The Puritan Smile.* Albany: State University of New York Press, 1987.

______. *Recovery of the Measure.* Albany: State University of New York Press, 1989.

______. Ed. *New Essays in Metaphysics.* Albany: State University of New York Press, 1987.

Nicolson, Majorie Hope. *The Breaking of the Circle.* New York: Columbia University Press, 1960.

______. *Mountain Gloom and Mountain Glory.* New York: Norton, 1960.

Nobo, Jorge Luis. *Whitehead's Metaphysics of Extension and Solidarity.* Albany: State University of New York Press, 1986.

Norris, Kathleen. *Dakota.* New York: Ticknor and Fields, 1993.

Oelschlaeger, Max. *The Idea of Wilderness.* New Haven: Yale University Press, 1991.

Peirce, C. S. *The Collected Papers.* Edited by Hartshorne, Weiss, and Murphy. Cambridge, Mass.: Harvard University Press, 1931–1958. 8 vols.

Plato. *The Symposium.* Translated by Nehamas and Woodruff. Indianapolis: Hackett, 1989.

_____. *The Republic.* Translated by H.D. P. Lee. New York: Penguin, 1987.

_____. *The Sophist.* Translated by Seth Bernardete. Chicago: University of Chicago Press, 1984.

_____. *The Statesman.* Chicago: University of Chicago Press, 1984.

_____. *Philebus.* Translated by Dorothea Frede. Indianapolis: Hackett, 1993.

_____. *Timaeus.* Translated by F. M. Cornford. London: Routledge and Kegan Paul, 1953.

Prigogine, Ilya. *From Being to Becoming.* San Francisco: W. H. Freeman, 1980.

Regan, Tom. *The Case for Animal Rights.* Berkeley: University of California Press, 1983.

Reynolds, Mary T. "The City in Vico, Dante and Joyce," in *Vico and Joyce.* Edited by Donald Verene. Albany: State University of New York Press, 1987.

Rolston, Holmes. *Environmental Ethics.* Philadelphia: Temple University Press, 1988.

Rorty, Richard. *The Consequences of Pragmatism.* Minneapolis: Univeristy of Minnesota, 1982.

_____. "Matter and Event," in *Explorations in Whitehead's Philosophy.* Edited by Ford and Kline. Bronx, N.Y.: Fordham, 1983.

Ross, Stephen David. *Art as Inexhaustibility.* Albany: State University of New York Press, 1982.

Ross-Bryant, A. "The Land in American Religious Experience," *The Journal of The American Academy of Religion* Vol. LVIII No. 3, Fall 1990.

Sachsteder, W. "Simple Wholes and Complex Parts: Limiting Principles in Spinoza," *Philosophy and Phenomenological Research,* Vol. XLV. No. 3, March 1985.

Schrodinger, Erwin. *What is Life?* New York: Cambridge University Press, 1967.

Seamon, David. *The Geography of the Life World.* New York: St. Martin's Press, 1979.

Singer, Peter. *Animal Liberation.* New York: Avon, 1977.

Smith, Barry, ed. "The Intrinsic Value of Nature," *The Monist,* Vol. 75 No. 2, April 1992.

Spinoza, Baruch. *Treatise on the Emendation of the Intellect*, in *The Collected Works of Spinoza.* Translated and edited by Edwin Curley. Princeton: Princeton University Press, 1985.

_____. *The Ethics.* Translated by Samuel Shirley. Indianapolis: Hackett Publishing, 1982.

Stone, Christopher. "Should Trees Have Standing?" *Southern California Law Review* 45, 1972.

Sullivan, William. *Reconstruction of Public Philosophy*. Berkeley: University of California Press, 1986.

Tao Te Ching. Translated by Addiss and Lombardo. Indianapolis: Hackett Publishing Co., 1993.

______. Translated by Witter Bynner. New York: Capricorn, 1962.

______. Translated by Stephen Mitchell. New York: Harper, 1989.

______. Translated by Ellen Chen. New York: Paragon House, 1989.

Taylor, Paul. *Respect for Nature*. Princeton: Princeton University Press, 1986.

Tu, Wei Ming. *Confucian Thoughts: Selfhood as Creative Transformation*. Albany: State University of New York Press, 1985.

Trimble, Stephen, ed. *Words From The Land*. Salt Lake City: Peregrine Smith, 1989.

Verene, Donald, ed. *Vico and Joyce*. Albany: State University of New York Press, 1987.

Wallack, F. Bradford. *The Epochal Nature of Time in Whitehead's Metaphysics*. Albany: State University of New York Press, 1980.

Westra, Laura. *The Principle of Integrity*. Lanham, Md.: Rowman and Littlefield, 1994.

Whitehead, Alfred North. *Adventures of Ideas*. New York: Free Press, 1967.

______. *Modes of Thought*. New York: Free Press, 1968.

______. *Process and Reality*. Corrected edition by Griffin and Sherburne. New York: Free Press, 1978.

______. *Religion in the Making*. New York: Meriden, 1974.

______. *Symbolism, Its Meaning and Effect*. Bronx, N.Y.: Fordham University Press, 1986.

______. *Science and the Modern World*. New York: Free Press, 1967.

Wienpahl, Paul. *The Radical Spinoza*. New York: New York University Press, 1979.

Yasuo, Yuasa. *The Body*. Albany: State University of New York Press, 1987.

INDEX